LIFEBOATS
—— OF THE ——
HUMBER

Two centuries of gallantry

NICHOLAS LEACH

AMBERLEY

Kenneth Thelwall, Humber lifeboat from 1987 to 1997, on service to the ketch Christian Brugge in severe conditions, 14 March 1989. The ketch, with five crew on board, got into difficulties seventeen miles south-east of Spurn Point. A helicopter located the ketch and stood by until the lifeboat arrived. The lifeboat then escorted the vessel to Grimsby during a service lasting nearly twelve hours, undertaken in force ten winds and rough seas. (By courtesy of Brian Bevan)

To the brave and dedicated lifeboatmen of Spurn Point, a unique breed

First published 2010

Amberley Publishing Plc
Cirencester Road, Chalford,
Stroud, Gloucestershire, GL6 8PE

www.amberley-books.com

Copyright © Nicholas Leach 2010

The right of Nicholas Leach to be identified as the
Author of this work has been asserted in accordance
with the Copyrights, Designs and Patents Act 1988.

ISBN 978 1 84868 875 9

British Library Cataloguing in Publication Data.
A catalogue record for this book is available from
the British Library.

Typeset in 9.5pt on 12pt Celeste.
Typesetting by Amberley Publishing.
Printed in the UK.

Contents

SPURN POINT AND THE HUMBER ESTUARY

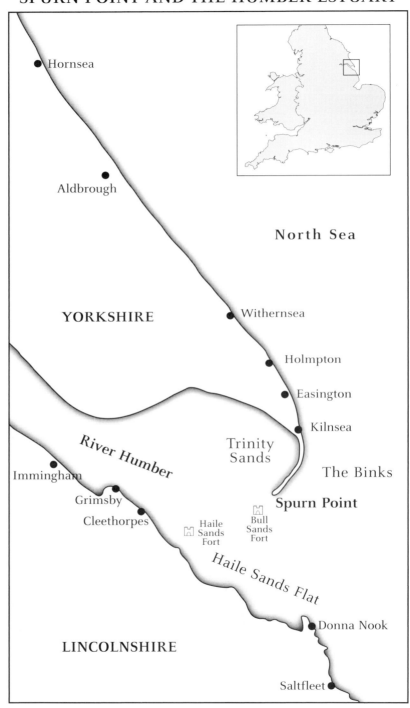

Hornsea

Aldbrough

North Sea

YORKSHIRE

Withernsea

Holmpton

Easington

Kilnsea

Trinity Sands

The Binks

River Humber

Immingham

Grimsby

Cleethorpes

Spurn Point

Haile Sands Fort

Bull Sands Fort

Haile Sands Flat

Donna Nook

LINCOLNSHIRE

Saltfleet

Introduction

In 2010 the Humber lifeboat station celebrated 200 years of life-saving. The unique station, at Spurn Point, has gained an outstanding record of gallantry during those two centuries, and its lifeboats have saved many hundreds of lives. It was managed and maintained independently of the Royal National Lifeboat Institution (RNLI) for more than a century, but between 1911, when the RNLI took over, and 31 December 2009 the station's lifeboats launched 2,268 times on service, saving 790 lives. Not only has it a gallantry record to be proud of, but its operation is unique, as Humber is the only station manned by a full-time paid crew, with other lifeboat stations crewed on a voluntary basis. A full-time crew has always been a necessity, and the lifeboatmen live at Spurn Point in purpose-built accommodation together with their families, with the wives and children being an important element to life on Spurn.

Spurn Point, made up of a series of sand and shingle banks open to the ravages of the North Sea, is a narrow sand spit on the tip of the coast of the East Riding of Yorkshire and forms the north bank of the mouth of the Humber Estuary. It is home to a national nature reserve, the Humber Pilots and Vessel Traffic Services, and of course the lifeboat. The peninsula is over three miles long, but as little as fifty

An aerial view of the Spurn peninsula and Spurn Point, showing the features of the headland in the foreground, including the Pilot Jetty and now demolished lifeboat house and slipway. The unique peninsula extends south for more than three miles into the mouth of the river Humber. (By courtesy of Brian Bevan)

yards wide in places. The area has been owned since 1960 by the Yorkshire Wildlife Trust, is a designated National Nature Reserve, and is part of the Humber Flats, Marshes and Coast Special Protection Area. Spurn's position, extending out into the Humber Estuary, has made it a natural waypoint for vessels navigating along the east coast, into Hull, or any of the other ports on the river. To mark the point, a series of lighthouses has been built, the first in the fifteenth century. The most recent lighthouse, which was built in 1895 to replace an old lighthouse that was positioned just to the south, was decommissioned on 31 October 1986, thus ending a long history of lighthouses at the Point. However, it remains standing and is one of the most notable landmarks at Spurn.

But Spurn Point is probably best known for its lifeboat, and I am very privileged to have been asked by Superintendent Coxswain Dave Steenvoorden to write this history for the station's bicentenary. I hope I have managed to capture some of the difficulties and dangers of life-saving off the Humber during the nineteenth century, the courage, bravery and skill of the lifeboat crews in the early motor lifeboats during the first half of the twentieth century, and the outstanding rescues performed during the late 1970s that made the station and its crews renowned the length and breadth of the country. For the nineteenth-century lifeboatmen and their families, life on Spurn was very harsh, and only relatively recently have conditions improved for the gallant men willing to risk their lives to rescue others.

ACKNOWLEDGEMENTS

I am very grateful to a number of people in the Humber area for their assistance with this book. Former Superintendent Coxswain Brian Bevan was extremely hospitable and helpful in supplying information and photos relating to his time on the crew. Local historians Jan Crowther and Mike Welton have assisted with information and historical images, and readily answered my questions and checked through the text to give me the benefit of their expertise, and I am very grateful to them both. The photographs in the Buchan Collection have also been very useful, and have considerably enhanced the book; this collection was scanned and thus preserved thanks to the Spurn, Kilnsea and Easington Area Local Studies Group (Skeals) through the efforts of Jan Crowther. A member of Skeals, Peter Martin, copied every one. At the RNLI, thanks to Brian Wead and the Service Information Section staff, who provided service details and listings, and to Nathan Williams, who efficiently supplied a variety of images. I gladly acknowledge the work of Jeff Morris, Honorary Archivist of the Lifeboat Enthusiasts' Society, whose previous books about the Humber lifeboats were very useful. I am also grateful to the following, who have all supplied photographs for possible inclusion: Syd Rollinson, Paul Richards, Paul Arro, Steve Medcalf, Cliff Crone and Tony Denton. And thanks to Superintendent Coxswain Dave Steenvoorden and the Humber lifeboatmen for their assistance during my many visits to Spurn, whose enthusiasm to mark the station's 200th anniversary knows no bounds. Lastly, thank you to Sarah for her continuing support and kindness during my researches, writing and photographic journeys.

Nicholas Leach
Lichfield, May 2010

BIBLIOGRAPHY

Benfell, Roy: *Spurn Lifeboat Station – The First Hundred Years* (Roy Benfell, 1994).

Crowther, Jan: *The People along the Sand: The Spurn Peninsula & Kilnsea, a history, 1800-2000* (Phillimore, Chichester, 2006).

Herbert, Barry: *Lifeboats of the Humber* (Hutton Press, 1991).

Morris, Jeff: *The History of the Humber Lifeboats* (2nd edition, 1997).

Storey, Arthur: *Trinity House of Kingston upon Hull* (Trinity House, Hull, 1967).

The First Rescuers

The entrance to the Humber Estuary, characterised by numerous sandbanks and shallows, can be a treacherous place for the unwary mariner. To reach the port of Kingston upon Hull, or any of the other smaller ports that line the Humber such as Grimsby, Immingham and Goole, vessels have to navigate the river, and for many the hazards proved too great. As the seas in and around the Humber have always been busy, shipwrecks were an inevitable occurrence. The first moves to provide a lifeboat for the estuary came in the early nineteenth century. In 1802 a newspaper in Hull began campaigning to get a lifeboat established at Spurn Point, at the mouth of the Humber. With this campaign underway, the South Shields-based boatbuilder Henry Greathead wrote to Hull Trinity House on 22 October 1802 offering to build a lifeboat for them. Greathead was responsible for designing and building the first craft intended for use as lifeboats, and completed a total of thirty-one lifeboats which served at ports throughout the British Isles. But his initial suggestions for providing a boat for Hull came to nothing.

However, the issue did not go away, and a few months later another attempt was made to remedy the situation and help safeguard shipping in the Humber. On 7 March 1803 William Iveson, agent of the Lord of the Manor of Spurn, Sir Francis Constable, wrote on behalf of Constable to Hull Trinity House urging that a lifeboat be provided at Spurn. But again nothing was done, mainly because it was believed that a lifeboat at Spurn would be almost impossible to operate unless the crew actually lived at Spurn, and this would have been economically unviable for Trinity House. As a result, nothing more happened and more than seven years passed before further proposals were put forward. Then, in April 1810 Iveson again contacted Hull Trinity House, reporting that Constable was still keen to see a lifeboat at Spurn, 'for humanitarian reasons only'. He had obtained the use of the shell of a former Barracks at Spurn and had offered to fit it out as a residence for the Master and crew of a lifeboat, with temporary accommodation for any survivors that may be landed. Constable also offered to build a boathouse if Trinity House told him the size required to accommodate the lifeboat and her launching carriage.

To crew the lifeboat, Constable had found eleven willing men during the previous year, and to ensure the Master could earn a living he would manage a tavern which was to be built in the old Barracks at Spurn. As well as income from this, he would sell provisions to vessels which stopped at Spurn to take on ballast. At least 500 ships called each year at the peninsula, so the Master was expected to earn more than £100 through this trade. As the problem of providing a crew at Spurn had been solved without their having to act, Trinity House accepted the generous offers made by Constable and immediately ordered a ten-oared lifeboat from Greathead, as Constable had indicated they should provide as he had provided its accommodation and crew. The boat, which cost £197, was 30ft in length, rowed by ten oars and painted white on the outside to make it visible to those in distress. The words 'Spurn Lifeboat' were painted on the hull in black lettering. The launching carriage, built locally by G. & W. Boyd at a cost of £84 2s 0d, was a somewhat large and bulky contraption, with wheels 16ft in diameter.

The funds to pay for the rescue equipment were provided through subscriptions given by the Corporations of the Town of Hull, the Dock Company, and Lloyd's insurers in London, as well as Trinity House. On 2 October 1810 the new lifeboat left South Shields and was towed south by the brig *Thomas* to Hull, where it was placed on display until the end of the month. The boat eventually reached Spurn Point on 29 October 1810. Robert Richardson was appointed the first Master of the lifeboat, a position equivalent to today's Coxswain. Richardson was a mariner from Hull, and he remained in his position at Spurn for thirty-one years. If his income from the Tavern did not reach £100 a year, the deficit would be made up by Constable, and the Lord of the Manor's role in establishing and supporting the lifeboat station at Spurn in its infancy cannot be understated.

Within a month of its arrival, the new lifeboat had proved its usefulness. On 15 November 1810, just over a fortnight after the lifeboat had arrived at Spurn, she was launched to the assistance of the ship *John and Charlotte*, of Newcastle, which came into the Humber waterlogged and had run aground on the Trinity Sands. The lifeboat crew helped get the ship off the sands and into Grimsby. Richardson stated afterwards, in a letter to Trinity House, that he was very pleased with the crew, who 'behaved with great courage and used every exertion'. This was the first of many rescues undertaken by the nascent Spurn lifeboat and its crew, who remained very busy and carried out numerous rescues during the first years of the service. However, as detailed records were not kept, the number of ships helped or accurate figures for lives saved cannot be reached. But the first lifeboat was launched seventeen times on service during 1820, making this her busiest year, and was called to help distressed vessels at least once every two months throughout her time on Spurn. In November 1813 she went to the ship *Sir Peter*, which had run aground off Stony Binks, and helped save the ship and her crew.

One of her most notable rescues took place on 8 June 1821. Just after midday, Robert Richardson saw a vessel aground on the Stony Binks. A strong north-easterly wind was blowing as the lifeboat was

A contemporary line drawing of the Greathead-built lifeboat, which had a rockered or curved keel and steering oars at either end. This engraving, which was drawn from a model presented by Greathead to the Admiralty, shows a ten-oared boat similar to that used at Spurn.

The two lighthouses at Spurn Point as depicted in a print from 1820. The first lighthouse at Spurn dates from the late seventeenth century. The high light was built in 1776 to the design of the engineer John Smeaton. The low light (on the left) was built by Shaw in 1816.

launched, but her crew managed to row through heavy seas, and found the troopship *Thomas*, with twenty-six soldiers and crew on board, as well as two women and a child. The lifeboat transferred some of the soldiers to the revenue cutter *Bee*, and then returned to stand by the troopship. As conditions worsened, everyone on board was taken off, except one of the women, who unfortunately drowned. As the lifeboat pulled away from the wreck, Richardson spotted one man still in the rigging. He immediately took the lifeboat to a pilot cutter, transferred the survivors and returned to *Thomas*. The last man was rescued and put aboard *Bee*, and the lifeboat returned to Spurn after more than eleven hours at sea.

One of the problems encountered during the first few years of the station's operation was the difficulty of getting crews to Spurn quickly enough. They lived at Kilnsea or Easington and thus had to travel several miles to go out with the lifeboat. In April 1816 it was suggested by Trinity House that proper houses be built for the crew so that they could live on Spurn. Constable provided sufficient land for the new cottages, and the Brethren raised sufficient funds for their construction. Twelve cottages were eventually completed in 1819 for the crew and their families. Having the crew on hand meant that launching was much faster, and the lifeboat could offer more immediate assistance.

Despite her good record of service, the first lifeboat came to a rather unfortunate end. She was often kept afloat during the winter months, so that launching at any state of the tide was easier, and had several times broken away from the moorings in bad weather. Previously she had been found undamaged and returned to service, but during a severe storm in December 1823, she broke adrift, overturned, and was wrecked. Seriously damaged but later salvaged, she was condemned for use as a lifeboat and was sold locally, subsequently being used as a shrimp boat. During her thirteen years as Spurn lifeboat, she is credited with assisting thirty-four vessels and saving about 120 lives.

Trinity House Lifeboats

Hull Trinity House wasted little time in finding a replacement for the first Spurn lifeboat after it had met its unfortunate end. A new lifeboat, ordered from local boatbuilder Thomas Mason at a cost of £190, was delivered in June 1824. The new boat was an oak-built non-self-righting type, 30ft 2in long, with a beam of 10ft, rowed ten oars and could be steered from either end, like her predecessor. She remained at Spurn until 1852, during which time she was as busy as the first lifeboat. In the late 1830s she was altered and improved when new air boxes, made from Baltic Redwood timber, were fitted, and the copper cylinders which drained the boat were also replaced, by cylinders made from elm. The boat was also fitted with a rudder, a mast 22ft long and 18in thick, and sails, which were found to be 'of the greatest utility'. These changes made the boat 'much superior in principle to the one formerly stationed at Spurn, and which was built by Mr Henry Greathead.'

One of the second lifeboat's early rescues involved assistance from a steamer, the first time that motive power was used for rescue work in the Humber. On 12 September 1830 the brig *Ann*, of Shields, went ashore on the Middle Bank. The lifeboat was immediately launched from her boathouse in a strong south-westerly wind and at about 9 a.m. reached the casualty. The crew helped to get the brig refloated and under sail again, although the vessel grounded on the Inner Binks. When the tide turned, at about 3 p.m., the brig got clear and by 10 p.m. she had been taken up to Kilnsea. The lifeboat had been towed to the casualty by the steamer *Prince Frederick* as her sails and mast had been carried away in the heavy weather. The steamer had also helped to tow the brig off the sands during the rescue.

In December 1841 Robert Richardson retired as Master of the Spurn lifeboat. During his time in charge he had helped to save more than 300 lives. He asked Trinity House if he could stay on another year so that he could clear his debts with the brewer, as he would otherwise be forced to sell all his possessions to find the money owed. Trinity House turned down this request, and the post was advertised, but what became of Richardson is not known. His plight, and the fact that he had got into debt, shows how precarious life was for those full-time crew members who manned the Spurn lifeboat.

Ten men applied for the post of Master, including three members of the crew, and twenty-eight-year-old Joseph Davey was appointed, taking up his duties on 4 December 1841. However, his tenure was somewhat short-lived and he was dismissed on 13 February 1843. It seems probable that he was in charge of the lifeboat on 19 February 1843 when the schooner *Elizabeth* ran aground on the Stony Binks in stormy weather. Her crew signalled for help, but no assistance from Spurn was forthcoming. So the schooner had to float off unaided, and she reached port safely. The subsequent enquiry found that the lifeboat had launched but been unable to reach the schooner due to the bad weather, but the dismissal of Davey suggests that he had not proved to be a particularly capable Master. His place was taken by Robert Brown, a Master Mariner, who was appointed on 25 February 1843, and took up his post the following month. He served until 1 November 1848, when he resigned, and was replaced by Michael Welburn.

The 1840s and 1850s were a time of great hardship for the Spurn lifeboatmen. Their income was badly affected by the decline in the gravel trade, and the difficulties of living at Spurn were exacerbated by the peninsula being broken and damaged by the action of the sea, often leaving the lifeboat station on an isolated island at the mouth of the estuary. On many occasions the Master wrote to Trinity House asking for relief, explaining the plight of the crews and himself, but the Brethren of Trinity House would not entertain an increase in pay. Many weeks went by with no earnings of any kind at all for the crews, with families often going hungry. Unsurprisingly, many left in search of better conditions.

However, despite the difficulties, the lifeboat crews continued the work of sea rescue and were ready whenever they might be needed. They were involved in a very difficult incident on 24 October 1850 when the brig *Cumberland* came ashore in very heavy seas, off Kilnsea, nearly four miles north of Spurn Point. The lifeboatmen went by land to the scene and, using rockets fired from the shore, succeeded in getting a line aboard. Using this in conjunction with the tender used to reach the lifeboat when she was at moorings which they had taken to the scene, they made several attempts to reach the shipwrecked crew. Initially they were unable to reach the ship because of the heavy seas, but on the fifth attempt they succeeded in getting alongside and got five of the crew off.

A sixth attempt failed, but, undeterred, the lifeboatmen tried again. However, on the next attempt to reach the brig, the small tender capsized and the three on board, Master Michael Welburn, the Mate, John Welburn, and one of the crew, John Branton, were thrown into the sea. The two Welburns managed to swim ashore, although John was injured, but Branton was drowned in the incident. As the tender was washed away, the other lifeboatmen took a small boat from a fishing smack on the beach and, using this, succeeded in saving the remaining nine members of the brig's crew. A public subscription was later set up to help Branton's widow and his five children, with the national body, the Royal National Lifeboat Institution, contributing £5 to the total of £42 11s 6d. In March 1852 John Welburn also died from the injuries he received during this service.

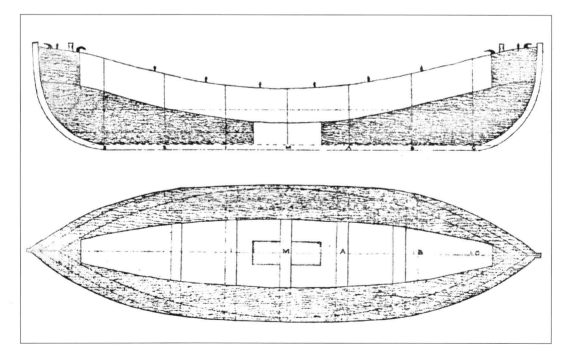

Plan of the lifeboat built for Spurn in 1853. The boat was 31ft in length, and was similar in design to the lifeboats then being built by the Royal National Lifeboat Institution.

On 7 August 1852 Trinity House decided to have a new lifeboat built for Spurn, as the old one was showing signs of deterioration, while at the same time the RNLI had developed a new design of self-righting lifeboat which saw widespread use and probably influenced the Brethren's decision to acquire a new boat. In July 1853 Edward Wilson, secretary of Trinity House, invited tenders from boatbuilders for the new lifeboat and several were subsequently received, resulting in an order being placed with the local yard of Hallett & Co. The new boat was 31ft in length, 9ft 4in in beam, and, unlike the previous two Spurn lifeboats, was a self-righter. She cost £112 18s 6d to build and arrived on station early in 1854, although the exact date is not recorded.

Three launches by the new lifeboat in 1855 demonstrated how difficult the Spurn lifeboat crew's work was, as they resulted in the boat being badly damaged and the loss of two lifeboatmen. The first of the three launches took place on 30 October 1855, when the lifeboat went to a barque, which was aground on the Inner Binks. The lifeboat was repeatedly filled during her passage to the sandbank, and as the boat went alongside the casualty, two oars were broken and some of her fenders were lost. The lifeboat crew went aboard the barque to help with bailing, and stayed on board throughout the night and into the following day to assist the crew, until the casualty had drifted ashore.

But the damaged lifeboat was not initially repaired, and less than a week later, on 5 November 1855, she went out again on service. She launched to the assistance of another barque in extremely heavy seas, and during the service one of the lifeboatmen, Thomas Holmes, was twice washed out of the boat but was hauled back aboard each time by his colleagues. Two weeks later, the lifeboat was called out again, launching on 19 November 1855 to the schooner *Zabina*, which had gone aground on The Binks, and on this occasion lives were lost. The lifeboat reached the stranded vessel and tied up astern of her, with all but two of the lifeboatmen going on board to help lighten her in an attempt to get her refloated. However, in the heavy seas that were running, the lifeboat capsized and the two lifeboatmen left on board, Henry Holmes and John Combes, were drowned. The crew got *Zabina* off The Binks and took her into Grimsby, while the fishing coble *York*, of Filey, towed the damaged lifeboat to the same port.

In the aftermath of the disaster, a public subscription was set up for Henry Holmes' widow, which raised £33 2s 6d, with a further £10 received from the RNLI and the Admiralty granting Mrs Holmes £10 on 12 January 1856. The lifeboat was inspected on 20 November 1855 by James Todd, the Trinity House buoy master, having been found 'laying bottom up on the White Chalk Stones, just below Grimsby Piers', very badly damaged. She was turned over the next day and taken to Hull for repairs, after which she was returned to Spurn to continue in service.

Life at Spurn remained very difficult for the lifeboat crew and Trinity House often had some difficulty in recruiting enough men to live there and form a full crew. Advertisements were placed in the local newspapers for men to fill the vacancies, and in about 1856 the number of crew had to be reduced from twelve to ten in response to the difficulty in finding sufficient men. However, life for the crew was improved in 1858 when new cottages were built, to the west of the lighthouse, by Ellis & Johnson, of Grimsby, at a total cost of £1,300. At the same time, at the request of William Willis, who had been appointed as Master in August 1857, a lookout tower was built with a bell to summon the crew when they were required. A new boathouse was also built, as the lifeboat, although usually kept afloat during the winter months, was brought ashore during the summer and keeping her under cover was desirable.

William Willis served as Master until 1865, when he was appointed keeper of the Killingholme lighthouse. The Mate, Fewson Hopper, was promoted to Master in Willis' place. Hopper remained until December 1877 when he was appointed keeper of the Saltend lighthouse, and his place as Master was taken by Thomas Winson, formerly the Mate. During the 1850s and 1860s, the crewmen were each paid £1 10s a month by Trinity House, which had also devised a scheme whereby they could supplement this with earnings from fishing in a smack provided for them. The crew earned extra money from driving piles for groynes to protect the cottages and lighthouse, and with the new cottages, which were occupied from early in 1858, and a reasonable income, the crew were more settled than at any time hitherto.

A painting showing the Trinity House lifeboat on service to a wrecked vessel hanging in the lifeboat crew room. In December 1850 Hull Trinity House stated that their lifeboat at Spurn Point had saved 729 lives since 1810. However, this painting is somewhat incongruous in that the cottages were built in 1858, and the lighthouse was never dark in colour.

The ten cottages built in 1858 for the lifeboat families were to the design of W. Foale. The Master's house was at one end of the row, the Mate's at the other, with the eight crewmen in between. The cottages remained in use until 1975, when they were demolished after new houses had been built. (By courtesy of RNLI)

One of the Trinity House lifeboats, probably the 32ft 6in non-self-righter built at Hull in 1881 which served at Spurn for twenty years. (By courtesy of Jan Crowther)

The work of sea rescue continued, though, and a particularly fine rescue was performed on Christmas Eve 1876 when the lifeboat was launched to the sloop *Grace Darling*, of Hull, which was wrecked in very heavy seas and an easterly gale on the Middle Binks. The lifeboat was towed part of the way to the scene by a pilot cutter, and then by the ship *Swanland*. The lifeboat got close enough to rescue two men, but the master of the sloop was clinging to the rigging and unable to let go. His hands were frozen in the bitterly cold wind and driving snow. One of the lifeboatmen, Edward Wheldrake, managed to get aboard the sloop, taking a line with him and, as heavy seas swept over the stricken vessel, succeeded in reaching the master. He helped him down from the rigging and into the lifeboat, which landed the survivors at Spurn. For his great courage during this rescue, Edward Wheldrake was awarded the RNLI's Silver medal.

The second Lifeboat Inn built at Spurn was made from the remains of the original cottages, and at this time James Hopper was the innkeeper. The income from running the Inn was used to supplement the keeper's Trinity House pay. (By courtesy of Jan Crowther)

In March 1881 Trinity House proposed that a new lifeboat be built for Spurn, and Thomas Winson responded to this proposal by saying that the crew at Spurn was 'very pleased that the old Boat is to be replaced by a new one'. In June tenders were invited from shipbuilders, and on 27 July the tender from John Edward Cooper, a boatbuilder based at Garrison Side, Hull, was accepted. The new lifeboat was a non-self-righter, 32ft 6in long, 9ft 8in in beam and rowing ten oars. She was copper fastened throughout, copper sheathed from the underside of the keel, and fitted with thirty copper air-cases. Built at a cost of £195, she arrived at Spurn in October 1881. The lifeboat of 1852 which was replaced had, according to a report by Trinity House in 1881, attended ninety-seven vessels in distress and saved seventy-seven lives since November 1854, giving the boat a respectable record of service.

During the winter of 1881/82, the new lifeboat was kept busy, and completed its first life-saving service on 18 December 1882, after which Winson reported that he was very pleased with its performance and capabilities. However, problems were encountered during the night of 11/12 December 1883 when, in severe westerly gales, she was almost lost. The strong winds whipped up extremely heavy seas, and the lifeboatmen stayed on watch throughout the night in case they were needed. However, no signals of distress were seen, but, as the storm eased at first light and the crew prepared to return home, they realised the lifeboat was missing. The boat had been at moorings, rather than in the boathouse, and during the night, with the storm raging and in the pitch dark, the moorings parted and it had been swept away. Fortunately, the old lifeboat was still in the boathouse and so was readied for possible use. As it turned out, she was not needed because, a few days later, the missing lifeboat was found by Dutch fishermen drifting off the island of Texel and she was towed to Nieu Dieppe in Holland. Arrangements

An unusual postcard showing the lighthouse and lifeboat at Spurn in the early years of the twentieth century. The lifeboat is the 1903-built craft, the last to be funded and built by Trinity House and taken over by the RNLI in 1911. The high light lighthouse depicted was built in 1895 and, although deactivated on 31 October 1985, remains standing as one of Spurn's more notable landmarks. The crab illustration was used on a number of postcards from this era, as crab fishing was one of the main occupations for local people. (From an old postcard in the Gordon Campbell Collection, by courtesy of the RNLI)

The lifeboat crew at Spurn Point, circa 1894, wearing cork life jackets similar to those used at the time by RNLI lifeboat crews. Robert Little, a crew member from 1894 to 1898, is on the left of the second row, but names of the other crew members are not known. The first life jackets were provided in November 1841, when Hull Trinity House bought twelve life-preservers for the crew from A. G. Carte at a total cost of £7 4s 0d. (Supplied by Mrs Tillott, by courtesy of Jan Crowther)

were made to bring the lifeboat back to Spurn and she was brought back on board the steamship *European*. Arriving at Hull on 7 January 1884, the lifeboat had a complete overhaul, including the fitting of a new rudder, and was then towed back to Spurn Point to resume service.

Four years later, in January 1888, during another severe storm, a similar incident resulted in the small tender, used to reach the lifeboat, breaking from her moorings. The small boat was washed out to sea in strong winds and eventually came ashore near Great Yarmouth. It was so badly damaged that it was beyond economical repair and so a new craft was ordered in February, 21ft long by 7ft 6in broad, from Lewis Emery, of Sheringham, at a cost of £21. The tender was delivered on 23 May 1888.

The lifeboat continued to undertake rescues throughout this time, and was successful in helping many vessels that got into difficulty, although no outstanding services were undertaken. In February 1894 Thomas Winson resigned as master of the lifeboat, and was succeeded initially by his son, Thomas Charles Winson, who the outgoing Coxswain recommended serve as his replacement. However, this caused outrage amongst the other crew members, who opposed the appointment from the outset. They argued that as the younger Winson had only been on the crew for two years he lacked the necessary experience, and in a letter sent to Trinity House they stated that 'no man of the crew has any confidence in him whatsoever in such a position of trust'. The post was therefore advertised, and David Pye, a fisherman from Easington, was subsequently appointed at a salary of £80 per annum. The Mate received £52 per annum, and each member of the crew 13s per week, out of which they had to pay one shilling a month in rent for their cottage.

David Pye took up his post in March 1894 having spent twelve years fishing in the vicinity of Spurn, and also serving on the Withernsea lifeboat. Pye remained in the post until July 1912, during which time

The Grimsby lifeboat Manchester Unity was loaned to Spurn for a few weeks in 1901 before the RNLI actually took over the station. This lifeboat was built in 1890 and served at Harwich for a year before coming to Grimsby in 1893. She was broken up in 1904. (By courtesy of Mike Welton)

considerable changes took place at the station. In 1897 the RNLI proposed the stationing of a steam lifeboat in the Humber and discussed the matter with the Board of Trinity House. Although Spurn was the ideal location for such a boat, Grimsby had better facilities for accommodation of crew members, firemen and supplies of coal, oil and water, so that was where the boat was located. Ordered in January 1898, *James Stevens No.3*, the fourth steam lifeboat to be built, was one of two screw-powered steam lifeboats built by J. S. White at Cowes. She arrived at Grimsby in October 1898, but spent less than five years there, as she was seldom called upon and only answered six calls, suggesting that the lifeboat to cover the Humber estuary had to be based at Spurn, which was closer to most of the casualties.

Some of the lifeboat crew outside the lookout building, circa 1900. The first wooden hut, which was built on top of the dune ridge and equipped with a bell to summon the crew, lasted until 1884 when it was destroyed in a storm. Its replacement was this hut, a larger building set on piles. Among those pictured are George (Dod) Hopper, second from right. His grandfather, Fewson Hopper, and father, William Fewson Hopper, were lifeboatmen at Spurn, and George became a member of the crew in the 1930s. (J. Collins, by courtesy of Jan Crowther)

The Spurn lifeboat crew standing by the 1902-built lifeboat on the beach in front of the cottages. This is one of the few images from the pre-RNLI era showing the Trinity House lifeboat. The boat, which has the words 'Trinity House Hull' on her bow, arrived at Spurn on 1 January 1903 but was beset with problems during its short career, particularly with corrosion of the copper sheathing and some of the water discharge pipes. The crew at that time were David Pye, William Hogg, David Craske, George Stephenson, Richard Major, William Curtis, Frank Raspin, Robert Cross, George Liversedge and one other, but the order of them in the photo is not known. (By courtesy of RNLI)

While the RNLI were engaged, only partially successfully, in pursuing steam-powered lifeboats at Grimsby and elsewhere, by the turn of the century the Spurn lifeboat was starting to show her age and in January 1901 it was reported that she was in need of urgent repairs. When the steam lifeboat at Grimsby became operational, the pulling and sailing lifeboat *Manchester Unity*, which had been stationed there, was withdrawn from service. She left in October 1900 and then the RNLI agreed to loan this lifeboat to Hull Trinity House, 'for use at Spurn while their own lifeboat is away being repaired'. This lifeboat, which had been built in 1890, only spent two weeks at Spurn, from the end of January to 8 February 1901, before being returned to the RNLI. She was not called on while at Spurn, and once the Spurn lifeboat had been repaired and returned to her station, *Manchester Unity* was taken away.

Although the 1881-built lifeboat had been successfully repaired, a replacement boat was still needed. David Pye wrote to Trinity House in January 1902 explaining that a new lifeboat was urgently required as the repaired boat 'cannot clear herself of water in a fresh breeze', and, if called on in a gale, he added 'I shall not be surprised at the crew refusing to go in her.' Trinity House therefore began the process of inviting tenders for a new lifeboat, and an order was placed with Earle's Shipbuilding and Engineering Co. of Hull, for a new boat. The boat, which cost £700 to build, was delivered to Spurn on 3 January 1903 and was another non-self-righter, measuring 34ft 6in by 9ft 10in, fitted with water ballast and two masts with sails. This lifeboat continued the work of rescue off Spurn for a further five years, at which point the station's operation underwent major changes which ultimately lead to the RNLI taking over.

The RNLI Takes Over

T he lifeboat built in 1902, which entered service the following year, remained under the control of Trinity House until 1 January 1908, operating as her predecessors had done, with similar manning arrangements. Then the Humber Conservancy Board, a body constituted by the Humber Conservancy Act of 1907, assumed responsibility for the navigation and pilotage of the Humber Estuary, taking over these duties from Trinity House. As a result, the Board became responsible for the lifeboat, its maintenance and operation, as well as the crew. However, the Board's involvement lasted just three years, and these proved to be years of bitter wrangling and arguing.

When the Humber Conservancy Board was created, its members assessed what was involved in the management, and found that included amongst their responsibilities was the lifeboat station. As soon as they realised that the station was manned by a full-time crew, the members of which had to be paid, they became determined to rid themselves of it and the associated responsibilities for maintenance and upkeep as soon as possible. It cost about £480 a year to maintain the station, money which the Board believed it should not be spending on what was perceived to be a 'philanthropic object'. The members of the Board, led by Chairman W. S. Wright, argued that the lifeboat was not necessary, it should not be under their remit, and that the RNLI was the natural body to operate such an establishment.

So the RNLI was immediately approached and asked in 1908 whether it would take over the station. But they refused to get involved, partly because having a paid full-time crew, rather than a volunteer one like at all the other RNLI-operated lifeboat stations round the country, was against their charter. They seemed to agree with the Board that paying a crew was unnecessary. Such attitudes on the part of both the Conservancy Board and the RNLI suggest that neither organisation appreciated or understood the nature of Spurn Point, the isolation and remoteness of which meant that full-time paid crew was the only viable option for operating the lifeboat.

Discussions between the Conservancy Board and the RNLI continued for the best part of three years, throughout which the Board continually threatened to close the station. In 1910 the Board sent notice to the crew to leave their cottages, together with termination of their employment as lifeboat crew members. Although the Board had continued, albeit reluctantly, to pay their wages, the crew's situation had been made extremely difficult through no fault of their own, and brought considerable anxiety to them and their families. But despite the instability of their position, to their great credit they continued the work of life-saving, performing a number of rescues during this time.

With the Conservancy Board threatening to close the station, the Board of Trade became involved in the situation, and eventually managed to persuade the RNLI to agree a take-over. The decision was reached at a meeting of the Institution's Committee of Management on 9 February 1911, and Thomas Holmes, Chief Inspector of Lifeboats, visited Spurn on 23 March 1911 to meet the crew. He agreed new contracts with them so that they would serve under the RNLI from 1 May, when the take-over was

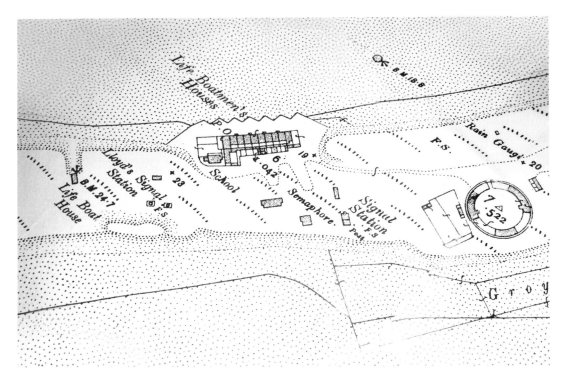

A map from 1910 showing some of the buildings at the end of the Spurn peninsula, including the lifeboat crew's cottages and a lifeboat house. Exactly when this lifeboat house was built is uncertain, but it could be the one of 1854 which Trinity House funded. By the time of this map, it might have been used to house a boarding boat.

formalised. And so, on that date, the Institution became responsible for the station, ending more than a century of independent operation, and three years of bitter arguing and unnecessary disagreements over the station's running, manning and funding.

The RNLI immediately looked at improving the station's facilities, and by the end of 1911 plans for the construction of a new boathouse and roller slipway were being made. The new building was intended to house a new motor lifeboat, which could be launched easily and quickly into the river. However, although in 1913 a new motor boat was allocated to the station following the District Inspector's recommendation that such a craft was needed at Spurn, its construction was considerably delayed by the First World War, as was the erection of the planned boathouse. The RNLI had first introduced motor power to the lifeboat fleet in 1904, and as experience and knowledge of motor lifeboats were gained during the following decade, more motor lifeboats were ordered. In February 1914 the RNLI announced that nineteen motor lifeboats were in service, and four new ones have been ordered for Arklow, Fraserburgh, Teesmouth, and Sunderland. New motor boats had also been approved for St Mary's, Scilly, Baltimore, Spurn, Blyth, and the Lizard. However, the war intervened in these plans, and many stations, including Spurn, were forced to wait before their new motor craft was ready.

As a result of the delay, the 1902-built boat remained in service. She carried out her first rescue under RNLI auspices on the evening of 12 January 1912 after the steam trawler *Agatha*, of Grimsby, ran aground on The Binks in heavy seas and an easterly gale. The lifeboat launched at 9.45 p.m. and the crew found the trawler full of water, with heavy seas breaking over her. Coxswain David Pye took the lifeboat alongside the casualty, the trawler's nine crew were rescued and landed at midnight.

When the RNLI took over, David Pye, who had been Coxswain since March 1894, was placed in full charge of the administrative duties of the station by the Institution, which recognised that this position was crucial to the operations of such a remote station. When he resigned as Coxswain in July 1912, having overseen one of the most difficult periods in the station's history, he was succeeded the following month by Robert Cross, who was appointed as Superintendent Coxswain and went on to become one of the most famous lifeboatmen in the RNLI's history. The additional title of Superintendent was given to the Spurn Coxswains, because, unlike at other stations, no Honorary Secretary was in post to undertake administrative duties, which thus became the Coxswain's responsibility.

Cross had first joined the crew on 11 October 1902, but left six years later after buying a share in a local herring drifter. But in 1909 he had gone out as crew in the Flamborough lifeboat to assist several cobles caught in a sudden gale. In the terrible conditions, two cobles and their crews were lost and among those who drowned were Cross's brother and the brother's two sons. As a result, Cross decided to devote himself to service in the lifeboats and so, when the post of Coxswain at Spurn became vacant in 1912, he applied. Once appointed to the post, he sold his fishing boat and moved to Spurn. His appointment was welcomed by the crew, who felt that he was one of them, with all the necessary leadership qualities.

One of the earliest rescues in which Cross was involved as Coxswain took place on 13 January 1913, when the lifeboat launched to the assistance of a vessel which had been heard signalling for help. In dense fog, a prolonged search was undertaken by the lifeboat, but the casualty could not be found and so the lifeboat crew returned to Spurn at 5 p.m. When the fog lifted, however, the lifeboatmen spotted the vessel and put out again to find the steam trawler *Cancer*, of Grimsby. She was not in fact aground, but she required a tug, as she had lost her propeller while homeward bound from Iceland with her holds full of fish. The lifeboat stood by until the trawler was safely anchored and then returned to Spurn. A tug subsequently went to the trawler and towed it safely to port.

In July 1913, although a motor lifeboat had been ordered for the station, the RNLI supplied a reserve lifeboat as a temporary measure to replace the Trinity House-funded boat of 1902. The reserve boat was

The Spurn lifeboat and her crew in 1909, just before the RNLI took over the station. The crew at this time were David Pye, Frederick Hopper, William Curtis, Frank Raspin, William Holborn, James Bishop, William Hopper, Richard Major, George Curtis and Thomas Blythe, but the order of them in this photo is not known. (J. Collins, by courtesy of Jan Crowther)

the former St Agnes lifeboat *Charles Deere James*, a 38ft Liverpool non-self-righting sailing lifeboat built in 1903 by Thames Iron Works and which had been designated Reserve No.9 by the RNLI for her stint in the Reserve Fleet. She stayed at Spurn much longer than was originally intended because of the delays in building the new motor lifeboat, but gave good service in and around the Humber, launching more than thirty times on service during her six years at the station. She was well liked by her crew and, according to Coxswain Cross, 'was in every way superior to the old [boat]'.

The first service undertaken after *Charles Deere James* arrived involved the boarding boat rather than the lifeboat herself and it was a somewhat routine affair. At 7.30 a.m. on 8 December 1913 , during a dense fog, the watchman reported that a vessel was ashore on the beach, a mile to the east. The crew immediately assembled and took the boarding boat out to help the motor fishing boat *Pat*, of Grimsby, which was bound for the fishing grounds. The vessel was refloated with the assistance of the lifeboat crew, and she then made her way back to Grimsby unaided. *Charles Deere James'* first actual service was on 7 February 1914, when she launched to the steamship *Belvenie*, of Glasgow, which had stranded on the Inner Binks, while outward bound from Grimsby to Grangemouth with a cargo of pig iron. *Charles Deere James* was launched at 6 a.m. and, with the weather worsening, stood by the steamer until she refloated at 1 p.m. The vessel then proceeded on her way, by which time a moderate gale was blowing. Her Captain later sent a letter of appreciation to the lifeboatmen for their help.

At 8 p.m. on 25 March 1914 *Charles Deere James* launched within ten minutes of the Bull lightvessel firing rockets. On reaching the lightvessel, the lifeboatmen were informed of a collision between the

Spurn lifeboatmen of circa 1890-1 wearing cork life jackets standing with the 1881-built lifeboat. The crew in this photo are Coxswain Thomas Winson, William Bacchus, Seaman Davinson, James Bishop, Francis Day, John Spauls, Edward Curtis, Thomas Jarratt, and Joseph Norman. Thomas Jarratt is on the back row, second from the right, and Coxswain Winson is at the front on the left, but of the others, who is who is not known. (By courtesy of the RNLI)

Spurn lifeboatmen on the sail-powered bogie which was used to travel along the peninsula until the mid-1930s. The sail trolleys and bogies, often constructed by the lifeboatmen, were informal vehicles with the railway mainly used by, firstly, steam engines and later railcars. The line was closed in 1951, with the military using it in the Second World War. (By courtesy of the RNLI)

Norwegian steamer *Norris*, which had been outward bound, and the brigantine *Jean Anderson*, of Hull, with a crew of six, which was bound from London to Hull with a cargo of lubricating oil. The collision had occurred quite close to the lightvessel, and one of the vessels involved had actually come into contact with the lightship, although was little damaged as a result. Coxswain Cross proceeded to the brigantine, which had badly damaged bows and was rapidly taking on water, and the captain asked the lifeboat to stand by. Four lifeboatmen were transferred across to help with the pumps, while the lifeboat stood by. A towline was then rigged between the brigantine and *Norris*, which towed the brigantine slowly towards Grimsby. A tug met them in the estuary and took over the tow to Hull. The four lifeboatmen stayed on the brigantine until she had been safely berthed, while the lifeboat returned to Spurn.

On several occasions the lifeboat crew used the small boarding boat to effect a rescue when necessary, as was the case on 9 September 1914 after the sloop *Chesterfield*, of Kings Lynn, stranded on the Inner Binks, while bound for Hull with a cargo of gravel. The lifeboatmen launched the boarding boat at 5.50 p.m. and proceeded to the casualty, which had waves breaking over her and was rapidly filling with water when the boarding boat reached the scene. Coxswain Cross realised the urgency of the situation and so the sloop's three crew were immediately taken off and landed at Spurn. The sloop subsequently broke up, becoming a total wreck within hours.

After standing by the schooner *Union*, of Portsmouth, which had run aground on the Middle Binks, in heavy seas and south-easterly gale on 29 October 1914, and then standing by the steamship *Elantsobe*, of Bilbao, which went aground on the Middle Binks during the night of 2/3 December 1914, the lifeboat was called out at 1.15 p.m. on 15 February 1915 to help the Government steamer *CT8*, which had run aground a mile north-west of Donna Nook. The lifeboat crew stood by and assisted in trying to get the vessel afloat, but it remained aground so the lifeboat returned to station.

During December 1915 the lifeboat was called out no fewer than five times. On 3 December she helped to refloat the steamship *Freidig*, of Bergen, which had stranded on the Middle Binks and, on 6 and 7 December went to the steamship *Lady Ann*, of Sunderland, and eventually helped to refloat her. On 9 December she went to the steamship *Florence*, of Stockton, a rescue which is described in detail below, and the final service of the month took place on 10 December and lasted for ten days. The lifeboat went to the steamer *Minsk*, of Copenhagen, which had been abandoned after hitting a mine. The lifeboat crew and others tried to save the vessel, with the lifeboat standing by in case she was needed during the salvage work. The prolonged efforts proved to be successful, and the vessel was eventually towed into safety.

The outstanding service of the month, and indeed the most notable rescue carried out in *Charles Deere James*, took place on 9 December 1915. During the evening the steamship *Florence* went aground on the Middle Binks in a heavy gale with terrible seas running across the sands. The lifeboat was launched at 11.15 p.m. and her crew battled their way out to the casualty. Although Coxswain Cross took the lifeboat as close as he could to the casualty, she ran aground on the sands some distance away. The waves were already breaking over the stranded steamer as her crew shouted for help. The only option was for a lifeboatman to go overboard and take a line across the sands to the casualty. Despite the bitter cold and intense darkness, Coxswain Cross himself jumped overboard, taking a line with him and struggled through the water, over the sands, towards *Florence*. But the heavy seas prevented him from reaching her and so the lifeboatmen hauled him back to the lifeboat. He asked for a volunteer to go with him onto the sandbank and pay out the line while he made another attempt and G. Martin, inspired by the Coxswain's example, volunteered to assist. So the two men set off into the dark, wading towards the steamer.

This time, Coxswain Cross succeeded in getting close enough to throw a line up to the shipwrecked men. The two lifeboatmen, standing on the sands and at times completely covered by water, helped the eight crew from the steamer get into the lifeboat. When they were all safely aboard, and the two lifeboatmen had also climbed on board, the lifeboat returned to station, reaching Spurn in the early hours of the following day. The RNLI's account of this rescue concluded that 'the splendid behaviour of Robert Cross met with commendation on every side, and the Captain of the vessel described his action as heroic [and] ... stated that he and his crew could not speak too highly of the bravery and self-sacrifice of the Life-boat's crew'. For the outstanding bravery and courage demonstrated during this rescue, Coxswain Cross was awarded the Silver medal by the RNLI and a special monetary award was made to lifeboatman Martin, with the other lifeboat crew members getting additional monetary awards.

Of the four services undertaken during 1918, the final year that *Charles Deere James* was at Spurn, two were completed using the boarding boat. On 29 January 1918 the lifeboat went to the aid of the steam trawler *Crystal*, of Hull, which was stranded on the Inner Binks and stood by until the vessel refloated seven hours later. The boarding boat was used on 5 July 1918 to help the smack *Amy King*, which had sprung a leak just off Spurn and had to be beached to prevent her sinking. Less than two weeks later the boarding boat was again in action, being used to help a seaplane which had nose-dived into the sea and stuck in the mud. The boat was used to take off the plane's two occupants.

What proved to be the last service by *Charles Deere James* at Spurn took place on 6 October 1918. She was launched at 10 a.m. to help the schooner *Amy*, of Newcastle, with its five crew, after the vessel had gone aground on the Trinity Sands. Heavy seas were breaking over the schooner when the lifeboatmen reached the scene. They battled against a strong westerly gale, standing by until the tide rose and then, with assistance from a tug and the lifeboatmen, the schooner refloated and was towed into port. In 1919 *Charles Deere James* left Spurn and served briefly at the Winterton No.2 station in Norfolk and then as a Reserve lifeboat, until being sold out of service in 1927.

The First Motor Lifeboat

S oon after the RNLI took over at Spurn, they planned to send a motor lifeboat to the station. At a Committee of Management meeting on 8 May 1913 the Deputy Chief Inspector proposed an 'improvement of the lifeboat service near the entrance to the Humber', and the Committee approved his recommendation that 'a powerful Motor Lifeboat be stationed at Spurn'. The boat allocated to the station was a 40ft Watson-class non-self-righting type, fitted with a single 40bhp Tylor C2 petrol engine, which gave a top speed of seven and a half knots. However, the outbreak of war a year after the new lifeboat had been ordered considerably delayed the boat's arrival at Spurn, and not until 1919, after hostilities had ceased, was the boat ready. The delay was caused largely because the boatyard initially instructed to undertake the building work, Summers & Payne, went out of business during the early stages of construction, and so the boat had to be finished by S. E. Saunders at Cowes.

A further delay was caused when an explosion took place on board the boat on 10 January 1919. She was in a shed at Saunders' Cornubia Yard awaiting completion after trials, and was being filled with water to test the deck, when the explosion occurred. Three men were on board at the time, but fortunately none were seriously hurt, and afterwards they stated that they had no indication of anything unusual happening prior to the explosion. Although the explosion badly damaged the deck, the engine was undamaged. The exact cause of the explosion could not be determined, although it was thought that some petrol had been spilled on the deck when filling up the tanks and this may have ignited. Repairs were immediately put in hand, but these took several more months to complete, and not until November 1919 was the boat ready to go to her station.

The problems experienced with *Samuel Oakes* were typical of the many difficulties the RNLI had to surmount to successfully operate motor lifeboats, with war and explosions almost the least of their worries. Although the first powered lifeboat had been introduced in 1904, during the second decade of the twentieth century motor lifeboats were still very much at the experimental stage and the Institution's technical and design staff had much to learn. Numerous technical problems had to be overcome to successfully operate an engine on board a lifeboat, including keeping the engine dry even in the event of a capsize, ensuring it was totally reliable both when starting and when running, and providing the propellers with protection from damage when in the water. But as the problems were gradually surmounted, lifeboats powered by the internal combustion engine began to be built in significant numbers and they pointed the way ahead. The motor lifeboat offered considerable advantages over its pulling and sailing counterpart, not least of which was its far greater range, something that would be particularly beneficial at Spurn Point, and the stationing of a motor lifeboat at the mouth of the Humber was something of a priority for the RNLI as they planned for the future of the station, newly under their control. The new boat eventually got to the station in December 1919, after a passage from Cowes under her own power during which the engine broke down a number of times due to its 'faulty installation'.

The lifeboat house and slipway under construction in 1923 ready for the station's second motor lifeboat. (A. Eldon, by courtesy of Jan Crowther)

Built at a cost of £7,156, the new lifeboat was provided out of a legacy from the late Mrs Elizabeth Mary Laing, of Barnes, in London, and was named *Samuel Oakes*. One of the earliest motor lifeboats on the east coast, with others stationed at Tynemouth, Teesmouth and Seaham Harbour, she stayed at Spurn for just four years, during which time she saved twenty-five lives. The first service she performed took place on 16 December 1919, when she launched to the steam trawler *Prince Victor*, of Grimsby, which had gone ashore off Kilnsea. She stood by the trawler, which had seas breaking over her, until after high water, at which point the vessel floated off safely and the lifeboat returned to station.

Although a new motor lifeboat was at Spurn, problems with crewing at the station were experienced at about this time. In 1918 the crew was short after vacancies could not be filled, and in July 1918 the Coxswain was given permission to take the lifeboat out with reduced crew if necessary. The problems did not improve, and in January 1919 the station was temporarily closed after the Second Coxswain and five of the crew left Spurn because of a reduction in their wages caused by the removal of the war bonus, which had been raised 25 per cent in view of the fishing restrictions imposed during the conflict. The matter was referred to the RNLI's Special Salaries Sub Committee and in February 1919 the crew were offered £130 per annum. This proved to be acceptable and in April 1919 the station reopened.

During 1920 and 1921 the new motor lifeboat undertook a number of services and 1920 was her busiest year, during which she performed her first life-saving service. On 18 May 1920 she went out late at night to the ketch *Wellington*, of London, bound from the capital to Newcastle, which was in distress on the Middle Binks. The lifeboat battled through very heavy seas and gale-force south-westerly winds and found the stranded vessel with 'the seas making a clean breach over her, and her position ... dangerous'. Once on scene, with Coxswain Cross at the helm, the lifeboat was taken alongside and the ketch's crew of three were saved, with great difficulty in the severe conditions. At dawn the next day the ketch floated clear of the sandbank so the lifeboat went out again, and several lifeboatmen went aboard to move the ketch to a safe anchorage. Later that same day, the lifeboat went out to the ketch for a third time to take the three rescued men back to their ship. As the weather was steadily improving by this time, they were able to weigh anchor and the ship proceeded on her way north to Newcastle.

Amongst the routine services undertaken by *Samuel Oakes* during the early 1920s, the lifeboat and her crew were severely tested on 3 December 1920. She launched at 8.30 a.m. that day to go to the aid of the schooner *Julia Maria*, of Riga, which had gone ashore at Kilnsea in a westerly gale. The sea was so heavy that attempts by two motor fishing vessels to tow the casualty had failed. The lifeboat arrived on the scene, and after Coxswain Cross had assessed the situation, he alerted the tug *Condor*, which was nearby, and requested assistance. A tow was rigged but the cable soon parted and the tug made for shelter. Another tug, *Lynx*, then came to the aid of the casualty, and towed *Julia Maria* towards the Humber. The lifeboat stood by until 3 p.m., and then headed back to Spurn. But when she reached the moorings, the crew was found it impossible to moor the boat as the sea was so rough, while the boarding boat had sunk. So the lifeboat put out again and made for Grimsby, arriving there at 8 p.m. with the crew drenched to the skin and numb with the cold. They remained at Grimsby overnight, and while they were away, their wives salvaged the boarding boat, which had been swamped, and made it usable again. A Letter of Appreciation, as well as a payment of 10s each, was sent to the women by the RNLI in appreciation of their efforts.

Despite only serving at Spurn for four years, *Samuel Oakes* was involved in a good number of services. The most difficult was that undertaken on 18 October 1922, when she put out in an easterly gale that had inflicted much damage on Yorkshire's coastal settlements. With heavy seas accompanied by rain squalls and hail, and in bitterly cold conditions, two vessels had gone aground on The Binks. Huge seas were breaking over the sandbanks, but *Samuel Oakes* was launched and headed towards the nearer of the two casualties, a fishing vessel. By the time the lifeboat was on scene, however, the vessel had sunk and only her mast remained above the waves with her crew, clinging desperately for their lives to the rigging, shouting for help. Violent seas were breaking over the sandbanks, lifting the fishing vessel and then smashing it down onto the bank. The lifeboatmen later said that it was the worst conditions they had seen on The Binks and made their task of rescue particularly difficult. Cross manoeuvred the lifeboat towards the shipwrecked men, but just as the lifeboat approached the casualty, an enormous wave struck her, pushing her forward and against the submerged fishing vessel. The next wave then lifted the lifeboat right over the sunken hull, and away from the stranded fishermen.

The first motor lifeboat at Spurn Point was the 40ft Watson Samuel Oakes, which served from 1919 to 1923, and was powered by a single 40hp Tylor petrol engine. She was replaced by a larger and more powerful lifeboat, and was transferred to Weymouth. (By courtesy of the RNLI)

The survivors had lashed themselves to the rigging so that they would not be washed overboard, but as a result they could not jump into the lifeboat as she passed the submerged hull. By this point, the lifeboat was herself in heavy broken seas, full of water and the lifeboatmen were having to cling to the boat's mast and rigging so that they were not washed overboard. Before Cross had brought the lifeboat into position to make another approach from leeward, the fishing vessel's mast crashed down into the sea, taking the survivors with it. Despite a thorough search, the lifeboatmen saw no sign of the men or of any wreckage. Coxswain Cross took the lifeboat south, towards the second casualty, the steam trawler *Mafeking*, of Hull. However, she had been abandoned and, it was later learned, her crew had taken to the ship's boats and been picked up safely by a pilot cutter. The lifeboat returned to station at 2.10 a.m., but put to sea again at first light to search the area in case any fishermen had survived, but nothing more was found.

This extremely difficult and dangerous service had been carried out with great courage and determination by every member of the lifeboat's crew, and for his outstanding skill and tremendous courage, Coxswain Robert Cross was awarded a Bronze medal by the RNLI. The Institution's Thanks on Vellum was accorded to each of the other members of the crew. They were Second Coxswain F. S. Kendall, Bowman G. W. Martin, Mechanic W. A. Neal and crew members G. M. Crimlisk, W. J. T. Hood, C. Robinson, W. A. Lewis, W. R. Jenkinson and C. H. Howes.

A more routine but nevertheless challenging service was undertaken on 6 December 1922. *Samuel Oakes* launched at 12.50 p.m. to the schooner *Hosanna*, of Thurso, which was aground on the Middle Binks in a north-westerly gale. As the lifeboat reached the stranded vessel, the crew saw heavy seas crashing right over it, so Coxswain Cross took the lifeboat as close as he could and a line was thrown to the shipwrecked men. One by one the five crew were then hauled through the waves and onto the lifeboat, which landed them at Spurn. A little later, the schooner refloated so the lifeboat went out again, some of the lifeboatmen boarded her, and they managed to take the vessel to a safe anchorage.

When she was called out on 29 August 1923 *Samuel Oakes* was involved in a rescue notable for being the first occasion that the line-throwing gun was used on service. The equipment had been supplied about a month previously and was seen as a more effective way to get a line across to a stranded vessel than if thrown by a lifeboat crew. For the service on 29 August the lifeboat put to sea at 5 p.m. after the sloop

Launching Samuel Oakes from the boathouse at Spurn. The house was built for the motor lifeboat, and the slipway was altered during the 1920s, after Samuel Oakes had left the station. The two lighthouses can be seen in the background. (By courtesy of the RNLI)

The first motor lifeboat to serve at Spurn Point was Samuel Oakes, a 40ft Watson-class lifeboat built in 1919 and one of the RNLI's first motor lifeboats. (By courtesy of Jan Crowther)

Spring, of Hull, with three on board, had gone aground on the Inner Binks in heavy seas and a southerly gale. With huge waves sweeping the sloop, Coxswain Cross took the lifeboat to within fifty yards of the vessel but could get not get any closer because of the shallow water. Then, using the line-throwing gun, the lifeboat crew fired a rope to the sloop which enabled the lifeboat, eventually, to pull the vessel clear. According to the account in *The Lifeboat* journal for December 1923, 'In the opinion of the Coxswain, she [the sloop] could not have stood much longer the pounding of the seas, so that it was this prompt use of the Line-throwing Gun which saved the crew of three men ... and the vessel from destruction.'

Although *Samuel Oakes* was involved in a number of good rescues during her time at Spurn, she proved not to be the most reliable of boats, and in June 1920 the RNLI decided that a larger and more powerful lifeboat would be more suitable for the rigours of rescue work off the Humber. At the same time, having reached agreement with the Humber Conservancy Board on 28 January 1921, the Institution was at last able to proceed with the construction of a lifeboat house and slipway for the new boat.

Samuel Oakes was launched at 11.15 p.m. on 25 September 1923 for what proved to be her last effective service at Spurn. The steam trawler *Portsmouth*, of Grimsby, was seen aground on the Inner Binks, in rough seas and a near gale-force south-westerly wind. The casualty, with a crew of nine, had been homeward bound with her cargo of fish when she got into difficulties. The lifeboat was launched and the lifeboatmen helped to refloat the trawler, which was then taken to Grimsby.

After leaving Spurn Point in November 1923, *Samuel Oakes* was reallocated to Weymouth, where she served from May 1924 to July 1929, saving nine lives during that time. She then went to Shoreham Harbour, where she spent just over three years before being replaced by a newer motor lifeboat. At all the stations she served she was the first motor lifeboat to be operated, but she was never the best of lifeboats and experienced further problems in 1925 when an engine-room explosion caused damage to her hull, which although repaired had been weakened. She was sold in January 1933, after fourteen years with the RNLI, and was converted into the pleasure boat *Grey Gull* based in the South East. However, after several changes of owner, she became semi-derelict and her hull was burnt at Rochester in the 1980s.

The First City of Bradford

The new lifeboat allocated to Spurn to replace *Samuel Oakes* was a 45ft Watson non-self-righter, a larger and more powerful craft which the RNLI had decided to place at the station in 1920. The 45ft Watson was developed in the years after the First World War and was one of the RNLI's first standard motor types. Although later boats of the class had small cabins giving some measure of protection for the crew, the boat allocated to Spurn did not have a cabin and was essentially open, with end boxes at stem and stern, although in 1929 she was fitted with a rudimentary shelter. She was powered by a single 80bhp Weyburn DE6 petrol engine, which developed 796rpm to give a top speed of just over eight knots, and was equipped with a drop keel and full sailing rig in case the engine failed.

To accommodate the new boat, a boathouse and roller slipway were constructed to the south of the crew cottages, with the slipway facing the river, something the RNLI had been planning since taking over the station. Hitherto the lifeboats had been kept afloat and reached by boarding boat, which could be

Although somewhat blurred, this photograph gives a good idea of the layout the the first City of Bradford lifeboat to serve at Spurn, a single-engined 45ft Watson motor type. (Vera Cross, by courtesy of Jan Crowther)

The first City of Bradford being hauled up the roller slipway into the lifeboat house, which was built at Spurn Point in 1923 to improve launching arrangements at the station. The new house and winch were, like the lifeboat, funded by the Bradford Branch, which held a three-day bazaar to help raise the necessary funds. The event was opened by Lord Barnby, supported by George Shee, the RNLI Secretary, and the Archdeacon of Bradford. On the third day, Coxswain Robert Cross was to be presented with the Bar to his Silver medal for the rescue of the crew of the steamer Whinstone on 25 November 1925, but bad weather on the coast meant he could not leave the station to come and receive the award. (Vera Cross, by courtesy of Jan Crowther)

dangerous in rough weather and strong winds. The new building, completed in 1923, made it much easier and safer for the crew to board the lifeboat, which could then be launched quickly into the mouth of the river. The building was partly funded out of money raised by the RNLI's Wharfedale Branch, and the rest was raised by a special bazaar held in Bradford. This boathouse remained in use until 1977, when moorings were once again taken up in the river, and it was eventually demolished in 1995.

Built by J. S. White, of Cowes, at a cost of £12,758, the new lifeboat was provided out of funds raised in Bradford, and was the first of four Humber lifeboats funded by the Yorkshire city which served at Spurn between 1923 and 1987. The station enjoyed close affiliations with Bradford throughout this time, and the Bradford Branch saw the station as its own. One of the earliest involvements the Spurn lifeboatmen had with the city came on 30 May 1923, when they were invited to the city to form a guard of honour for HRH Prince of Wales during his visit. The lifeboat crew had travelled to Bradford the previous day and were met by the Lord Mayor and Lady Mayoress, as well as officials from the local branch. According to *The Lifeboat*, the Spurn crew 'played a prominent part in the welcome given to him, and were themselves warmly welcomed by the people of Bradford'.

A few months later, on 14 November 1923, the new lifeboat arrived at Spurn. Just before her arrival, however, she had been, unintentionally, involved in a special review of the Atlantic Fleet held at Spithead for the Dominion Prime Ministers attending the Imperial Conference. On the day of the review, *City of Bradford* was carrying out her trials, and her appearance among the Fleet was described in the *Yorkshire*

City of Bradford is formally named by Lady Priestley at the end of the boat's inauguration ceremony at Scarborough on 25 May 1924. (Vera Cross, by courtesy of Jan Crowther)

Evening Post: 'In the morning, as the *Princess Margaret* slowly steamed down the line of ships, there appeared on the starboard side a Motor Life-boat, her oil-skinned crew swept repeatedly by the dancing seas, the craft itself being almost smothered at times by the exuberant waters. Eventually, I made out her name. It was the Spurn Lifeboat, and on her side was painted *City of Bradford*. It is well that the people of the northern city who brought her into being should know that their Lifeboat is not afraid of the tempest.' A few days later *City of Bradford* arrived at Spurn Point after a passage up the east coast from Cowes to take up her duties as the new Humber lifeboat. In 1924 the RNLI's Committee of Management decided that the name of the station should be changed from Spurn to the Humber, to more accurately describe the station's scope of operation, and so *City of Bradford* became the first Humber lifeboat.

Because of the remoteness of the station at Spurn, the new lifeboat was officially named at Scarborough. The ceremony, held on 25 May 1924, was a double inauguration, with the new Scarborough lifeboat being named at the same time and thousands of supporters and well-wishers in attendance. A special train had been laid on to bring people from Bradford, and lifeboats from Whitby and Filey were also present. The Scarborough lifeboat *Herbert Joy* was christened first, being named by Mrs Alexander Joy, wife of the donor. For the Humber ceremony, the Rt Hon the Lord Mayor of Bradford Alderman H. M. Trotter, President of the Branch, presided, with Sir Henry Whitehead, a Vice-President of the Branch, speaking about Bradford's long connection with the lifeboat service and the fine record of the Bradford lifeboats at Ramsgate, which between them had saved nearly 900 lives. He also described how the present *City of Bradford* was the result of a visit by the Secretary of the Branch to the naming ceremony of the Whitby motor lifeboat, after which the Bradford Branch resolved that their city should provide a similar boat. Sir William Priestley, Chairman of the Branch, formally presented the boat to the Marquess of Graham, and said: 'We of Bradford seldom see the sea, but we can raise £10,000 in three years for a Life-boat, a proof that we have great imagination, and great sympathy with the magnificent men who are manning the boats.' After a Service of Dedication conducted by the Bishop of Bradford, the Right Rev Dr Perowne, the boat was named by Lady Priestley, wife of Sir William.

The first service by the new lifeboat took place on 6 July 1924, when she was launched at noon after a small boat, with three people on board, as seen drifting near the Haile Sands Fort. The lifeboat put out into moderate seas and a north-westerly gale and her crew began a search of the area. During the search, a small steamer off Donna Nook signalled to them, and on reaching the vessel, it was found that the small boat had drifted down onto the steamer and was tied up astern of her. The three occupants of the boat were taken aboard, the boat was taken in in tow, and the lifeboat made for Grimsby, where the survivors were put ashore. Because of the prevailing weather, it would have been impossible to rehouse at Spurn, so the lifeboat remained at Grimsby overnight and returned to station the next day. The only other service of the year was undertaken on 16 October, when *City of Bradford* went to the aid of two vessels, the steamship *Harlech* and the steam trawler *Elf King*, which had been in collision. The steamer

The first City of Bradford leaving Scarborough at the end of her naming ceremony, passing the lighthouse in the harbour. This photograph gives a good indication of the deck layout of the early motor lifeboats, on which no protection was provided for the crews. The single engine was housed in a small box in the middle of the deck. (Vera Cross, by courtesy of Jan Crowther)

had stranded on the Middle Binks, and her fourteen crew had been taken on board the trawler. The lifeboat took them off and landed them at Grimsby.

A particularly fine service completed during November 1925 involved lifeboatmen from both the Humber and Donna Nook, who showed outstanding bravery and endurance to effect a rescue. Just before 8 a.m. on 25 November signals of distress were seen coming from a vessel aground off Saltfleet, and so the pulling and sailing lifeboat *Richard* was launched from Donna Nook, in Lincolnshire, to investigate. Conditions could not have been worse, with a hurricane-force northerly gale blowing and tremendous seas running, accompanied by snow squalls. Coxswain John Dobson took the Donna Nook lifeboat as close as he could to the stranded vessel, the steamship *Whinstone*, of Preston, which was on passage from Hull to Berwick. Despite the violent seas which were pounding the casualty, but Dobson was told by the crew of the steamer that they required a tug, rather than a lifeboat. So Dobson took the lifeboat back to Donna Nook, which itself involved a dangerous journey, as the conditions were so difficult that preventing the lifeboat from capsizing required great skill. Once the lifeboat had been beached, a message was sent to Grimsby requesting the help of a tug, even though it was thought that a tug would struggle to reach the steamer in the appalling conditions.

Before the RNLI's Annual General Meeting in London on 14 April 1926, the medal-winning lifeboatmen went to the Cenotaph to lay a wreath there with the inscription 'In memory of the men of Boulmer who fell in the Great War. From the inhabitants of Boulmer, Northumberland'. This photo was taken outside Lifeboat House, Charing Cross Road, as they were on their way and shows, from left to right, Coxswain Robert Cross, Miss N. Stephenson (daughter of the Coxswain at Boulmer), Mrs Slanton (wife of the Second Coxswain at Boulmer), Coxswain Fleming (Gorleston) and Coxswain John Dobson (Donna Nook). In the background on the right is George F. Shee, Secretary of the RNLI. The two women from Boulmer represented the thirty-five women launchers of Boulmer. (Vera Cross, by courtesy of Jan Crowther)

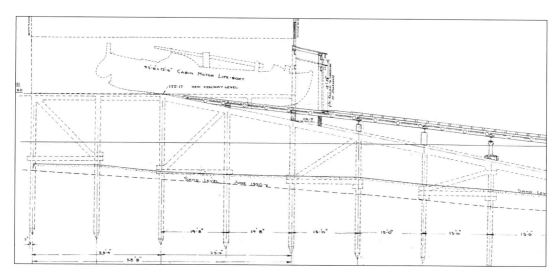

Diagram of the lifeboat house showing the extension at the front needed so the house was large enough for the 45ft 6in Watson cabin motor lifeboat. The original slipway, which was never dismantled, is included on this drawing. The house had to be altered in the late 1920s so that City of Bradford's successor could be accommodated. (By courtesy of the RNLI)

Despite being almost totally exhausted from their efforts to reach the steamer, the Donna Nook lifeboatmen prepared to put to sea again. But the Honorary Secretary refused to let the tired men go out and instead telephoned Coxswain Robert Cross at Spurn Point to explain the situation. So *City of Bradford* launched at 9.30 a.m. to help the steamer. Huge waves were sweeping the stranded vessel by the time the lifeboat reached her, but a line was got aboard and the breeches buoy rigged by the Humber lifeboatmen. With huge seas repeatedly covering the lifeboat, the steamer's six crew were hauled through the waves one by one and into the lifeboat, which then landed them at Grimsby. For his outstanding seamanship and courage, Coxswain Cross was awarded a Silver medal, while Coxswain Dobson, of the Donna Nook lifeboat, received a Bronze medal for outstanding seamanship and courage, and both crews were given extra monetary awards. *The Lifeboat* journal noted that 'the courage and skill shown by the Donna Nook Coxswain and Crew are the more remarkable since they are most of them farm labourers, who only go to sea on service in the lifeboat and for the quarterly exercises'.

The Humber and Donna Nook coxswains were presented with their bravery medals at the RNLI's Annual General Meeting in London on 14 April 1926 and the trip to London proved an eventful one for the lifeboatmen. They met two women from Boulmer, in Northumberland, who were representing thirty-five women launchers of Boulmer and who were the guests of the Duke and Duchess of Northumberland at their house in Prince's Gate. On the morning of the meeting the lifeboatmen accompanied the two women during the laying of a wreath at the Cenotaph, and after the meeting they were taken by Mrs Hilton Philipson, MP for Berwick, to the House of Commons. In the evening, together with Coxswain Cross, Coxswain Dobson and Coxswain Fleming, they were the guests of Sir Oswald Stoll at the Coliseum, where the recipients of RNLI gallantry medals attending the Annual Meeting had been entertained. The previous evening Coxswain Cross and Coxswain Dobson were entertained at the Polytechnic, where they saw Major Court Treatt's film *Cape to Cairo*.

The following year, 1926, proved to be the busiest for *City of Bradford*, with the first service coming on 9 February 1926 when she was launched at 9.40 a.m. after a vessel had been reported aground on the Haile Sands. The casualty, the trawler *Dinorah*, had been returning to Grimsby, her home port, loaded

The 45ft Watson motor lifeboat City of Bradford pictured at Southend-on-Sea in the later stages of her career after an aft shelter had been fitted. She served in the Reserve Fleet of the RNLI until 1952, and was sold out of service in October 1952. Among the stations she temporarily operated at were Ramsgate, Lowestoft, Torbay, New Brighton, Holyhead, Baltimore, Fenit, Courtmacsherry Harbour and Galway Bay, making her one of the most travelled Humber lifeboats. (Grahame Farr, by courtesy of the RNLI)

with fish. In rough seas and a strong easterly wind, the trawler was found to be leaking badly, so the lifeboat went alongside, rescued the crew of eleven and landed them at Grimsby.

During her last full year of service, 1928, she launched only three times, of which two proved to be effective services. The first of these came on 16 March, when she assisted the steam trawler *Night Hawk*, of Grimsby, which was in difficulty on the Inner Binks in south-easterly winds and moderate seas. The second service was during the early hours of 6 June. *City of Bradford* launched at 2.30 a.m. to the steam trawler *Abelia*, of Grimsby, which had been caught out in heavy seas near the Inner Binks Buoy. The vessel, with a crew of nine, was aground, so the lifeboat stood by until she refloated.

By the time of this service, the RNLI had decided to send another new motor lifeboat to Spurn even though *City of Bradford* had only been on station for less than six years. During that time she saved thirty-seven lives, a creditable total, and undertook a number of fine rescues, but a lifeboat offering better crew protection was needed. After she had been replaced by a new and larger lifeboat in 1929, *City of Bradford* was allocated to the Reserve Fleet, becoming the first motor lifeboat to serve in this fleet. As her replacement was named *City of Bradford II*, so she was renamed *City of Bradford I*. She did return to Spurn for a further period of service, described below, and then spent two decades as a Reserve boat.

The Second City of Bradford

The development of motor lifeboats continued apace during the interwar years, and in 1923 the first twin-engined lifeboat, a 60ft Barnett-class, was completed. Two propellers and twin engines gave the boat much more power and manoeuvrability and meant that sails, carried in case of engine failure, were no longer needed. However, the 60ft Barnett was too large for most stations, and too large for boathouses, such as the one at Spurn, so smaller twin-engined designs were produced, and in 1927 the first twin-engined 45ft 6in Watson-class lifeboat was built. As Humber was regarded as an important station, it was allocated a new twin-engined Watson almost as soon as the design had been developed. As well as twin engines, the design also incorporated a cabin which,

The new 45ft 6in Watson motor City of Bradford II on trials before coming to Spurn Point. She was also equipped with sails in case of engine failure. (By courtesy of the RNLI)

City of Bradford II at Newhaven in February 1929 in freezing conditions with iced handrails during her passage from her builder's yard on the Isle of Wight up the east coast to Spurn Point. (By courtesy of the RNLI)

according to its designer James Barnett, was 'very useful for immediately treating rescued people, who may have suffered severely from exposure or accident'.

Built by S. E. Saunders at a cost of £8,662 17s 9d, the new lifeboat for Spurn was provided out of funds raised in the city of Bradford, and the Airedale and Wharfedale districts of Bradford, together with a legacy of £5,000 received from the late Mr Moss Howson, of Harrogate. She was driven by two 40bhp Weyburn CE4 petrol engines, which gave her a speed of just over eight knots. The new boat arrived at the Humber on 13 February 1929 in freezing conditions, visiting Grimsby Docks with her handrails covered in ice. Because of Spurn Point's remoteness, the naming ceremony was held at Bridlington on 6 July 1929. Lord Deramore, the Lord-Lieutenant for the East Riding of Yorkshire, presided, and among those in attendance for the ceremony were the Lord Mayor of Bradford Alderman H. Thornton Pullan; Sir William Priestley, a Vice-President of the RNLI and Chairman of the Bradford Branch; Sir Henry Sutcliffe-Smith, Honorary Secretary of the Bradford Branch; and the Mayor of Bridlington Alderman C. H. Gray. About 150 members of the Bradford Branch and Ladies' Lifeboat Guild were also present to witness the naming of the second lifeboat which they had been involved in funding.

At the start of proceedings, the Lord Mayor of Bradford formally presented the lifeboat to the RNLI on behalf of the two donors, Mr Moss Howson and the city of Bradford, stating that the inhabitants of the city were 'glad to do all that they could to support those who were ever ready to help their comrades in peril on the sea'. The lifeboat was accepted by Sir William Priestley and the service of dedication that followed was conducted by the Rural Dean of Bridlington. At the end of the formalities, Mrs Moss Howson named the lifeboat *City of Bradford II*, after which various votes of thanks were proposed, and the lifeboat took a number of the visitors for a short trip to sea.

By the time of her naming ceremony *City of Bradford II* had already completed a number of rescues, although none of the casualties had needed her assistance. Her first effective service was undertaken on 19 September 1929, when she was launched at 5.15 a.m. to the motor boat *Curlew*, which had two people on board and was in difficulty in choppy seas and a stiff north-westerly wind. The boat's engine had broken down and she had drifted onto The Binks. The lifeboat reached the casualty, pulled her off the sand and saved the two men, then towed the boat to Grimsby. The other three effective services of 1929 were all to local steam trawlers, which the lifeboat stood by.

From January 1930, for two and a half years, Spurn was served by two lifeboats after the station's former lifeboat, which had been renamed *City of Bradford I*, returned to the Humber. After being replaced in 1929, she had been placed in the RNLI's Reserve Fleet, and served temporarily at St Mary's and Ramsgate. However, she returned to the Humber on 9 January 1930 to become the Humber Emergency Lifeboat, or No.2 lifeboat, and stayed until the summer of 1932. At about the same time, to improve launching arrangements, a new and longer slipway was built for *City of Bradford II*. As she was slightly larger than her predecessor, the boathouse at Spurn had to be modified to accommodate her. This work was funded from of a legacy from the late S. Crabtree Helm, of Bradford and Ilkley, and to mark the donation a memorial tablet was unveiled at the boathouse on 11 July 1931 by Alvin Whiteley,

The naming ceremony of City of Bradford II was held at Bridlington on 6 July 1929, enabling supporters to get to the event far more easily than if it had been held at Spurn. This photograph shows the boat being blessed and dedicated by the Rural Dean of Bridlington. She was named by Mrs Moss Howson, whose late husband left £5,000 to augment the Bradford Lifeboat Fund. The girl in the cloche hat holding the flowers, to the right of the steps, is Vera Cross aged eleven. (Vera Cross, by courtesy of Jan Crowther)

Spurn lifeboat crew on board City of Bradford II at Bridlington for her naming ceremony in July 1929. They are, from left to right, William J. T. Hood, George Voller, Coxswain Robert Cross, Charles Howes, George Crimlisk, Charles Robinson, Mechanic William Augustus Neale and Frederick Stephen Kendall. (Vera Cross, by courtesy of Jan Crowther)

one of the executors of the late Mr Helm's estate. A short ceremony was held to formally dedicate the new building, after which Sir William Priestley, Chairman of the Bradford Branch and a Vice Chairman of the Institution who had been at the lifeboat's naming ceremony two years previously, presented a Centenary Vellum to the station. Although the station had been in existence for longer than 100 years, the Vellums had only recently been introduced, and so the award was made retrospectively.

During her second period at Spurn, *City of Bradford I* was kept at moorings in the river just off the lifeboat house, and completed seven services during that time. The effective services included a launch on 1 November 1930 to the steam trawler *Kingston Olivine*, of Hull, which was in difficulty just off Spurn Point. The lifeboat spent almost six hours at sea, assisting the vessel to safety. On 7 March 1931 *City of Bradford I* landed the two crew members from the steamship *Tern*, of London, which had been caught out in a very rough sea. During the afternoon of 1 December 1931 she stood by the steam trawler *St Irene*, of Hull, which had stranded on the Inner Binks in dense fog. The trawler refloated at 4.40 p.m. and, after the skipper had thanked the lifeboat crew, proceeded up the Humber.

The last service by *City of Bradford I* at Spurn took place on 27 January 1932, when she towed in the lifeboat's boarding dinghy with two crew members on board. The incident began at 9 a.m. when the mechanic and bowman went out in the boarding boat to run the engines on *City of Bradford II*, which was at moorings, as well as hang out riding lights on her in the mist. But as they rowed out, the mist turned to dense fog causing them to miss the lifeboat and begin drifting out to sea. When it was realised they had not returned, the other lifeboatmen searched the beach in case they had come ashore. But they could not be found, so *City of Bradford I* was launched from the boathouse and headed off in the direction of The Binks. A thorough search was made for the missing men, but nothing was found. When the fog eventually began to lift at 2.30 p.m., a steam trawler was seen making for the river with the boarding boat in tow. The trawler's crew had found the boat drifting eight miles north of Spurn lightvessel and had taken the two lifeboatmen on board. They were transferred to the lifeboat, which then headed out to sea to follow up reports that two steamers had been in collision, but nothing was found.

Meanwhile, *City of Bradford II* undertook many services during the 1930s, and was one of the busiest lifeboats in the UK. On 23 August 1930 she launched to the auxiliary sloop *Dakar*, of Hull, which was aground on the Inner Binks in rough seas, and saved her crew of two. Her two services of 1931 were both to local fishing boats, which she stood by and escorted, during May and June respectively. Only one effective service was completed during 1932, but in January 1933 *City of Bradford II* undertook a couple of more difficult services. At 8.47 p.m. on 13 January 1933 the Royal Naval Signal Station reported that a vessel was ashore a mile and a half north-east of the station. *City of Bradford II* launched and found

Civic dignitaries visited Spurn Point on 11 July 1931 to mark the opening of the new, longer slipway which had been built to improve launching arrangements at the station. The improvements had been funded from the legacy of Mr S. Crabtree Helm, of Bradford and Ilkley, who left more than £2,000 to the RNLI. To mark the gift, a memorial tablet was unveiled in the boathouse. The ceremony was attended by about forty members of the Bradford Branch, as well as the Easington vicar, the Rev Holt, who is pictured in the centre. Alvin Whiteley, one of the executors of the late Mr Helm, unveiled the tablet, and it was dedicated by the Rev Canon R. Whincup, Vicar of Heaton, Bradford. After the dedication, Sir William Priestley, a Vice-President of the Institution and chairman of the RNLI's Bradford Branch, presented Coxswain Robert Cross (in cap to left of keelway) with a Vellum certificate signed by the Prince of Wales, President of the Institution, in recognition of the station's centenary. Before the ceremony the lifeboat had been launched, and after it the guests were given tea by the lifeboat crew and their wives. (Vera Cross, by courtesy of Jan Crowther)

that the steam trawler *Teanio*, of Hull, had stranded while bound from the Faroes to Hull, manned by a crew of thirteen. A light wind was blowing with a slight ground swell, but a dense fog reduced visibility considerably. The lifeboat stood by at the request of the captain, and later ran out a kedge anchor to be picked up by the tugs which had been requested. However, because of the fog, the tugs were unable to find the trawler, which refloated on the flood-tide without assistance and made her own way to Hull. The lifeboat returned to station at 7 a.m. having been on service for ten hours.

City of Bradford II was out again the following day after the Spanish steamship *Arantzazu*, of Bilbao, stranded six miles south of Haile Buoy, while bound from Bilbao to Immingham with a crew of twenty-nine on board. The steamer called for help using her wireless, and the lifeboat launched at 11.45 p.m. into a strong and increasing south-westerly breeze, with a rough sea and patches of fog. The lifeboat stood by the steamer and, at the request of the master, ran out a kedge anchor. This enabled the steamer to refloat on the flood-tide, and then the lifeboat escorted the vessel up the Humber. The lifeboat had been out for over nine hours by the time she returned to station at 9 a.m.

Early on the morning of 8 September 1934 the lifeboat watchman saw rockets in the direction of Kilnsea, and *City of Bradford II* launched at 5 a.m. into a south-easterly breeze with moderate seas. The lifeboat found the Danish motor fishing vessel *Noordstjernan*, of Frederickshaven, ashore two and a half miles north of the lifeboat station. She had four crew on board and was returning from the fishing grounds. At the request of her skipper, the lifeboat ran out an anchor and stood by until after high water. The lifeboat then returned to her station, reaching Spurn at 7.45 a.m., while the fishing vessel was subsequently towed off by a tug and taken into the Humber.

Just over a week later, on 19 September 1934, the lifeboat was called out again. During the afternoon, the pleasure boat *Sunbeam*, with two crew, went for a trip with a party of twelve from Cleethorpes to Spurn. They left again at about 4.30 p.m. but shortly afterwards the boat was seen to get into difficulties, so *City of Bradford II* was launched. She put off at 5 p.m. and found the pleasure boat lying broadside on in choppy seas shipping a lot of water. The twelve passengers and one of the crew, all of whom were soaked through, were taken aboard the lifeboat and a towline was secured by the remaining crewman so that the lifeboat could tow the boat to safety. The craft was brought back to Cleethorpes, after which the lifeboat returned to station.

Launch of City of Bradford II down the slipway at Spurn Point. (By courtesy of the RNLI)

City of Bradford II in Hull Docks. (Vera Cross, by courtesy of Jan Crowther)

A long service was undertaken on the evening of 22 January 1935 after the Royal Naval Shore Signal Station telephoned the Coxswain Superintendent to say that a vessel about the size of a trawler appeared to be aground on Spurn Point, south of the military pier. Two of the lifeboat crew went to investigate and reported that a trawler was ashore by a steeply sloping beach. *City of Bradford II* was launched at 9.05 p.m. and, in good conditions, found the Icelandic trawler *Havardour Isfirdingur*, of Isafjordur, had got into difficulties while bound from Grimsby to the fishing grounds with a crew of sixteen aboard. Soon after the lifeboat got alongside the casualty, it started listing to port. The crew were afraid that she would capsize and asked to be taken off. However, they stayed on board while the lifeboat stood by. At low water the lifeboat ran out an anchor, which was hove in tight on the trawler's winch, and at about 7 a.m. the following day the trawler hauled herself off and put to sea. The lifeboat returned to her station at 7.03 a.m., having been on service for ten hours.

More routine services were undertaken in 1936 to help vessels in difficulty. Early on the morning of 17 February *City of Bradford II* launched to the motor barge *River Witham*, of Hull, which had stranded on the beach at Mablethorpe. She stood by in case her help was wanted, but *River Witham* was washed high up on the beach by the flood-tide, so the lifeboat returned to station after six hours. On the morning of 18 August she went to the trawler *Runswick Bay*, of Hull, which was aground on the Middle Binks. Once on scene, *City of Bradford II*'s crew ran out an anchor for the trawler and then stood by. At half flood-tide the trawler heaved on the anchor and eventually floated clear.

At about 4.35 a.m. on 21 February 1937 a vessel was reported to have run ashore about a quarter of a mile north-east of Spurn lightvessel. She was the steam trawler *Rose of England*, of Grimsby, which was badly holed after colliding with another trawler. Five of her crew of ten had been taken off by a third trawler, and the remaining five had run her ashore to prevent her sinking and these men were still on board. The lifeboat crew initially thought they could reach *Rose of England* along the shore, but when they realised this was impossible, *City of Bradford II* was launched at 5.45 a.m. By the time she arrived on scene, the trawler's decks were awash, so the five men were rescued and taken to Grimsby.

In the summer of 1938 *City of Bradford II* went away for overhaul, so the reserve lifeboat *J. W. Archer*, a 1924-built 45ft Watson motor, was placed on temporary duty at Spurn, and she completed two services during her stint at the station. On 7 August she stood by the trawler *Capricornus*, of Grimsby, which had gone ashore at Dimlington Heights, and the lifeboatmen eventually helped to refloat her. Then, on 29 August, she was used to help refloat the steamship *Salerno*, of Hull, which had come ashore near Saltfleet, in a dense fog. The vessel, bound laden from Oslo for Hull was lying broadside on to the sea, which was breaking into her, but the lifeboat managed to get under her lee and two lifeboatmen were transferred across. The lifeboat then ran out an anchor from her, and using this, *Salerno* refloated on the flood-tide.

Just before the outbreak of the Second World War, several services were performed to steam trawlers or steamships, as well as one motor vessel. The service to the motor vessel *Peterborough Trader*, of Wisbech, bound for the Humber, took place on 20 January 1939. *City of Bradford II* went to the vessel after it had been seen on the Middle Binks at about 11.30 p.m. The lifeboat found the vessel bumping hard on the bottom in a nasty ground swell, so stood by until it refloated on the rising tide.

At 5.30 a.m. on 14 February 1939 the lifeboat watchman reported that a vessel had run ashore on the end of Spurn Point. The Coxswain went to the beach and saw the steam trawler *Hausa*, of Hull, stranded. Although only a light westerly wind was blowing and the sea was smooth, it was realised that the trawler was probably going to roll onto her beam ends as the tide ebbed. So *City of Bradford II* was launched at 6.05 a.m., and stood by until the tide had ebbed and the vessel was safe, and then returned to station. A tug got a wire aboard the trawler and, when the tide flowed, as there was a possibility of the sea going over *Hausa*'s bulwarks, the lifeboat put out again and stood by the trawler until she refloated safely.

City of Bradford II taking a group of Spurn visitors for a trip. (By courtesy of Paul Richards)

Wartime Service and the Post-war Era

During the Second World War the demands made on the Humber lifeboat crews were greater than ever. In the first eight months of the war, the station's lifeboat rescued more lives than any other, according to Charles Vince in *Storm on the Waters*, an account of the lifeboat service during the war. During the six years of hostilities, the Humber lifeboat crews are credited with answering seventy-three calls and saving 244 lives, and many outstanding rescues were performed in the course of the conflict. Wartime rescue work was often undertaken in extremely difficult and dangerous conditions, and the lifeboat crews had to deal not only with the usual hazards such as wind and tide, but were faced with the constant threat of mines in the area, as well as enemy aircraft and warships. The Humber Estuary was of great strategic importance, and so was well defended with two steel forts built on piles above the sandbanks at its mouth, anti-aircraft guns, a three-mile line of iron buoys and various other measures.

Despite the dangers and difficulties, the Humber lifeboat crew faced up to the risks and several rescues brought formal recognition from the RNLI. The first of the notable war services took place on 10 October 1939 after the trawler *Saltaire*, of Grimsby, went aground just off the beach at Spurn. A gale had been blowing for several days, and although the wind had dropped the seas were still very rough. *City of Bradford II* was launched at 4.55 a.m. and reached the trawler to find its gunwales under water and waves breaking over it. To reach the casualty, Coxswain Robert Cross anchored the lifeboat to windward and veered down towards it, and then manoeuvred the lifeboat alongside the trawler. Skilfully using the engines and the rudder, Coxswain Cross held the lifeboat in position while the nine crew jumped across. At one point one of the survivors fell between the lifeboat and the trawler, but he was quickly pulled to safety by the lifeboat crew just before the two boats were flung against each other by the heavy seas.

The lifeboat returned to station at 6.30 a.m. with the survivors. When the wind dropped at low water, it was possible to walk out to *Saltaire*. So her crew and the ship's agent laid a buoyed wire from her to be picked up by a tug. However, as the tide rose again and the wind picked up, the trawler was again caught in rough seas. The vessel swung round, broadside to the waves, heeled over forty degrees with waves breaking over her, forcing the crew to shelter in the wheelhouse. With further help needed, the lifeboat was launched again. Once on scene, Coxswain Cross and his crew found that the depth of water between trawler and beach was insufficient for a leeward approach, while on the windward side the trawler's masts prevented the lifeboat from getting close. Cross therefore dropped anchor to windward and took the lifeboat towards the trawler stern first. Another rope was made fast from the lifeboat's starboard stern bollard to the anchor cable, and this was used as a bridle. By going astern, Cross managed to keep both the rope and anchor cable taut while the crew fired a line over the trawler. The fishermen made this fast, rigged the breeches buoy, and three fishermen were hauled across to the lifeboat.

However, with the seas crashing over the trawler, the fishermen found it difficult getting into the breeches buoy. Matters got worse when the trawler's nets and gear, which had been washed overboard, fouled the lines of the breeches buoy, so a second line had to be fired across and a second breeches buoy rigged, which enabled four more men to be hauled through the waves and onto the lifeboat. Throughout the rescue, the seas continued to pound both boats and the lifeboat was often totally engulfed in water. Hauling the seven men through the water and into the lifeboat had been extremely hard work for the lifeboat crew, while both Coxswain Cross and Mechanic John Major worked together to keep the lifeboat in position. The last three men on the trawler decided not to risk being hauled through the sea to the lifeboat, and instead requested to be hauled ashore by soldiers using ropes from the beach, but two were badly hurt as they were dragged through the surf. With all the fishermen safe, the lifeboat's anchor was recovered, she cleared the wreck at 3.30 p.m., and the seven survivors were landed twenty minutes later.

For his outstanding skill and courage during this service, Coxswain Cross was awarded the Silver medal by the RNLI, Mechanic Major received the Bronze medal and the rest of the lifeboat's crew were accorded the Thanks Inscibed on Vellum. They were Second Coxswain William Jenkinson, Bowman William Hood, Assistant Mechanic Samuel Hoopell and lifeboatmen George Hopper and Walter Biglin.

Less than a month after this service, the Humber lifeboatmen were involved in another excellent service, this time helping a war casualty. On 3 November 1939 the steamship *Canada*, of Copenhagen, was holed by enemy action twenty-one miles north-east of the Humber, and one of her holds filled with water. Forty of her crew left in three ship's boats and were picked up by the Norwegian steamer *Ringhorn*, leaving just the Captain and thirteen others aboard the damaged vessel. *City of Bradford II* launched at 5.45 p.m., headed into rough seas and a strong south-easterly wind and found the steamer two hours later, anchored off Holmpton. The lifeboat stood by the vessel throughout a bitterly cold night and, at daybreak, transferred the Captain to a tug, which was returning to Hull. But as the weather got worse, the steamer started listing, and the crew remaining on board signalled for lifeboat assistance. Coxswain Cross had great difficulty in getting the lifeboat close to the vessel, with its forty-five degree list and the timber cargo washed overboard floating around the ship. The lifeboat did get damaged going alongside, but she was held in position long enough to enable the thirteen men to get off. By 10.30 a.m. all had been rescued, and five minutes later *Canada* heeled over and sank. The lifeboat landed the men at Grimsby and arrived back at Spurn at 12.30 p.m., having been at sea in dreadful conditions for over eighteen hours. For this fine service, Coxswain Robert Cross was accorded Thanks Inscribed on Vellum by the RNLI.

This was the first of five outstanding services carried out by the Spurn lifeboatmen during November 1939 with the next coming just over a week later, on 11 November 1939, when *City of Bradford II* went to the steamship *Dryburgh*, of Leith, which had collided with the sunken wreck of the Danish steamer *Canada*. The lifeboat went alongside *Dryburgh*, rescued the crew of sixteen and then stood by until the tugs *Yorkshireman* and *Superman* arrived on scene. The following day, the lifeboat was out again, launching to the steamship *Fireglow*, of London, which had gone aground on the wreck of *Canada*. Her boats had been lowered and the crew were preparing to leave, but instead all eighteen were taken aboard the lifeboat, which then stood by to see what would happen to the steamer. While standing by, the lifeboat crew received another request for help, this time from the 5,000-ton steamship *Deerpool*, which was aground on the Middle Binks, had a heavy list to starboard and was leaking badly. One of her crew had been injured so the lifeboat took him to Spurn at about 3.30 a.m., and then returned to *Deerpool*. As conditions had worsened and the steamer was striking the bottom, the captain asked the lifeboat to take off his crew. Although the tide was creating a whirlpool under *Deerpool*'s lee, the lifeboat was able to get alongside, albeit with great difficulty, and took off twenty-nine men, leaving the captain and four others on board. As the crew of *Fireglow*, who were still on board the lifeboat, wanted to find out the fate of their own ship, the lifeboat left *Deerpool* and searched for *Fireglow*.

It was now 6.30 a.m., and the lifeboat had been out for nearly twelve hours. *Fireglow* was found to have slipped off the wreck, and was afloat about a mile and a half away, so her crew reboarded. The lifeboat stood by to ensure *Fireglow* was seaworthy, and then returned to *Deerpool*. The five men left on board this vessel had abandoned her in the ship's boat and were on board a tug, so the lifeboat returned to station at midday and anchored. At 3.30 p.m. it was decided to take the crew of *Deerpool* back to her, but attempts

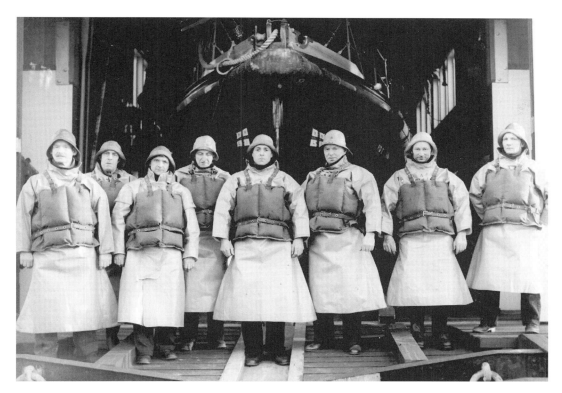

Spurn lifeboat crew in about 1938-39, around the start of the Second World War. They are, from left to right, George (Dod) Hopper, Samuel Hoopell, John Major, Walter Hood, Samuel Cross, Coxswain Robert Cross, Walter Biglin, and William Jenkinson. (Vera Cross, by courtesy of Jan Crowther)

to save her by the tugs were impossible in the heavy seas, and four men from a tug, who had got aboard her, had to be rescued. The men had to jump into the lifeboat as she went alongside at full speed, but all were got off safely. *City of Bradford II* finally returned to her station at 6.30 p.m., nearly twenty-four hours after being called out. For this long service, a special reward of £1 was made to each man in the crew.

On 14 November, three days later, the lifeboat was in action again. She launched at 8 p.m. to the steamer *Georgios*, of Piraeus, which had hit the wreck of *Canada*, but the lifeboatmen found no one on board when they reached the scene, so they searched for the missing crew in very rough seas. Eventually twenty-one men from *Georgios* and a North Sea pilot were found drifting helplessly in two of the ship's boats, by when the wind had risen to gale force. Coxswain Cross placed the boats were under the lifeboat's lee, enabling the twenty-two men to quickly scramble to safety. During the five-hour passage to Grimsby, the lifeboat was frequently washed by heavy seas, soaking all on board, but once at Grimsby the rescued men were landed. The lifeboat returned to station at 8 a.m. having been out for twelve hours. The RNLI later sent a Letter of Thanks to Coxswain Cross for this service, and monetary awards of £1 to the crew.

The last of the November 1939 services took place on the 24th. At about 9.05 a.m. a loud explosion was heard near the Lower Middle Buoy, where a vessel was on fire. *City of Bradford II* launched seven minutes later and found the steamship *Mangalore*, of Liverpool, in trouble. Her crew had been thrown into the sea by the explosion, but by the time the lifeboat arrived they had got aboard one of the ship's boats. From this boat the lifeboat rescued about thirty men, numb with cold and covered in oil. She then rescued about twenty more men from another boat, while a further seventeen were saved by a pilot cutter. As the captain wanted to stand by his ship, the lifeboat transferred a number of men to the pilot cutter, which took them to Grimsby, and then, with the captain and seventeen officers on board, stood by for an hour and a half until the steamer broke in two. She then landed the eighteen men at Grimsby and returned to station at 1.30 p.m.

During the first two weeks of February 1940 the Humber lifeboatmen undertook several services. On 2 February *City of Bradford II* was launched to the steam trawler *Barbados*, which was stranded two miles north-west of Donna Nook. She stood by while attempts were made to tow the trawler off, but the vessel remained stuck fast, and the lifeboat was out to her on successive days up to 7 February. On 5 February the lifeboat had to take off the crew after the weather worsened, and so she went in under the trawler's lee, rescued the eleven men on board and transferred them to the tug, which took them to Grimsby.

A few days after this prolonged rescue, on 12 February 1940, the Humber lifeboatmen took part in a service which was one of the most outstanding of the Second World War. The steam trawler *Gurth* was homeward bound for Grimsby when she was caught in bitter winter weather, a gale-force wind from the north-east and heavy continuous snow. When flares were seen south-east of Donna Nook, a message was sent to Spurn requesting the lifeboat. *City of Bradford II* was launched just after 6.30 p.m., but with only five crew on board, rather than the usual eight crewmen, because two of the regulars were ill and one of the crew posts was empty. So Coxswain Robert Cross, with his reduced crew, set course just outside the Haile Buoy. When he reached the Buoy, he saw a glimmer of light to the south, and realised it was coming from the steam trawler *Gurth*, which was drifting and, before the lifeboat could reach her, went aground. As surf swept the vessel, only her fo'c'sle remained above water with her nine crew clinging to it in desperation. Once on scene, Coxswain Cross realised how difficult it was going to be to effect the rescue: if he approached the trawler from the starboard side, to get a slight lee, the flood-tide would carry the boat on top of the casualty as it was running across the seas. If the lifeboat anchored to windward and dropped down before the gale, the tide, which was running across, would push her off course.

Nevertheless, Cross anchored the lifeboat 160 yards to windward of the trawler and, with his engines working slowly, began to edge stern first towards the casualty. When he thought that a wave was about to break over the lifeboat, he called on the mechanic to go full speed ahead to meet it, and rode over it before it broke. The Bowman was tending the cable but the heavy seas made it impossible for him to stand forward to do this, so two turns of the cable were taken round the samson post and two more round the bollard in the forward cockpit. This enabled him to work the cable from the cockpit. The seas were breaking continuously over the lifeboat and both cockpits were full of water throughout. The Mechanic, standing in the after cockpit at his engine controls, was only just able to keep his chin above water, while the crew were repeatedly thrown on the deck by the seas. They were bruised and shaken, but stayed on board by clinging to the handrails. The Coxswain dropped down until the lifeboat was almost in the surf, but the tide carried her 150 yards down from the casualty, leaving her almost as far from the trawler as when she had anchored. He then told the Second Mechanic to make a line fast to the cable and to bring it to the starboard after bollard, so the lifeboat was held fore and aft. The cable itself held her head on to the seas, but by hauling on the quarter line the Coxswain could bring her beam on to the seas and head into the tide, so that she could steam up against it towards the wreck, employing a method which Coxswain Cross had used before with great success.

These arrangements made, the Coxswain told the Second Coxswain and last remaining member of his crew to stand forward and be ready to seize the men on the wreck as the lifeboat came alongside. The two absent crew members were much needed at this point as the Mechanic was alone at the engine controls, the Coxswain alone at the wheel, and nobody was free to work the searchlight. By now it was 8.15 p.m., and, in pitch darkness, the Coxswain had to watch for the best opportunity to get alongside the wreck.

By working the engines and hauling on the cable and the line, the Coxswain succeeded in nosing the bow of the lifeboat against the tide up to the trawler's fo'c'sle. One of the trawler's crew was pulled aboard by the two lifeboatmen positioned on the bow, and the lifeboat had to go astern. Again and again the Coxswain brought the lifeboat alongside the trawler using the same technique. Several times the seas, lifting her higher than the trawler, nearly threw her onto the casualty's deck, but each time the

An unusual photo taken on board City of Bradford II during the Second World War with a canvas displaying the word 'Lifeboat' on the cabin. (By courtesy of Paul Richards)

A party of VIPs on board City of Bradford II during the war. (By courtesy of Paul Richards)

City of Bradford II in her wartime guise, with the canopy across her windscreen identifying her as a lifeboat. (By courtesy of Paul Richards)

City of Bradford II launching at Spurn Point during the war. (By courtesy of Paul Richards)

Coxswain went hard astern to get clear. Even when the lifeboat was alongside, Coxswain Cross could sometimes only hold her in position long enough for one man to be taken off, before having to repeat the manoeuvre. After twenty attempts, which had taken an hour, six men had been rescued. Then the lifeboat's port engine stopped after a rope, which had been washed out of the after-cockpit, got wrapped round the propeller. It was impossible to attempt to clear it, so with only one engine running the Coxswain had no choice but to continue with the rescue, with, according to *The Lifeboat* journal, 'his confidence unshaken although the danger was doubled' as three men still had to be rescued. Several more attempts were made to get alongside before, one by one, the men were taken off. In the course of rescue attempts, the lifeboat's bow fender and its iron support were carried away, the port wale was split, and further damage was inflicted on the lifeboat.

Once the nine men had been saved, the difficult task of taking the lifeboat out of the broken water, with only one of her engines functioning, had to be completed. The line attached to the cable was let go and her stern swung towards the shore, but before she could move seawards her stern hit the bottom several times, which left her rudder split and the stern post damaged, although the rudder was still usable. Severely damaged but under control, the lifeboat was taken towards her anchor, which was weighed. When she was well clear of the broken water, the scuttle above the port propeller was lifted, and Coxswain Cross spent ten minutes cutting the rope away using a knife which he had invented.

With both engines working, the lifeboat made for Grimsby, where she arrived at 10.35 p.m. She had been out for three and a half hours while the actual rescue had taken an hour and a quarter. The Honorary Secretary of the Grimsby lifeboat, who welcomed rescued and rescuers, found the lifeboatmen more exhausted than the men they had saved, and suffering from being badly bruised and the exposure to the severe conditions. Although the lifeboat looked, as one eyewitness described her, 'like a battle-scarred warrior', she had not taken on any water and the damage was largely superficial.

The account in *The Lifeboat* journal concluded, 'The courage, endurance and skill of the Coxswain were beyond praise, and the unfailing confidence of his crew in him, and their unhesitating obedience to his every order, enabled them, shorthanded though they were, to carry out successfully one of the most difficult and gallant rescues in the history of the lifeboat service.' In recognition of their efforts, the RNLI awarded Coxswain Robert Cross the Gold medal for gallantry; John Major, the Mechanic, received the Silver medal; and the other members of the crew each received the Bronze medal: Second Coxswain W. R. Jenkinson, Bowman W. J. T. Hood, Second Mechanic S. Cross, and S. Hoopell. A special award of £10 was also made to each of the six men, and Coxswain Cross was awarded the George Medal.

Temporary repairs were made to *City of Bradford II* to ensure she remained operational, and she was called out again just two days later, on 14 November 1940, to the steamship *Castor*, of Bergen. The steamer, with a crew of eighteen, had been holed when she struck a submerged wreck on the Haile Sands, and the captain was afraid that water might reach the cargo, which contained carbide. *City of Bradford II* stood by the casualty for over seventeen hours, until noon on 15 November, and eventually returned to station at 12.05 p.m. She went out again later, but no further help was needed.

Throughout 1941 wartime casualties continued in the seas around the Humber and the Spurn lifeboatmen remained ready to help any vessels in difficulty. Early on the morning of 27 February 1941 the Royal Naval Signal Station reported that a mine had exploded in the convoy anchorage and the lifeboatmen were asked to stand by. Ten minutes later another message was received stating that a vessel had sunk and so *City of Bradford II* launched at 3.20 a.m. into the pitch dark to help. It was snowing heavily and a full south-easterly gale was churning up extremely heavy seas as Coxswain Cross made for the vessel. Once on scene, the lifeboatmen found the steamship *Venus*, of Rotterdam, which was in difficulty having fouled the boom defences. Her master wanted tugs to assist, so Coxswain Cross went to the gate vessel and asked the crew to telephone for tug assistance.

He also asked for the position of a vessel reportedly sunk, which was given as about half a mile to the north. The lifeboat found nothing there, but as she was searching, the lifeboatmen saw rockets a little way to the north-east. Although a large number of mines had been dropped by enemy aircraft only a

A painting showing the dramatic rescue of the steam trawler Gurth on 12 February 1940. (By courtesy of the RNLI)

The visit to Spurn Point of HRH The Princess Royal on 16 April 1940. Coxswain Robert Cross is standing to the left of the Princess, while the rest of the crew are William Jenkinson, Walter Hood, Samuel Cross, George Stephenson, Samuel Hoopell, Walter Biglin and John Major. (Vera Cross, by courtesy of Jan Crowther)

day or two earlier, Coxswain Cross took the lifeboat straight towards the rockets despite the risk presented by the mines. The lifeboatmen found the air-raid balloon ship *Thora* aground on the edge of the Trinity Sands with her anchor cable caught round her propeller, and she had fouled the balloon cable. Out of control, the vessel had struck the sands, and when the lifeboat reached her just before 5 a.m., heavy seas were sweeping right over her. After assessing the situation, Coxswain Cross took the lifeboat through the heavy surf and round the vessel's bows to reach her lee side, but the water there was so shallow that the lifeboat repeatedly struck the bottom. The eight men on board *Thora* threw a rope to the lifeboatmen and using this together with the engines, Cross held the lifeboat in position long enough for all eight to jump onto the lifeboat. Heavy seas repeatedly swept her, but fortunately the actual rescue only took a few minutes. Once all the men had been rescued, the lifeboat was brought clear and a course was set for Grimsby where the men were landed after the pier lights had been shown to help guide the lifeboat in. The lifeboat returned to station at 9.30 a.m. after a demanding and difficult rescue, which the RNLI's account summed up as 'not only a skilful, but a very courageous rescue, in circumstances of great danger.' For his great skill and courage during this rescue, Coxswain Robert Cross was awarded the Bronze medal and, with each of the seven members of the crew, a special reward of £2.

An unusual wartime incident occurred on 7 August 1942. At 5.20a.m. the lifeboat watchman saw a large bomber crash near the gate vessel, leaving the sea ablaze with burning petrol. Coxswain Robert Cross rang up the Port War Signal Station and was told that two steel boats had gone out to search for the plane's crew, but permission to launch the lifeboat was refused until after the flames had died down, as she was wooden hulled. At 5.40 a.m. the lifeboat launched, but the crew found only wreckage. The bomber's crew, believed to be nine in number, had lost their lives, although only four bodies were recovered by one of the patrol vessels. Coxswain Cross later spoke to the naval officer in charge, who agreed in future to leave it entirely up to the coxswain to decide whether or not it was advisable to launch the lifeboat.

Although 1942 had, on the whole, been a relatively quiet year for the Humber lifeboat and its crew, another outstanding service was completed on 6 January 1943. At 7.57 p.m. Coxswain Cross was informed that the Phillip's Defence Unit No.1, a large anchored craft mounted with anti-aircraft guns, had broken away from its moorings and gone ashore inside the boom defence on the north side of the Trinity Sands. *City of Bradford II* was launched twelve minutes later into very rough seas and an easterly gale. The night was very dark and bitterly cold, with frequent heavy snow showers, but ten minutes after launching the lifeboatmen were informed by the crew of the boom defence vessel that a tug had gone to the aid of the Phillip's defence unit so the lifeboat returned to station.

Just as the lifeboatmen had finished rehousing the lifeboat, Coxswain Cross received a telephone call in the boathouse reporting a vessel aground on The Binks. On the ebbing tide, the Coxswain knew that the lifeboat would not be able to get close to the stranded vessel so he decided to wait for the tide to turn. Then at 10.50 p.m. the Port War Signal Station reported that the Phillip's Defence Unit No.3 had broken adrift and was entangled on the inner side of the boom defence. When those manning the unit were seen firing red rockets and signalling for help, *City of Bradford II* was immediately launched to assist.

The defence unit was entangled in the boom and Coxswain Cross had to approach cautiously from seaward, with searchlights illuminating the scene, but at times also blinding the lifeboatmen. The Coxswain took the lifeboat bow first to the boom four times and all five men on the defence unit jumped to safety. But, during the rescue, the lifeboat sustained significant damage after striking the long steel spikes along the outside of the defence units intended to prevent boats from going alongside. However, once she was clear of the casualty the lifeboat landed the rescued men at 11.20 p.m. and then was tied up alongside a patrol vessel to wait for the flood-tide before going to the aid of the vessel on The Binks.

The lifeboatmen put out at 3.10 a.m. on 7 January 1943 and found HM Trawler *Almondine* lying on her port side with heavy seas pouring over her, and a strong spring tide swirling across the sands at about six knots. Coxswain Cross made his first approach at 3.35 a.m., taking the lifeboat head-to-tide to go

City of Bradford II on service during the Second World War, approaching an armed fishing vessel. (By courtesy of the RNLI)

alongside the trawler's lee side. A rope was thrown to the shipwrecked men and quickly secured, but the tide swung the lifeboat round and the rope snapped. The lifeboat's mast then fouled the trawler and broke, but Coxswain Cross was able to bring the lifeboat round and he then took her in again and again, twelve times in all, while heavy seas swept clean over her. On a number of occasions the lifeboat was smashed against the hull of the trawler, and 5ft of her stem was splintered down to the planking, which was holed in several places. But by 4.20 a.m. nineteen of the trawler's crew had been rescued.

As the tide rose, the trawler gradually righted herself and appeared to be afloat again. Her captain hailed Coxswain Cross asking if he and the boat's officers should also abandon ship, or remain on board. But before Coxswain Cross could reply, the trawler's lights went out and in the driving snow and pitch dark the vessel disappeared. The lifeboatmen, using their searchlight, and aided by searchlights on the shore, scoured the area looking for the missing trawler. But after ninety minutes no sign of her had been seen and so at 6.15 a.m. the lifeboat returned to her boathouse and landed the nineteen survivors. Coxswain Cross immediately telephoned the Port War Signal Station and was told that a tug had found *Almondine* drifting off the mouth of the Humber and had taken her in tow.

The rescue of the men from *Almondine* had only been made possible by the fine seamanship and great determination of the Coxswain, who was ably supported by his crew, and for his outstanding seamanship and tremendous courage during this most difficult rescue Coxswain Cross was awarded the Gold medal by the RNLI. George Richards, Reserve Mechanic, was awarded the Silver medal, and the other members of the crew each received a Bronze medal; they were Bowman George Stephenson, Assistant Mechanic Samuel Cross, Signalman William Major and lifeboatmen Sidney Harman and George Shakesby.

Though damaged from this rescue, *City of Bradford II* remained seaworthy and four days later she went out, though her broken stem had not been repaired. She launched at 8.45 a.m. on 11 January to the Belgian steamer *Anna*, of Nieuport, which had ten men on board, including a pilot. In the early

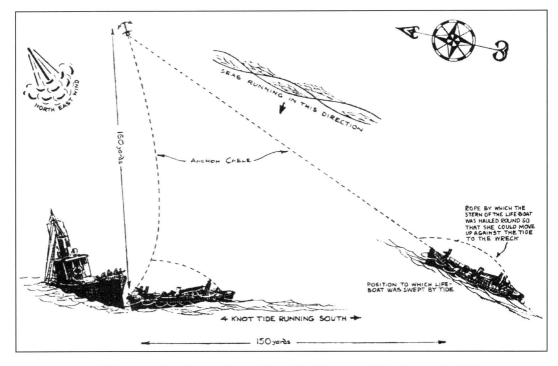

Diagram of the rescue from the trawler Gurth, produced by L. F. Gilding from a sketch by Coxswain Robert Cross.

54

The dramatic sight of City of Bradford II being launched down the slipway at Spurn Point.
(Vera Cross, by courtesy of Jan Crowther)

morning in a dense fog she had been in collision with the Danish steamer *Sparta* and had sunk. The lifeboat rescued the crew of eight, but the captain and pilot decided to stay on board, as the bridge and after part of the ship were above water. The lifeboat landed the rescued men at Grimsby and then, at the request of the naval authorities, went out again to look for *Sparta*, but failed to find her as the steamer was making for Goole. So the lifeboat went to *Anna*, but her services were not needed until the tide rose, and then she stood by until after high water. A naval salvage party had boarded the casualty, pumped her out, and on the high tide the steamer refloated. Although leaking, she had sufficient pumps to control the water, so the lifeboat returned to station at 11.15 p.m.

In 1943 Robert Cross, then aged sixty-seven, retired as Coxswain and in February 1944 he and his wife Sarah left Spurn after an association spanning more than four decades. At sixty-seven he was over the normal retirement age for Coxswains, but he had been asked to stay at Spurn until a suitable replacement had been found. During his time in the post, Cross had become one of the most famous lifeboatmen in the country and in December 1941 he had talked about the wartime work of the station in the one o'clock news in the Home and Forces programmes. His wartime exploits have become legendary, and during the period of the conflict he took part in the rescue of 244 lives, and won the Gold medal twice, the Silver medal, the Bronze medal and the Thanks on Vellum, as well as being awarded the George Medal. In the thirty-one years he was Coxswain, he took part in the rescue of 403 lives.

Having first served on the lifeboat crew from 1901 to 1908, he returned as Coxswain in 1912 and his time at Spurn was remarkable for many reasons. Not only had he been involved in some outstanding rescues, which brought fame to him and the station, but he had overseen the transfer of the station to the RNLI, seen the lifeboat house and slipway built, and worked with his wife, Sarah, to nurture the small settlement at Spurn. He introduced a policy, followed by Coxswains ever since, that the wives and families of the crew must be as settled and happy about living on the Point as their husbands. Cross met his wife Sarah Hood at Flamborough, where she was the principal lightkeeper's daughter. They married in 1902, the year they first came to Spurn, and had a son who sadly died aged four months; they then had to wait until 1918 before their daughter, Vera, was born. Both Robert and his wife Sarah loved Spurn's unique way of life and were involved with all aspects of it, with Sarah delivering babies, providing medical aid when needed, and supporting the other wives.

The retirement of Cross was the end of an era, and his replacement, John Mason, lasted only six years. Mason had served on a minesweeper during the war and was then offered the job of Coxswain at Spurn. Before he moved to the small community, he gave his wife Lily a very positive account of life there. However, the reality proved somewhat different for Lily, who did not enjoy living at Spurn, where she was faced with a completely different way of life to what she had known. To reach Spurn from Hull at the time involved a bus journey from Hull of two and a half hours and then a half hour railcar journey down the peninsula. The Masons stayed until 1949, at which point Captain William Anderson, a master mariner from Tyneside, was appointed and, with his wife Ethel, he came to live at Spurn.

The final three services of the war by *City of Bradford II* all came in 1944. On 22 April she went to the steam trawler *Chandos*, of Grimsby, which had gone aground on The Binks while returning from the fishing grounds. Two lifeboat crew went aboard to help, but the vessel eventually floated with the tide. On 14 October *City of Bradford II* went to the Danish fishing vessel *J. N. Fibiger*, whose skipper did not know his way into the river, so two lifeboatmen boarded to help pilot her. On 24 December the lifeboat launched the landing craft (G)110, which had been in collision with another vessel and was sinking. The lifeboat crew reached the scene to find the craft, with 125 men on board, being towed by HM trawler *Arlette*, so the lifeboat escorted the craft into Grimsby Docks.

With the end of war in 1945, a year in which the Humber lifeboat undertook no effective services, the station returned to relative normality and left behind the considerable difficulties of wartime operation. The first service in peacetime came on 18 January 1946, when *City of Bradford II* was launched at 2.45 a.m. to help one of the crew of the Humber lightvessel who had been injured. The man was taken aboard the lifeboat and landed at Grimsby, and the lifeboat returned to station at 9.30 a.m.

Flood damage in January 1953 caused by severe weather and high tides, with rubble mounted up outside the lifeboatmen's cottages. (Robertson Buchan Collection)

A formal portrait of Coxswain Robert Cross, recipient of the Gold, Silver and Bronze medals, in his oilskins, sou'wester and kapok lifejacket. Cross retired in 1943, after thirty-one years as Coxswain, and was replaced in the post by John Mason, who served until 1949. (By courtesy of the RNLI)

At about 9.25 a.m. on 16 August 1947 *City of Bradford II* launched after reports that the steamship *Keila*, of Glasgow, had collided with the 527-ton steamship *Lady Anstruther*, also of Glasgow, in fog about twenty-two miles north-east of Spurn Point, and that *Lady Anstruther* was sinking. In a light north-easterly breeze and moderate sea, the lifeboat put out, but soon received a wireless message that she was not needed and so returned to station and anchored off at 11 a.m. At 3.15 p.m. the Filey coastguard asked her to take off *Lady Anstruther*'s crew from *Keila*, which had picked them up, and she found *Keila* eleven miles north-east of Spurn Point in dense fog. The lifeboat went alongside so that *Lady Anstruther*'s fourteen crew and her badly injured captain could be taken aboard and then given rum and biscuits. The lifeboat then made for Grimsby, where the men were landed at 8.30 p.m. It was too foggy for the lifeboat to return to station so she remained in Grimsby, and went back to Spurn at 6.45 a.m. the following day.

During 1948 the reserve lifeboat *Milburn* was on duty at Spurn while *City of Bradford II* went for overhaul, the first she had had since before the war. *Milburn*, built in 1925 for the Holy Island station in Northumberland, performed two services while at Spurn. The first was on 13 June 1948, when she launched at 8.30 a.m. to the cabin cruiser *Alisdair*, which was aground two and a half miles north-west of Donna Nook. The lifeboat crew passed tow ropes across to prevent the casualty being carried further in by the flood-tide and, when the water was deep enough, pulled her clear. The other service was on 7 July 1948 when *Milburn* towed in the motor yacht *Dawn Patrol*, which had broken down and whose crew, although in no immediate danger, asked for a tow, as they wished to spend the night ashore.

Back on station towards the end of 1948, *City of Bradford II* undertook several routine services during 1949, 1950 and 1951. On the morning of 28 January 1949, in dense fog, the motor vessel *Northgate*, of Hull, went ashore close to the lifeboat station. Although she was not initially in need of any help, her owners and captain later asked the lifeboat to assist in refloating her, so at 3.20 p.m. *City of Bradford II*

City of Bradford II after being sold out of service became a privately-owned pleasure craft based in Northern Ireland. She is pictured at Cushendall in April 2000. (Nicholas Leach)

launched and towed her clear. On 6 July 1950 the lifeboat brought ashore injured man from the Danish fishing vessel *Kutter*, which was alongside the Bull lightvessel, and took him to Grimsby for treatment. On 14 January and 8 August 1951 *City of Bradford II* assisted further crews, landing a sick man at Grimsby from the Humber lightvessel on the former occasion, and bringing ashore a man with an injured eye from the steamship *Afterglow*, of London. During the early months of 1952 another reserve lifeboat was on station, *Edward Z. Dresden*, a 1929-built 45ft 6in Watson motor lifeboat which had just been replaced at Clacton-on-Sea. She undertook a couple of services before the station lifeboat returned from overhaul.

City of Bradford II undertook what proved to be her last effective service at the Humber on 21 October 1953. She was launched at 9.48 a.m. after the crew of the steamship *Nestos*, of Piraeus, had reported that three of their colleagues were adrift in a small boat, which was being swept by the tide towards the mouth of the Humber. The lifeboatmen found the boat and another boat, with nine men in it, which had also put off from *Nestos* to search for their ship mates. Both boats were found tied up to the Middle Light Buoy, as neither had been able to make any headway against the strong tide. The lifeboat towed both boats back to *Nestos* and returned to station at 1.15 p.m.

By the time she was replaced at Spurn in November 1953 by a new Watson motor lifeboat, *City of Bradford II* had gained a magnificent service record, and had saved more than 300 lives in twenty-four years at the station, while being involved in some of the most dramatic rescues in the history of the lifeboat service. After leaving Humber, she served another fifteen years in the Reserve Fleet, before being sold out of service. As a Reserve lifeboat, she spent just over two years at Amble as well as a year at Broughty Ferry from December 1959 after the lifeboat there had been wrecked on service. She was sold out of service in December 1968 and was renamed *Spurn* for use as a pleasure boat, before becoming *Frieda* in the 1980s. Since leaving service and going into private ownership, she has been based in Northern Ireland and has reverted to her lifeboat name. In 2009 she was kept at Ringhaddy Pier, Strangford Loch.

The Last Watson Lifeboat

D uring the early 1950s, as the RNLI continued to rebuild and modernise the lifeboat fleet following the six years of war when no new lifeboats were completed, Humber was allocated a new lifeboat. Built by J. S. White at Cowes, the new boat was a 46ft 9in Watson motor type, driven by twin 40bhp Ferry VE4 four-cylinder diesel engines, which gave a top speed of eight and a half knots. The 46ft 9in version was the latest development of the Watson type, and the latter boats of this type had a redesigned deck layout. This incorporated an aluminium superstructure, with the cockpit positioned amidships to give the Coxswain better overall visibility when at the wheel, as well as an aft cabin for crew and survivors. The 46ft 9in Watson was suited to slipway launching and had propellers protected in tunnels. The boat built for the Humber was the nineteenth of the class, and upon completion in late 1953 she was sent up the east coast from Cowes, arriving at Spurn on 27 January 1954. Her first service took

The 46ft 9in Watson motor City of Bradford III was built in 1953 with an open midship steering position. She served at Humber for more than twenty-three years, and was the last slipway-launched lifeboat at the station. (By courtesy of the RNLI)

The scene at York during the naming of City of Bradford III, with the lifeboat moored on the river Ouse, and supporters crowding the banks. The boat was dedicated by the Lord Archbishop of York, the Right Hon and Most Rev C. F. Garbett, and she was named by Lady Croft.

place on 5 May 1954, when she launched at 4.05 p.m. to take a sick man from the Humber lightvessel to Grimsby, being called on as no other boat was available. In rough seas and a strong south-westerly breeze, the lifeboat took the patient on board, landed him at Grimsby, where an ambulance was waiting to take him to hospital, and returned to station by 10 p.m.

The new lifeboat was, like her two predecessors, provided by the City of Bradford Lifeboat Fund and for her inauguration ceremony on 24 July 1954 she was taken up the River Ouse to York to be named. The Lord Mayor of Bradford, Alderman H. J. White, oversaw the ceremony, which began with Lieut-Cdr H. H. Harvey, district inspector of lifeboats, describing the new boat. Sir Arthur Croft formally presented her to the RNLI on behalf of the Bradford and District branch, and she was accepted by Captain the Hon. V. M. Wyndham-Quin, RN, a member of the Committee of Management. The service of dedication was conducted by the Lord Archbishop of York, the Most Rev C. F. Garbett. At the end of the ceremony, Lady Croft named the lifeboat *City of Bradford III*, making the boat the seventh to bear the name Bradford.

During the first three years of her service at Humber, *City of Bradford III* undertook a series of routine services, mostly to help sick or injured crew members of passing ships. On 14 November 1954 she took out a doctor to a seriously sick man on board the steamship *Caronte*, of Rouen, which was at anchor a mile and a half south-east of Spurn Point, but the doctor was not required. At 9.24 p.m. on 15 August 1955 *City of Bradford III* took out a doctor after a crew member of the steamship *Atlantic Sea*, of Panama, had been seriously injured by a falling derrick. Within fifteen minutes of launching, the lifeboat was alongside the casualty and the doctor was transferred across, but a few minutes later the injured man died.

City of Bradford III had to wait until 6 June 1958, more than four years after arriving on station, before undertaking a first life-saving service. At 9.57 a.m. the Spurn Point coastguard reported that a man had tied his small boat to a float of the Admiralty boom half a mile north of the lifeboat house. He was baling continuously and clearly in need of assistance. *City of Bradford III* launched at 10.02 a.m. in calm seas

60

Spurn Point from the lighthouse, with the lifeboatmen's cottages to the right and the lifeboat house and slipway visible in the background to the right. (Robertson Buchan Collection)

The crew of City of Bradford III in the lifeboat house in the mid-1950s, soon after the boat had been placed on station; left to right Mechanic Leslie Willis, Robertson Buchan, Coxswain William S. Anderson, S. Cross, W. Major, Bob Appleby and H. Harris. (By courtesy of the RNLI)

The crew of City of Bradford III on board their lifeboat in about 1956; left to right R. Stork, Bob Appleby, B. Major, Robertson Buchan, S. Cross, Coxswain William S. Anderson, D. Fox and L. Welles. (Robertson Buchan Collection)

with a light easterly wind and soon reached the rowing boat. The man was taken on board and the boat was towed to the beach. The lifeboat was rehoused at Spurn at 10.45 a.m.

Another life-saving service was undertaken on the morning of 1 January 1959 after three red flares had been seen about six or seven miles off Withernsea. *City of Bradford III* was launched at 7.47 a.m. in rough seas accompanied by a strong south-westerly wind. While she was making for the casualty's position, the crew received a radio message from a helicopter, which had joined the search, that a boat with two men on board had been seen two or three miles off Withernsea. At 10.15 a.m. the lifeboat found the fishing vessel *Excelsior* of Hull, which had collided with a Royal Air Force target buoy. As the vessel was leaking and her engine was flooded, the lifeboat towed her to Grimsby, reaching the docks at 4 p.m.

In 1959 Robertson Buchan took over as Superintendent Coxswain when William Anderson retired, aged sixty. Married to Doris Anderson, Coxswain William Anderson's daughter, he had come to Spurn in 1952 as Second Coxswain. After William Anderson died, his wife Ethel moved back to Spurn and stayed with her daughter Doris Buchan in the Coxswain's cottage.

In 1960 the station celebrated its 150th anniversary. A service of rededication, conducted by the Bishop of Hull the Rt Rev G. F. Townley, assisted by the Rev L. F. Erving, Vicar of Easington, was held at the boathouse on 22 June. The ceremony was concluded with the presentation of a certificate inscribed on vellum, signed by HRH Duchess of Kent, by Admiral Sir William R. Slayter, a member of the RNLI's Committee of Management. Among the many people who attended the event were the Lord Mayor and Lady Mayoress of Hull, as well as former Coxswain Robert Cross, aged eighty-four. At the time of the anniversary, establishing the exact record of service was not possible because of incomplete records of lives saved before 1911, although more than 760 lives had been saved between 1810 and 1854. But between 1911, when the station came under the control of the RNLI, and 1960, the Humber lifeboats had gained a fine record of service, launching 400 times on service and rescuing 414 lives.

At 7 p.m. on 20 November 1961 the Coastguard informed the Coxswain Superintendent that a cargo vessel and a trawler had been in collision and that the trawler's skipper needed medical attention urgently. The trawler, *Jules Deyne,* of Ostend, had sunk, and the motor vessel *Fulham VIII*, which had collided with her, had rescued her six crew and was making towards the Humber lightvessel. *City of Bradford III* launched twenty-five minutes later with a doctor on board and reached *Fulham VIII* two miles east of Spurn lightvessel. The doctor was put aboard, but found that the skipper had died. The motor vessel and the lifeboat then made for the Bull lightvessel, where the sea was calmer, and the doctor, the six rescued seamen and the body of the trawler's skipper were transferred to the lifeboat and landed at Grimsby. The lifeboat left at 12.35 a.m. on 21 November and reached her station an hour later.

While *City of Bradford III* was away undergoing overhaul between January and April 1962, the station's former lifeboat *City of Bradford II,* from the Reserve Fleet, served on temporary duty, and she completed six services during her short stint. On 18 January 1962 she took a doctor to the steamship *Bencruachan*, of Leith, to tend to an injured man who had a broken neck and fractured skull, and who was found to be dead. Then on 16 February, the Reserve lifeboat saved the crew of two from the yacht *Star Song*, of Colchester, which had broken down and was dragging her anchor in bad weather. Seven days later she landed a sick man from the Bull lightvessel in a strong north-westerly gale.

Dedication of City of Bradford III inside the lifeboat house during the 150th anniversary of the Humber lifeboat station, 22 June 1960. (Robertson Buchan Collection)

*City of Bradford III alongside the
slipway taking guests for a trip at the
end of the service to mark the station's
150th anniversary on 22 June 1960.
A certificate inscribed on vellum, signed
by HRH the Duchess of Kent, President
of the Institution, was presented to
the station by Admiral Sir William
R. Slayter, a member of the RNLI's
Committee of Management.*

Coxswain Robertson Buchan on board City of Bradford III in the Royal Dock Basin, Grimsby, after the service to the yacht Yacht Sthoreen on 14 July 1960. (Robertson Buchan Collection)

(Below) City of Bradford III being hauled up the slipway ready for rehousing, 1960. (Robertson Buchan Collection)

City of Bradford III towing the yacht Toad into the Royal Dock Basin at Grimsby on 20 September 1960. The yacht had got into difficulty off Easington after her propeller had been fouled by a rope in gale-force winds. The tow rope parted twice during the passage to Grimsby, where the lifeboat remained until the next tide, by which time the wind had moderated. She reached Spurn at 5 p.m. having been on service for ten hours. (Robertson Buchan Collection)

City of Bradford III returned to station in April 1962 and was soon in action. She launched on 12 May 1962 to the motor fishing vessel *Monbretia*, which was in difficulty off Spurn with a fouled propeller. The casualty was drifting seawards, so the lifeboat crew rigged a tow and took the craft to Grimsby dock in the mid-afternoon. Less than two weeks later the lifeboat was out again, on 23 May 1962, to the yacht *Valhalla*, which had engine trouble three miles north-east of Spurn. The trawler *Notts Forest* had unsuccessfully attempted to take the yacht in tow, so the lifeboat was called. When the lifeboat reached

(Above) City of Bradford III in Princes Dock, Hull, on 3 June 1961, for a publicity visit to the city. (Robertson Buchan Collection)

(Right) On board the lifeboat for the visit were, from left to right, Bob Appleby, B. Gerrard, E. Davies, C. Alcock, Coxswain Roberston Buchan, E. Stott, T. Alcock and (at front) R. Stott. (Robertson Buchan Collection)

The lifeboat crew and their families at Spurn Point in the early 1960s. With Coxswain Robertson Buchan (on left), the lifeboat crew are, left to right, Barry Sayers, Thomas Alcock, Elvin Stott, Bob Appleby, G. Sayers, Cliff Staves and R. Stott. The three standing are, left to right, Doris Buchan (wife of Robertson Buchan), L. Staves and G. Appleby. (Robertson Buchan Collection)

the casualty she found that another vessel, the fishing boat *Peggy III*, had taken the yacht in tow. So the lifeboat stood by until both vessels had entered the river safely, and she then returned to station.

City of Bradford III performed an unusual service in October 1964. The Reserve lifeboat *The Cuttle*, a single-engined 35ft 6in Liverpool-type which had served at Filey and Skegness, broke down off Withernsea while on passage along the Yorkshire coast on 4 October, so *City of Bradford III* was called out to help. She launched at 1.35 p.m. and towed the lifeboat back to Spurn Point, where she was placed on moorings. However, two days later, it was noticed that *The Cuttle* appeared to be dragging on her moorings and so the lifeboat again launched to her, and this time the crew faced a westerly gale with very rough seas. By the time the lifeboat had been launched at 7.50 a.m., *The Cuttle* had broken from the moorings and was quickly drifting out to sea. She was in broken water when *City of Bradford III* reached her, but Coxswain Robertson Buchan manoeuvred the Spurn lifeboat close enough for Second Coxswain Thomas Alcock to jump across to the drifting boat. Alcock took a line with him and, once this was secured, *The Cuttle* was then towed to Grimsby, where she was moored at 11 a.m. The lifeboat remained at Grimsby, as it was not possible to rehouse *City of Bradford III* in the prevailing conditions, but before returning to Spurn another call was received. At 3.45 p.m. the lifeboat put to sea, taking a male nurse to the cargo vessel *Thorpe Grange*, of London, which had radioed for medical assistance. Somebody on the vessel had been injured, so she was transferred to the lifeboat and landed at Grimsby at 6.25 p.m. The lifeboat eventually returned to station the following day once conditions had improved.

The reserve lifeboat City of Bradford II on service to the yacht Star Song, of Colchester, on 16 February 1962, with an RAF helicopter also on scene. The yacht was in difficulties two miles north-east of Grimsby with a broken-down engine. The casualty was pitching and veering considerably in the conditions, and the lifeboat had to make three attempts to get alongside to take the two men off the yacht. The survivors were landed at Grimsby at 12.20 p.m. and the yacht later went ashore. (Robertson Buchan Collection)

In January 1962 City of Bradford III was taken away for an overhaul, during which an echo-sounder was installed and a wheelhouse was fitted over the previously open centre cockpit. She is seen here on 19 November 1964 from a helicopter of 202 Squadron, RAF Leconsfield. (Robertson Buchan Collection)

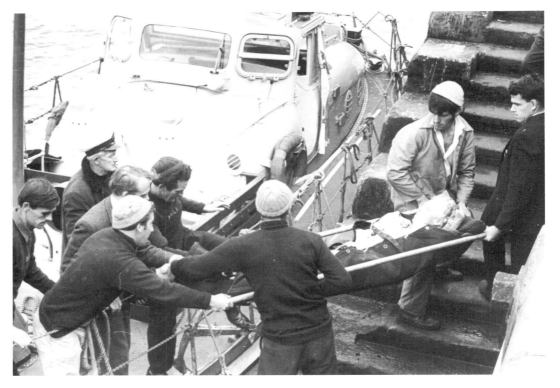

Bringing ashore an injured woman at Grimsby on 6 October 1964 from the motor vessel Thorpe Grange, of London. (Robertson Buchan Collection)

Just over a week after the service to the Reserve lifeboat, *City of Bradford III* was called out again. She launched at 10.30 a.m. on 14 October 1964 to the Russian cargo vessel *Jushnij Bug*, on board which was a severely ill woman who needed immediate medical attention. The lifeboat set off with a doctor on board, and as soon as she arrived on scene was taken alongside the Russian vessel so that the doctor could board it and attend to the woman. Twenty minutes later the doctor returned to the lifeboat with the woman, and both were transferred across. She was brought ashore by the lifeboat and taken to hospital by ambulance while *City of Bradford III* returned to station at 12.15 p.m.

On 19 August 1965 *City of Bradford III* was involved in another medical emergency when she took a doctor to an injured man on board the Russian steamship *Smolensk*. The lifeboat launched at 11.55 a.m. with a doctor and made for the vessel, which was in Spurn anchorage. The doctor went aboard the steamer and attended to the injured man, who had broken an ankle. He wanted the man to come ashore, but the vessel's captain refused, saying that the vessel would be in Hull the next day, so the lifeboat returned to station in the early afternoon and landed the doctor.

However, in the early evening of the same day Coxswain Buchan received a message from the doctor that the agents of the Russian vessel had informed him that *Smolensk* would be at anchor for another seven days and wanted the lifeboat to bring the injured man ashore so that he could get hospital treatment. The doctor asked to be taken out the next morning and at 10.30 a.m. on 20 August *City of Bradford III* was launched with the doctor and a bone specialist on board. The injured man was transferred onto the lifeboat and his ankle was set in plaster by the doctors during the passage to Spurn. The injured man was accompanied by a Russian interpreter and another crew member requiring dental treatment, and the three Russians were eventually taken to hospital by ambulance.

Launching City of Bradford III on 22 July 1965 during a visit by the Lord Mayor of Hull, and (below) recovering the boat after the trip. (Robertson Buchan Collection)

The lookout post at Spurn Point, with Coxswain Robertson Buchan raising the RNLI house flag. Trinity House records state that in 1858 the master, Willis, drew attention to the difficulty of keeping a lookout during gales and rain storms and suggested the provision of a lookout hut and a bell to summon the crew when required. Trinity House Brethren soon agreed and a wooden hut was built and a bell provided. The hut was subsequently maintained by the RNLI when it took over the station, and became known to the crew as the watch box. It was eventually removed in 1974 and taken to the garden of crew member Bob White, when the crew moved to the new houses. It had been made to replace an earlier one by the Easington joiners Stothards. Up until it was removed, the lifeboatmen used it regularly, and it was equipped with a telephone. (Robertson Buchan Collection)

The Humber lifeboat crew had to undertake a difficult search on 30 August 1965 after a small vessel got into difficulty and began firing red flares a mile and a half east of Withernsea. *City of Bradford III* launched at about 5.30 p.m. into a fresh westerly wind, and when abreast of Dimlington her crew saw a red flare about five miles to the east. The lifeboat altered course and a few minutes later a helicopter was seen coming from the direction of the flare. When the helicopter reached the lifeboat, one of its crew was lowered on board and told the Coxswain the location of the boat, which had a broken-down engine and had lost her anchor. The lifeboat found the motor fishing vessel *Pandora* with a crew of three and so towed it to Grimsby, returning to station at 9.45 p.m.

On 27 December 1965 the Spurn lifeboatmen were involved in a major incident after the oil rig *Sea Gem* collapsed and sank while drilling in the North Sea. *City of Bradford III* was one of four lifeboats which launched to help search for survivors. The rig was forty-seven miles north-west of Cromer and thirty-six miles north-east of Spurn Point. On board were thirty-two men, of whom nineteen were picked up by the steamship *Baltrover* and five were known to have died, leaving eight missing. *City of Bradford III* was launched at 2.40 p.m. on 27 December to join the massive search, and did not return to station until 4.25 a.m. two days later, but failed to find anything in that time. She was at sea continuously for almost thirty-eight hours, and her crew were tested to the limit. Lifeboats from Cromer, Wells and Skegness also helped in the search, but unfortunately no survivors were found.

Another testing service was undertaken on 2 April 1966 after the Coastguard reported to Coxswain Robertson Buchan that two red flares had been seen off Donna Nook, so *City of Bradford III* launched at 11.50 p.m. into very heavy seas and a severe north-easterly gale. Within an hour of launching, the lifeboatmen had found the motor vessel *Anzio I*, which had heeled over broadside on to the waves, with water already halfway up her deck and huge seas sweeping over her. Conditions around the vessel were extremely bad, with very heavy breaking seas on the sandbanks; Coxswain Buchan realised that getting alongside the stranded motor vessel would be impossible. So he dropped anchor and the lifeboat was veered down towards the casualty, with the anchor cable being tended by Second Coxswain Thomas Beverley, Bowman Clifford Staves and lifeboatman Edgar Knaggs.

As the lifeboat was veering down to the casualty, an enormous wave suddenly crashed over her bows, throwing the three lifeboatmen onto the front of the wheelhouse. All were injured, but they returned to the foredeck and continued to veer the anchor cable until the lifeboat was within thirty yards of the wreck. Using the searchlight, the lifeboat crew scanned the motor vessel for any survivors, but nobody could be seen. In the very heavy seas, *Anzio I* was slowly sinking and the lifeboat and her crew were taking considerable punishment, with the cockpit and aft cabin filling with water at least three times. For over twenty minutes, Coxswain Buchan held the lifeboat close to the wreck but no sign of life could be seen on the vessel, so the anchor was recovered and the lifeboat was brought clear. A thorough search downtide was then made, but no survivors were found, and the lifeboat finally left the scene at 8.35 a.m., by which time mast and top of the funnel of *Anzio I* could be seen. An hour later the lifeboat reached Spurn and was rehoused. For this service, carried out under extremely difficult conditions, Superintendent Coxswain Buchan was accorded the RNLI's Thanks Inscribed on Vellum.

City of Bradford III being recovered, being held in place at the top of the slipway.
(Robertson Buchan Collection)

The lifeboat crew in 1968, including Robertson Buchan (on left), D. Bailey, C. Staves, G. Sayers, B. Sayers, and Edgar Knaggs. (Robertson Buchan Collection)

In April 1968 City of Bradford III was sent for overhaul and re-engined with twin 70hp Barracuda diesel engines and also fitted with radar. She is pictured off Spurn with the radar mast visible on the aft cabin, and the lifeboat cottages background right. (Robertson Buchan Collection)

The boarding boats at Spurn have often been used for rescues near the station, and they performed many other duties. Even when the boathouse had been built, the station was still supplied with boarding boats. The 1957-built BB.109 was a 16ft by 6ft craft fitted with a Seagull 100 outboard engine, and launching involved the crew physically dragging the boat across the beach. (Grahame Farr, by courtesy of the RNLI)

From 1967 to May 1968 the Reserve lifeboat *Edward and Isabella Irwin* was on station while *City of Bradford III* was sent for a major overhaul, during the course of which she was fitted with new engines. The Reserve lifeboat, which had been built in 1935 and was stationed at Sunderland for almost thirty years, performed several services during her stint at Spurn, most of which were fairly routine. Probably the most significant life-saving service she undertook was on 7 October 1967, when she launched at 1.55 p.m. in a fresh north-westerly breeze to go to the fishing boat *Sea Venture*, of Immingham, which had four people on board. The boat had broken down and was drifting a mile south-east of Chequer buoy when the lifeboat arrived on scene. The lifeboat crew rigged a tow and took the vessel to Grimsby, where they arrived at 4.45 p.m. The lifeboat left Grimsby fifteen minutes later and returned to station at 6.30 p.m. In gratitude for the lifeboat's help, the fishing boat's owner sent a gift to the lifeboat crew.

City of Bradford III returned in May 1968 and was soon in action, standing by the trawler *Guidesman*, of London, on 17 May. On 12 June she saved a small boat which had broken adrift from the motor vessel *Delphic Eagle*, of Monrovia, at the Bull anchorage. The lifeboat found the drifting boat, with three men on board, half a mile east of Haile Sand Fort, so towed it back to *Delphic Eagle*. The next day she went to the same vessel as one of the crew was sick and needed medical assistance. *City of Bradford III* launched with a doctor on board at 9.20 p.m., reached the vessel at 10 p.m., and half an hour later the doctor and patient were transferred to the lifeboat, which took them to Grimsby, and the man was taken to hospital.

During 1968 concern was expressed about launching the lifeboat, as problems with the slipway had been encountered at certain states of tide. The RNLI therefore decided to supply a second lifeboat to the station, which came from the Reserve Fleet, and was kept afloat at moorings off the boathouse as a trial to assess the viability of a mooring in the river. The 46ft Watson motor-class *The Princess Royal (Civil Service*

In September 1973 Robertson Buchan, pictured on board City of Bradford III, retired as Superintendent Coxswain and was succeeded by Neil Morris. Robertson Buchan, born in 1913, married William Anderson's (previous Coxswain) daughter Doris, had three children, Joe, Robbie and Stuart, and died on 10 October 1999 aged eighty-six. (By courtesy of the RNLI)

No.7), which had served at Hartlepool for most of her career, arrived at Spurn on 18 August 1968 for a twelve-month trial period. During her time, she only performed one effective service and was withdrawn on 27 August 1969 after it was realised that keeping two lifeboats at the Humber was not necessary. However, the trial had proved that a lifeboat could be moored in the river, even though launching the boarding boat from the beach was a difficult undertaking, particularly in strong westerly winds.

The only effective service by *The Princess Royal* at Spurn took place on 13 October 1968 after a boat, with five men on board, went ashore near Patrington Haven. It was low water so launching the boarding boat was quite difficult, but the lifeboat crew got aboard *The Princess Royal* and slipped moorings at 2 a.m. to head out in rough seas and a near gale-force westerly wind, taking the boarding boat in tow. They headed round the Point but in the darkness the lifeboatmen could not see the casualty. So the boat's crew was asked to fire a flare, and having spotted this the lifeboat was able to find the casualty, the barge *Reise*, which had been working with the dredger *Queen of Holland*.

The barge was in very shallow water, so the lifeboat was anchored and the boarding boat was prepared for use by two of the lifeboat crew. As they were about to cast off, however, a heavy sea smashed the boat into the side of the lifeboat, breaking the support brackets for the outboard engine, which fell into the sea. It was recovered, but the boarding boat then had to be rowed three-quarters of a mile to the barge. However, the five men on board refused to leave, so the boarding boat returned to the lifeboat, which stood by. With the weather worsening, the master of the dredger advised the five men to leave the barge, so the boarding boat was rowed back to the barge. Once the men had been taken off, they were put aboard the lifeboat, which in turn transferred them to the dredger, before returning to station at 10.40 a.m.

(Above) The Lord Mayor of Bradford Councillor
T. E. Hall (on the right) with Lord Mayor of
Hull Councillor L. Johnson and Superintendent
Coxswain Neil Morris standing next to City
of Bradford III during a publicity visit to the
publicity station in the mid-1970s. Morris left the
post after less than two years, and was replaced
by twenty-eight-year-old Brian Bevan (right) on 16
February 1975. (By courtesy of the RNLI)

City of Bradford III was used for all the services
undertaken during 1969. At 9.20 a.m. on 13 April she
launched at 9.28 a.m. in a fresh north-westerly wind
after two red flares had been sighted off Donna Nook
and found the fishing boat Elaine drifting in broken
water a mile and a half south-west of the Haile Sand
buoy. Her engine had broken down, and a helicopter
had winched off two of the six crew. Once the lifeboat
was on scene, a line was made fast and the fishing boat
was towed to safety, with the remainder of her crew.

A yacht in difficulties about half a mile offshore
on 28 June 1971 led to the Humber lifeboat City of
Bradford III launching at 12.25 p.m. in a fresh to

A view looking towards the lifeboat house and old jetty at Spurn Point from on board City of Bradford III in August 1976. (By courtesy of Brian Bevan)

City of Bradford III returning to station with Second Coxswain Dennis Bailey, Snr, putting out fenders and Brian Fenton on the port side. (By courtesy of Brian Bevan)

City of Bradford III afloat off the lifeboat house in August 1976, shortly before she left the station. In September 1972 she had been fitted with an air-bag, mounted on her aft cabin, to give her a one-off self-righting capability in the event of a capsize. (By courtesy of Brian Bevan)

strong north-westerly wind and rough sea. The lifeboat found the catamaran *Shidajo* a mile east of the coastguard lookout, laid over to port with her anchor down, her mast broken and her sail lying across the deck. As the lifeboat reached the catamaran, two cold and wet crew members appeared from under the sail where they had been sheltering. They were both taken aboard the lifeboat and wrapped in blankets. The catamaran's anchor was recovered and she was taken in tow and beached at the lifeboat station at 3.17 p.m. The survivors were given tea in the second coxswain's house and their clothes dried out.

On the evening of Christmas Day 1972, with the lifeboat crew and their families at Spurn enjoying the festive season, the Coastguard rang Coxswain Robertson Buchan to report that one of the crew on board the motor vessel *Scottish Wasa*, of Bristol, which was in the Bull Anchorage, had attempted to commit suicide and a doctor was urgently needed. The station's honorary medical adviser at Easington was called, and he hurried to Spurn as fast as possible. Despite the cold night, with a near-gale-force south-easterly wind creating rough seas in the anchorage, the lifeboatmen left their families and the comfort of their homes, and hurried through the darkness to the lifeboat house. *City of Bradford III* was launched at 8.35 p.m. with the doctor, who was put aboard the motor vessel to treat the casualty. The man was then transferred to the lifeboat, along with the doctor, and the lifeboat headed for Grimsby, where doctor and patient were landed, and the lifeboat returned to Spurn at 8.50 a.m. on Boxing Day.

In February 1975 the twenty-eight-year-old Brian Bevan was appointed as Superintendent Coxswain and became the RNLI's youngest ever coxswain. Born in South Wales, Brian had moved to Yorkshire with his family aged five and was brought up in Scarborough and Bridlington. In 1966, while working as a fisherman, he joined the Bridlington lifeboat crew as a volunteer. Three years later a vacancy came up at the Humber station for a full-time crew member, and he spent a year at Spurn Point, but without a car he and his wife Ann found it rather remote and so Brian went back to fishing out of Scarborough for five years. When the role of Coxswain at Spurn became vacant Brian again applied and was appointed. His

The old lifeboat cottages at Spurn Point were used by the lifeboat crew for well over a century, from the 1850s until the mid-1970s, when they were demolished. Only their foundations can be made out today. (By courtesy of Brian Bevan)

first service as Coxswain took place soon after he had been appointed, on 27 February 1975, when the lifeboat launched in thick fog to land a sick man from the motor vessel *Hermes*.

At 4.40 p.m. on 30 May 1975 the Coastguard informed Superintendent Coxswain Brian Bevan that the fishing boat *Anina* of Grimsby was drifting with a net in her propeller just over eleven miles south-east of Spurn lighthouse. As no other boats were in the area and a heavy swell was endangering the vessel, *City of Bradford III* was launched ten minutes later in the strong north-westerly wind. While on the way to *Anina*, the lifeboat crew learnt that the boat's skipper was suffering from chest pains, which was diagnosed as a heart attack. As *Anina* was rolling too much in the swell for a helicopter lift, and a tow would take up to six hours, Coxswain Brian Bevan decided to take the skipper aboard the lifeboat and request a helicopter. This operation was carried out in very difficult conditions because the fishing boat had her trawl doors slung on both her quarters and loose net and wires were floating at her stern. She was broadside to the wind and rolling heavily, so the lifeboat approached her port side and transferred the sick man. The lifeboat then met the helicopter and at 7.15 p.m. the casualty was safely lifted off the lifeboat, which returned to help the drifting boat and her two remaining crew. *Anina* had been pushed by the wind and tide five miles south of her first position. At 7.48 p.m. she was taken in tow, but it was possible to make only two or three knots in the difficult conditions. After a tow lasting seven and a half hours, *Anina* and her crew were brought safely into Grimsby Docks at 3.22 a.m. on 31 May. The lifeboat left the docks at 5 a.m. after refuelling, and arrived back on station at 5.47 a.m. to be rehoused.

During her last full year of service, 1976, *City of Bradford III* was fairly busy and one of her last services proved to be particularly notable. On the evening of 1 October 1976 the Belgian trawler *Marbi*, heading for the Humber, reported to the Coastguard that two injured crewmen needed medical attention and requested that the lifeboat rendezvous with her to put a doctor aboard. Dr James Busfield, the honorary medical adviser, was informed and Coxswain Brian Bevan and his crew stood by waiting for the doctor. In heavy rain and very poor visibility, the doctor drove along the narrow road to Spurn which, in places, was under water. When still a mile and a half mile from the lifeboat station, his car skidded off the road and got stuck in the sand. Undeterred, Dr Busfield began to walk to the Point, carrying his two bags.

In 1975 seven new houses were built at Spurn Point for the lifeboat crew and their wives and families. These houses, which cost a total of £100,000 and replaced the cottages which had been in use since 1858, remain in use today. (Both photos by courtesy of Brian Bevan)

City of Bradford III, in private hands, moored in the River Mylor, July 2004. She was kept in South Cornwall for more than twenty years after being sold out of service, and was maintained in excellent condition, with virtually no external alterations. (Nicholas Leach

Meanwhile, Coxswain Bevan had become concerned that the doctor had not arrived, so went to see if something had happened and found the doctor walking along the flooded road, so took him to the station. Although soaked to the skin, Dr Busfield insisted on no further delay and *City of Bradford III* launched at 10.23 p.m. into a light wind with heavy rain reducing visibility. The lifeboat found the vessel eighteen miles north-east of Spurn Point lighthouse at 12.45 a.m. on 2 October. A moderate easterly swell initially made it difficult to transfer the doctor across, so Coxswain Bevan asked *Marbi* to steam east at slow speed which made boarding easier. The lifeboat went alongside and Dr Busfield got aboard, accompanied by the lifeboat first-aider Bill Sayers. The two men stayed aboard *Marbi* to treat the casualties, while both boats headed for Grimsby at full speed. On arrival at Grimsby at 3.50 a.m. the lifeboat crew learnt that the two injured men had been taken to hospital accompanied by both Dr Busfield and Bill Sayers.

But half an hour after reaching Grimsby, the lifeboat crew were informed by Humber Coastguard that a red flare had been sighted off Immingham and asked that they investigate. Although a thorough search was made, no sign of any casualty was found and the lifeboat returned to Grimsby to refuel and pick up Dr Busfield and Bill Sayers. *City of Bradford III* sailed for her station at 7.17 a.m., arrived at 8 a.m., and was rehoused. In appreciation of his service, which involved a long spell at sea both on the lifeboat and then the trawler, a special certificate inscribed on vellum was presented to Dr Busfield by the RNLI.

The final few services undertaken by *City of Bradford III* at Humber were all routine in nature. She was asked on several occasions to assist with sick or injured men on board cargo vessels during the first three months of 1977. In March 1977, having been replaced by a new lifeboat, she left Spurn for the last time, a few days after the service by her successor on 28 March, and was taken to William Osborne's boatyard at Littlehampton for overhaul and survey. Having been reallocated to the Lytham St Annes station in Lancashire, she served there from March 1978 to May 1985, and in July 1985 was sold out of service to Graham Mountford, of Newquay, Cornwall.

City of Bradford IV

I n March 1977 a new lifeboat arrived at Spurn Point to replace *City of Bradford III*. The wooden displacement-hulled Watson and Barnett lifeboats were reaching the end of their operational lives by the 1970s, and the RNLI had been developing replacement designs to make life-saving faster and more efficient. New designs of lifeboat were constructed which were faster, more seaworthy and safer than the boats they replaced. Of the new designs that were developed at this time, the Arun class, built from glass-reinforced plastic, proved the most successful and in 1976 one of the 54ft Aruns then under construction was allocated to the Humber. As the Arun's hull shape and size prevented her from being kept in the boathouse, she was operate from a permanent mooring laid in the river. Built by Halmatic Ltd and powered by two 360hp Caterpillar D343 diesel engines, the new boat had a top speed of over eighteen knots, a range of 226 miles, and was completely different from the old Watson lifeboat.

The 54ft Arun City of Bradford IV, a new generation of lifeboat, was placed on station at Humber in March 1977. Prominent in this photo is the Y-class inflatable boat, and its launch davit, on the roof of the superstructure. (By courtesy of the RNLI)

The new lifeboat was named *City of Bradford IV*, having been funded like her predecessors by the people of Bradford, and when she had been completed, the crew spent a few days at the RNLI Headquarters at Poole training on her. Moving from the Watson to the Arun was a major step up, as not only was the new boat much more powerful but she also carried a far greater range of equipment. The new lifeboat arrived at Spurn in March 1977, having travelled from Poole with overnight stops at Dover, Lowestoft and Boston in Lincolnshire. Boston had never before been visited by a lifeboat on passage, so the call by the new Arun was a first, with the Humber crew meeting the local fund-raising branch as part of the goodwill visit. A few days after arriving at Spurn, the new lifeboat took up her operational duties.

An 18ft 6in McLachlan lifeboat, specially adapted as a boarding boat, was provided for the crew to get out to the moored lifeboat. The boarding boat was kept afloat off the Pilot Jetty, which had been built in 1974-75. The jetty made getting to the boarding boat much easier than hitherto, when earlier such boats had been launched across the beach using manpower. In strong westerly winds this was both difficult and dangerous, although getting aboard the floating McLachlan from the ladder on the jetty was not always easy. To improve matters and make the boarding procedure safer and easier, in 1992 a davit was installed on the north end of the Pilot Jetty. The installation was completed in August 1992, and greatly improved the situation, as the crew could climb onto the boarding boat before it was lifted into the water.

City of Bradford IV served at the Humber for just over a decade, during which time she achieved a remarkable record of service, launching 416 times on service and saving over a hundred lives. She was also involved in some of the most dramatic and daring rescues in the history of the lifeboat service, although she had a relatively quiet start. Her first call came on 28 March 1977, and even though the crew were still training on her, when the call came they went in her and soon proved her capabilities. She left Spurn at 5.13 a.m. after the Grimsby trawler *Sioux* was reported to be sinking near the North Outer Dowsing Buoy in rough seas and a northerly gale. Five of the trawler's crew were picked up by the rig standby vessel *Margaret Christina*, but one man was missing. Helped by a helicopter and HMS *Churka*, the lifeboatmen searched for the missing man. At 11.25 a.m. the warship radioed that her crew had spotted a life jacket and possibly a body in the water, but were unable to recover it, so the lifeboat headed for the spot and the crew recovered the body of the missing man, which was landed at Grimsby at 2.30 p.m.

City of Bradford IV arriving at Spurn Point in March 1977. (Grimsby Evening Telegraph)

City of Bradford IV moored in the King George Dock, Kingston-Upon-Hull, on 10 September 1977 for her naming ceremony. (By courtesy of Brian Bevan)

While the lifeboat was being refuelled at Grimsby, a message was received that one of the survivors on board *Margaret Christina* had collapsed and needed medical attention, so the Port Medical Officer was taken out by the lifeboat. He was put aboard the rig standby vessel, which was then entering the river, and the lifeboat returned to station at 5 p.m.

The speed and range of the Arun lifeboats enabled a much faster response time to incidents, many of which would have been beyond the range of conventional displacement lifeboats. Speed was of the essence on 22 June 1977 after Coxswain Brian Bevan had been informed that the trawler *Bermuda*, of Lowestoft, with a crew of seven, was taking in water seventy-five miles north-east of Spurn Point. Such a service in *City of Bradford III* would have been a major and time-consuming exercise. But *City of Bradford IV* slipped her moorings at 8.06 p.m. and headed out at full speed into calm seas ready for a long journey. A Nimrod aircraft and a helicopter were also tasked. At 9.45 p.m., when the lifeboat was twenty-five miles north-east of Spurn, her crew was radioed that the pumps on the trawler, which was heading slowly towards the Humber, were coping with the ingress of water and so the Mayday was cancelled. Coxswain Bevan brought the lifeboat round and headed back towards Spurn. However, at 10.56 p.m., just as the lifeboat was passing the Spurn lightvessel, the lifeboatmen intercepted another radio message from the trawler stating that the pumps had failed and the crew were having to bail using buckets. Coxswain Bevan immediately turned the lifeboat round and headed back towards the trawler. The casualty was reached at 1.45 a.m., thirty-five miles north-east of Spurn Point, and one of the lifeboatmen was transferred across with a portable pump. The trawler then set course for the Humber, escorted by the lifeboat, and the two vessels reached Grimsby Docks at 8.45 a.m., where the fire brigade took over the pumping. The lifeboat returned to her station at 10.30 a.m., having been at sea for nearly more than fourteen hours.

The new lifeboat was named at a ceremony held at the King George Dock, Kingston-Upon-Hull, on 10 September 1977, which was organised jointly by the Hull and Bradford branches. While a relief lifeboat and her crew gave temporary cover at Spurn, *City of Bradford IV* was brought by her regular crew to King

The seven lifeboat crew houses at Spurn Point built in the 1970s. (By courtesy of the RNLI)

George Dock, with wives and children following by road, meaning the whole Humber lifeboat community was at the dockside for the ceremony. The boat, which cost £163,453.48, was provided by the Metropolitan City of Bradford's Lord Mayor's appeal 1974-75, supported by Bradford and District branch, ladies' guild and ladies' luncheon club, Baildon, Bingley, Ilkley, Shipley, Keighley guilds and Keighley branch, together with the Sheffield lifeboat fund, a gift from the International Transport Workers' Federation, various legacies and a gift from the Phoenix ladies' club, Pinner. Sir Basil Parkes, OBE, JP, president of Hull branch, opened proceedings and Clifford Kershaw, chairman of Bradford Branch, presented the lifeboat to the RNLI. She was accepted by the Duke of Atholl, Deputy Chairman and a member of the Committee of Management. After the service of dedication, led by the Lord Bishop of Bradford the Right Rev Hook, and a vote of thanks, chairman of Hull branch, Councillor T. E. Hall, Lord Mayor of Bradford 1974-75 and patron of the appeal committee, accompanied by his granddaughter, named the lifeboat *City of Bradford IV*. The boat was the fourth lifeboat named *City of Bradford* to be stationed at the Humber.

City of Bradford IV had already undertaken a number of rescues before her naming ceremony, and she went on to have an outstanding career at the Humber. The first of many fine services she performed took place on 18 December 1978 after the fishing vessel *Falke*, on delivery passage from the Continent to Whitby, broke down sixty miles north-east of Flamborough Head with no power or steering. As no other ships were in the area and Humber Radio was having communication problems with *Falke*, it was decided to launch. *City of Bradford IV* slipped her moorings at 8.13 a.m., and set course through slight seas for the casualty's last known position in good visibility. The fishery protection minesweeper HMS *Stubbington* was also on her way to help and she sighted *Falke* at 12.27 p.m. and sent an engineer across in an inflatable to see if he could help. He was unable to get the engine started, however, and so the lifeboat, which arrived a quarter of an hour later, agreed to tow the boat to Bridlington. Although the casualty had no steering, Bridlington Harbour was reached safely at 8.56 p.m. and, after refuelling their boat and having a meal, the lifeboat crew returned to station. Following this service a letter of thanks was received from *Falke*'s owner together with two cheques, one to thank the Humber coxswain and crew, and the other a donation to the Institution.

Although she served the station for little more than a decade, *City of Bradford IV* was involved in some of the most memorable and outstanding rescues ever undertaken. The first of these took place on 30 December 1978 when the Dutch coaster *Diana V* got into difficulties seventy-four miles south-east of Spurn Point having been caught in rough seas near Well Bank, and her cargo of maize had shifted. When news of the coaster's distress call reached Spurn, *City of Bradford IV* slipped her moorings, at 2.10 p.m., and with Coxswain Brian Bevan at the helm headed out. Cromer lifeboat, the relief 46ft 9in Watson *William Gammon – Manchester and District XXX*, on temporary duty, also put out, and HMS *Lindisfarne* altered course to help.

As *City of Bradford IV* cleared the river, she ran into extremely heavy seas, whipped up by a violent easterly gale, with visibility reduced at times to less than 100 yards in very heavy snow showers. At 4 p.m., as Coxswain Bevan headed at full speed into the violent seas, having by then covered about twenty-five miles, *City of Bradford IV* suddenly lost speed after an oil supply pipe to the starboard engine fractured due to the pounding that the boat had been taking, and so that engine was shut down. Knowing that HMS *Lindisfarne* was standing by the coaster and that the Cromer lifeboat was on her way, Coxswain Bevan decided to return to Grimsby to make emergency repairs. On the way, Mechanic Barry Sayers and his brother Ronald, the Assistant Mechanic, managed to strip down the pump, despite having to work in the confined space of the engine room and cope with the extreme motion of the lifeboat.

The lifeboat reached Grimsby safely on one engine at 6.45 p.m. and, with waves breaking over the lock head, Coxswain Bevan skilfully took the lifeboat through the narrow Fish Dock gates and tied up alongside the quay. Coxswain Bevan knew that if they remained there, the lock gates would be closed when the tide turned and the lifeboat would be trapped in the Dock until 4 a.m. So, rather than risk being off service, and with a replacement piece of pipe having been obtained, Coxswain Bevan took the

City of Bradford IV bringing in the fishing vessel Falke to Bridlington on the evening of 18 December 1978. (By courtesy of Brian Bevan)

City of Bradford IV assisting the barge Almeco aground off Mablethorpe on 12 October 1982.
(By courtesy of Brian Bevan)

lifeboat out of the dock at 8.30 p.m. and returned to Spurn, where the lifeboat was refuelled. Meanwhile, the two mechanics were working as fast as they could to replace the damaged pipe and by 9.36 p.m. the lifeboat was again on her way to the casualty. Meanwhile, at 5 p.m. HMS *Lindisfarne* had downgraded the situation as *Diana V* had been able to get underway again and was heading for the Humber at about nine knots, so the Cromer lifeboat was recalled. But as *City of Bradford IV*, with both engines working, headed towards *Diana V*, HMS *Lindisfarne* reported that the situation was in fact getting worse, with the coaster taking in water, twenty-eight miles east of Spurn Point. To reach the casualty, the lifeboat had to battle her way through 25ft waves, which pounded both boat and crew.

The lifeboat was heading almost directly into the 25ft short, steep seas at full speed, at times taking off on one wave and then crashing down into the next wave. At 10.35 p.m., when still eight miles from the casualty, she crashed down from an exceptionally large sea and all lighting, window wipers and fans failed. Crew member Dennis Bailey, Jnr, was thrown against the wheelhouse bulkhead, injuring his right eye, as well as his knee and elbow. Speed had to be reduced to ten knots to give the mechanics a chance to find the fault and restore the lighting. While repairs were being made, HMS *Lindisfarne* radioed that the lifeboat was urgently needed to take off the coaster's four crew and two women, so Coxswain Bevan resumed at full speed towards the casualty. The coaster was reached at 11 p.m. and the lifeboat prepared to go alongside *Diana V*, which had a heavy list to port and was steering an erratic course at about five knots. With the wind at storm force ten gusting to fifty-six knots, the lifeboatmen tied fenders round the lifeboat's bow to reduce any impact. As they worked on the open foredeck, heavy seas repeatedly swept over them and, with the air temperature at minus four degrees centigrade, the sea froze on the deck and handrails, making their task exceptionally difficult.

Coxswain Bevan instructed the master of *Diana V* to have his crew on the port quarter, ready to jump and, with the crew of HMS *Lindisfarne* illuminating the scene with their searchlight, Bevan

The original boarding boat arrangement when City of Bradford IV arrived involved the 18ft 6in McLachlan A-505, which was kept afloat off the Pilot Jetty and hauled alongside the ladder when needed.

took the lifeboat towards the coaster. All the lifeboatmen, except for Coxswain Bevan and the two mechanics, were on the foredeck, with their lifelines fastened to the rails forward. As the lifeboat edged towards the coaster's port quarter, a heavy breaking sea struck *Diana V*, almost washing the crew off the deck. As the two boats were flung together, part of the lifeboat's rubbing strake was ripped away and the anchor-stowage was damaged. With the lifeboat's bow then 10ft above the deck of the coaster, Coxswain Bevan put both engines full astern and she pulled clear. A second approach was made, but this time a very heavy sea struck the lifeboat, smashing her starboard bow against the coaster with such force that one of the fenders exploded with a tremendous bang, and more of the rubbing strake was torn away. At one point, as the coaster heeled over, she was only three feet from Coxswain Bevan on the lifeboat's flying bridge. Again he quickly put the engines into reverse and the lifeboat pulled clear.

On the third run, the lifeboat's bow hit the coaster about five feet below where the crew were huddled and a twelve-year-old girl was dropped into the arms of the waiting lifeboatmen. Then, as the lifeboat rose up on the top of the following wave, the other woman and four men jumped across. The lifeboat's engines were put full astern and she was taken clear with the six survivors aboard. They were wet, cold and suffering from shock, and were immediately taken into the cabin to be looked after. Coxswain Bevan brought the lifeboat round again to take up station on the coaster's port quarter as her captain, his crew safe, had decided to stay on board to try and save his ship.

Escorted by the lifeboat and HMS *Lindisfarne*, *Diana V* then limped towards the Humber, twenty miles away, huge waves repeatedly sweeping her with, at times, only her fo'c'sle and bridge visible above the seas. But she struggled on and entered the Humber at 1.45 a.m. Fifteen minutes later, a pilot went on board and *City of Bradford IV* was able to return to Spurn, where ambulances were waiting to take the survivors to hospital. By 3.45 a.m. the lifeboat had been refuelled and was ready for service having been at sea for nearly fourteen hours in truly appalling conditions. For his outstanding seamanship, great courage and fine leadership during this service, Superintendent Coxswain Bevan was awarded a Silver medal by the RNLI. For their courage and bravery during this extremely demanding service, the RNLI's Thanks on Vellum were accorded to each of the other members of the crew: Second Coxswain Dennis Bailey, Snr, Mechanic Barry Sayers, Assistant Mechanic Ronald Sayers and lifeboatmen Michael B. Storey, Peter Jordan and Dennis Bailey, Jnr. A Framed Letter of Thanks, signed by Major-General Ralph Farrant, the Chairman of the RNLI, was sent to the commanding officer of HMS *Lindisfarne*, Lt Cdr A. J. C. Morrow, RN, for the considerable help given by him and his crew during this service.

Just six weeks after this outstanding service, the Humber lifeboatmen performed an even more dramatic rescue after the Panamanian motor vessel *Revi* was reported in distress thirty miles north-east of Spurn Point, and this rescue catapulted them into the spotlight of the national media. The call for help came just after midnight on 14 February 1979 and at 12.15 a.m. *City of Bradford IV* slipped her moorings and headed out into extremely rough seas and a north-easterly gale, with gusts up to force nine and increasing. By the time the lifeboat had cleared the river and was about two miles north-east of Spurn lightvessel, she was heading into very large seas. She crested one and then fell fifteen to twenty feet, hitting the next trough so hard that the electric breakers on the lights and window wipers opened. Speed was reduced to fourteen knots in the head seas, which were now estimated to be thirty-five feet high.

The lifeboat arrived on scene at 1.36 a.m. and found *Revi* heading slowly towards the Humber, making about six knots. The heavy following seas were lifting the coaster's stern out of the water, while her bows were almost constantly under water, and another vessel, the ship *Deepstone*, was standing by. The conditions at this stage were extreme, with the crew of a nearby gas rig recording winds of storm force ten from the north-east, with occasional snow showers. At 1.45 a.m. the master of *Revi* radioed that he was slowing down so that two of his crew could be taken off. At first, Coxswain Bevan thought that this would be impossible in the conditions and asked *Revi* to stop to see how she would behave in the violent seas. Stopped, she lay broadside to the weather with heavy seas breaking across her whole length, and the danger to survivors and crew members alike was so great that a rescue in that position had little chance of success. So Coxswain Bevan instructed *Revi* to steer a course southward at slow speed and to have the two men on the boat deck on her starboard quarter ready to jump.

With the lifeboat's port shoulder heavily fendered, Coxswain Bevan slowly took the lifeboat towards the coaster. But just as she came under the casualty's starboard quarter, a huge wave struck *Revi*, completely covering her stern and sending her crashing down towards the lifeboat. Coxswain Bevan quickly put both engines full astern and the lifeboat pulled clear, just avoiding being damaged. Nine attempts had to be made before the two men had been taken off *Revi*, whose stern at times was twenty-five feet above the lifeboat. The two men eventually jumped to safety as the lifeboat came up to *Revi* in blinding snow.

Revi's master still hoped to make it to the Humber, but five minutes later he radioed to say that the ship's accommodation was flooding and the situation was deteriorating rapidly. The cargo had shifted and the vessel had a forty-five degree list, so he had decided to abandon ship. He turned *Revi* to provide a lee

(Above) Cty of Bradford IV at moorings off the Pilot Jetty during the late 1970s. (Tony Denton)

(Right) The Humber lifeboat crew on the bow of City of Bradford IV, from left to right, Coxswain Brian Bevan, David Capes, Second Coxswain Dennis Bailey, Snr, Mechanic Bob White, Michael Storey and Syd Rollinson. These photos were taken during the filming of a television documentary about the lives of the full-time crew at Spurn Point. (By courtesy of the RNLI)

City of Bradford IV moored with the 37ft Oakely J. G. Graves of Sheffield, at the Pilot Jetty, Spurn, October 1979. The Oakely was on passage back from Staniland's boatyard, Thorne, having undertaken relief duties at Skegness. (By courtesy of the RNLI)

for the lifeboat on the port side, while the lifeboatmen moved the fenders into position, a difficult task in the violent seas with huge waves repeatedly sweeping them. As the lifeboat came alongside the casualty's heaving deck on the first approach, a large wave broke right over both vessels and swept the lifeboat away from the ship's side. The same thing happened again and again, and it took another twelve attempts before the lifeboat could be brought alongside at a moment when, with a reasonable height between the two decks, a man was able to jump.

With the lifeboat in position, the mate jumped six feet into the arms of the lifeboat's crew who broke his fall and hurried him below. *Revi*'s bows were now almost submerged, her No.1 hatch was completely awash and her stern was clear of the water, poised dangerously above the lifeboat. The last survivor, the master, was hanging on to the outside of *Revi*'s stern rails, ready to jump. On about the tenth attempt to get him off, as *City of Bradford IV* approached *Revi*'s quarter, the stricken vessel's stern rose twenty feet in the air and began to crash down towards the lifeboat's foredeck, where the crew were lashed to the rails with little or no chance to get clear. Seeing what was happening, Coxswain Bevan rammed the throttles full astern and the Arun's impressive power pulled her clear with only inches to spare.

As they prepared to go in again, three enormous waves completely covered *Revi* and it was feared that the master had been lost, but when the water cleared he was still clinging desperately to the outside of the stern rails. Coxswain Bevan realised that *Revi* was now on the point of capsizing, so he quickly took the lifeboat towards her in a trough between two waves, drove the lifeboat under the coaster's port quarter, striking her stern, and giving the master the opportunity to jump. He almost fell overboard as he left the stricken ship, but the lifeboatmen just managed to grab him and haul him to safety. It was 2.33 a.m. and just minutes later *Revi* rolled over and sank. Coxswain Bevan set course for Grimsby where the survivors were landed and the lifeboat left at 6.09 a.m. to be back on her moorings at Spurn just over an hour later.

For this truly outstanding rescue, during which the lifeboat had to be manoeuvred up to *Revi* thirty-five times, in the most appalling conditions, Superintendent/Coxswain Brian Bevan was awarded a Gold medal by the RNLI. It was a service demanding great skill and tremendous courage on the part of the whole, extremely gallant crew and the RNLI awarded a Bronze medal to each of the other crew members: Second Coxswain Dennis Bailey, Snr, Mechanic Barry Sayers, Assistant Mechanic Ronald Sayers and lifeboatmen Michael Story, Peter Jordan, Sydney Rollinson and Dennis Bailey, Jnr.

The day after this remarkable rescue, 15 February 1979, the Humber lifeboat was called out once again and, in the same severe weather, completed another outstanding service. The casualty on this occasion was the Romanian cargo vessel *Savinesti*, with twenty-eight people on board, which was in distress thirty-seven miles south-east of Spurn Point. She had engine failure and was dragging her anchor. The danger was that she might ground on either the Race Bank or the Docking Shoal, so the Wells lifeboat *Ernest Tom Neathercoat*, a 37ft Oakley type with an open cockpit and minimal shelter for the crew, was launched at 10.24 a.m. with the Humber lifeboat crew on standby to go to another casualty to the north as conditions had prevented the Bridlington lifeboat from launching.

As *Ernest Tom Neathercoat* crossed the bar at Wells Harbour, she encountered exceptionally heavy seas churned up by the violent north-easterly gale, which was gusting to storm force ten, and conditions were extremely cold with frequent very heavy snow storms. The lifeboat was hit repeatedly by enormous breaking seas and her radar, radio and echo-sounder were put out of action by the severity of the weather. The forward well was constantly full of water and her crew had to seek what shelter they could in the aft cockpit. The lifeboat was labouring heavily to clear the huge volume of water she was taking on board and her Coxswain, David Cox, had to reduce speed to stop her foundering.

The Bridlington lifeboat was eventually able to launch to the other casualty, so at 11.24 a.m. *City of Bradford IV* put out to *Savinesti*. Getting aboard the lifeboat from the boarding boat in the extremely poor

The crew involved in the two medal-winning rescues in February 1979 were, from left to right, Dennis Bailey, Peter Jordan, Mechanic Barry Sawyers, Superintendent Coxswain Brian Bevan, Second Coxswain Dennis Bailey, Sydney Rollinson, Assistant Mechanic Ronald Sayers and Michael Storey. (By courtesy of the RNLI)

conditions was a difficult and dangerous task, but once the crew were on the lifeboat Coxswain Bevan headed out at full speed. Visibility was reduced to less than seventy-five yards in the blizzard, with a three-inch layer of ice on the boat and her rails and the air temperature well below freezing. As the radar picture was very poor and the Decca Navigator did not appear to be working, Coxswain Bevan slowed down so that the scanners could be checked and they were found to be covered in ice, which was chipped away so the equipment could work. Once the lifeboat cleared Spurn Point, she again had to reduce speed because of the violent seas, with visibility down to almost nothing in the blizzard. The Decca Navigator could only be used if the lifeboat slowed right down during the infrequent pauses in the heavy snow.

With the tanker *Annuity* and the ferry *Norwave* standing by *Savinesti*, which had radioed that she had lost both anchors, *City of Bradford IV* battled on, although concern was growing for the safety of the Wells lifeboat in the appalling conditions. Coxswain Bevan radioed to the two vessels standing by the casualty asking if they could pick up the lifeboat on their radars, but neither could. However, a few minutes later the Wells lifeboatmen saw one of the ships and they reached *Savinesti* at 1.07 p.m. The Wells lifeboat and her crew had taken a terrible battering and all were suffering from the cold and wet, with waves up to forty feet high sweeping the sandbanks and often engulfing the lifeboat. The north-easterly gale was blowing a steady force ten, gusting to force eleven, with the spray off the waves reducing visibility further and heavy snow was still falling.

Several attempts were made to get a line aboard *Savinesti* from the other two vessels, but this proved impossible and so the Wells lifeboat continued to stand by, while the casualty just about held her own to the north of the South Race Buoy. By 3 p.m. the Humber lifeboat was only seven miles from the scene and so the Wells lifeboat was released to try and get ashore in the daylight. The wind had risen to hurricane force twelve and, with her drogue streamed astern to steady her, she set off for home. At half-speed because of the violent seas, she headed slowly towards the coast, with heavy snow blowing straight into the open aft cockpit. At 6.15 p.m. the Wells lifeboatmen fired a parachute flare to confirm their position, and an Auxiliary Coastguard saw the lifeboat just north of Brancaster Golf Club. Coxswain Cox therefore steered an easterly course for Wells, but those last seven miles took a further two hours, with the lifeboat having to be repeatedly brought round to head into the mountainous seas.

By 8.30 p.m., the lifeboat was off the entrance to Wells Harbour, but in the blizzard it was impossible for any of the crew to make out the leading lights to guide her over the bar. One of the local fishing boats therefore went down the channel towards the harbour entrance to act as a guide and help pilot the lifeboat by radio. At 9.10 p.m. the lifeboat crossed the bar, being buried by three enormous waves as she came in, but she made it safely across and was berthed alongside the Town Quay at 9.50 p.m., having been at sea in the most appalling conditions for more than eleven hours. Each of the crew was suffering greatly from exposure and exhaustion, and they had to be helped out of the lifeboat and onto the Quay, most being unable to walk unaided so bad had their ordeal been.

Back out at sea, further attempts were made by the Humber lifeboatmen to get a line aboard *Savinesti*, but without success. The tug *Lady Moira* reached the scene at 6 p.m., but in the terrible conditions her master decided it was too dangerous for any of his crew to work on the open deck. So, with the other vessels and the Humber lifeboat escorting her, *Savinesti* headed slowly north, making four knots at best. Shortly after midnight, as the snow finally eased and the wind dropped to force nine, *Savinesti* and the other ships, then about five miles north of the Dowsing lightvessel, turned to head for the Humber. They eventually entered the river at 3 a.m., and *City of Bradford IV* returned to her moorings at Spurn at 4.25 a.m. after over fifteen hours at sea.

For this long, extremely difficult and demanding service, undertaken in the worst weather for many years, Coxswain David Cox of Wells was awarded a Silver medal by the RNLI, with Medal Service certificates going to the rest of the Wells crew. Coxswain Bevan was awarded the Bronze medal, and Medal Service certificates were presented to the rest of the Humber crew: Second Coxswain Dennis Bailey, Mechanic Barry 'Bill' Sayers, Assistant Mechanic Ronald Sayers and crew members Michael B. Storey, Peter Jordan and Dennis Bailey, Jnr. Framed Letters of Thanks signed by Major-General Ralph

Line up of medallists at the RNLI's Annual General meeting of 1979 with Superintendent Coxswain Brian Bevan (on right). The other Humber crew are, from left to right on front row, Second Coxswain Dennis Bailey, Snr, Mechanic Bill Sayers, Assistant Mechanic Ronald Sayers, Michael Storey, Peter Jordan, Sydney Rollison, and Dennis Bailey, Jnr. The other lifeboat personnel pictured are (second row) Coxswain David Cox (Wells), Cyril Alcock (Plymouth) and Dennis Bailey, Jnr (Humber). The third row, left to right: Coxswain William Morris (St Davids), Coxswain Evan Jones (Barmouth), Coxswain/Mechanic William Rees Holmes (Angle) and Second Coxswain Patrick Marshall (Plymouth). On back row, from left to right: Coxswain Arthur Curnow (Torbay), Acting Second Coxswain Seamus McCormack (Rosslare Harbour), Coxswain/Mechanic Charles Bowry (Sheerness), Coxswain John Petit (St Peter Port) and Coxswain Fred Walkington (Bridlington). (By courtesy of the RNLI)

Farrant, Chairman of the Institution, were sent to the master of *Norwave*, Captain Wally Patch, and to the skipper of motor fishing vessel *Strandline*, John Ward, in recognition of their assistance.

The winter of 1978-79 had seen some of the worst weather in living memory along the east coast, and the feats of the Humber lifeboatmen, led by Coxswain Brian Bevan, were as considerable as any performed in the history of the lifeboat service, including rescues by their predecessors under Robert Cross during the Second World War. Recognition for the lifeboat crew's courage came in the spring when, in May 1979, the Humber lifeboatmen with their wives and families went to London to attend the RNLI's Annual General Meeting at the Royal Festival Hall. A relief crew was sent to Spurn to cover operational requirements, and had two calls in the three days they were at Spurn.

At the AGM on 22 May the Humber lifeboatmen received their medals for gallantry from the President of the RNLI, HRH The Duke of Kent. The presentation was particularly notable, as Brian Bevan became the first lifeboatman in the history of the RNLI to receive Gold, Silver and Bronze medals at the same medal ceremony. In the space of forty-six days during the winter of 1978/79 the Arun lifeboat had carried out three outstanding rescues and the feats of seamanship shown by Coxswain Bevan and his crew were unparalleled in the history of the RNLI. The new lifeboat, which had been on station at Spurn for less than two years, had shown what a capable craft she was and how her speed, power and crew protection had brought a new dimension to life-saving at Spurn Point. For the service to *Revi*, Coxswain Brian Bevan was later presented with the Maud Smith Award, which recognised the most outstanding act of life-saving by any lifeboatman during 1979.

The interest shown by the media and public in the extraordinary rescues of that winter was considerable, and resulted in Brian Bevan being invited to attend many functions, such as the Earl's Court Boat Show in January 1980, which he formally opened. In March 1980 he was invited to the exhibition 'In Danger's Hour' at the Kodak Photographic Gallery, at High Holborn in London, and there he was surprised by the waiting TV presenter Eamon Andrews, who greeted him with the famous words 'Coxswain Brian Bevan, This Is Your Life'. For the programme, they were joined at the TV studios by Brian's wife Ann, their son, the lifeboat crew and their wives, and by coxswains and friends from many other lifeboat stations around the country, while a relief crew was provided to 'look after things at Spurn'. The programme was watched by about eighteen million people, and inevitably Brian became a nationally known figure.

Following the events of 1978-79, the Humber lifeboatmen continued to be busy, answering on average one call a week, and during the 1980s, further notable services were performed. In October 1980 *City of Bradford IV* was taken to Robson's boatyard, at South Shields, for overhaul, and the relief 52ft Arun *Edith Emilie* was placed on temporary duty at Spurn, remaining until summer 1981. While on station, she was involved in a very fine service on 6 December 1980 after the tug *Lady Debbie* had radioed that a small boat, the converted ship's lifeboat *Nicholas*, was aground on Foul Holme Sands, near Immingham. Shallow water prevented the tug from getting any nearer than three-quarters of a mile from the casualty, so the lifeboat was called. *Edith Emilie* slipped her moorings at 8.19 p.m. into force six north-westerly

Drawing of City of Bradford IV on service to the coaster Revi on 14 February 1979, one of the most dramatic rescues in the history of the lifeboat service.

The lifeboat house and slipway built in 1923, with the longer second slipway added in 1931. The original slipway remained in place beneath the later slipway, and this photograph provides a good view of both slipways. The house was used until 1977, when the lifeboat was placed on moorings. (By courtesy of Brian Bevan)

During the summer of 1995 the lifeboat house and slipway, which had been built at Spurn in 1923, were dismantled and removed. The whole structure was removed and this photo was taken on the day that demolition work began. (Photos by courtesy of Brian Bevan)

The station's last slipway-launched lifeboat, the 46ft 9in Watson motor City of Bradford III, with the old crew cottages in the background. City of Bradford III served at Spurn from 1954 to 1977 and saved 107 lives, launching 351 times on service. (By courtesy of Brian Bevan)

The crew houses constructed in the 1970s form a small community at Spurn Point, close to the pilot station and the lifeboat's moorings. There are a total of seven more or less identical houses, with the Superintendent Coxswain's on the far right. (Nicholas Leach)

54ft Arun City of Bradford IV at sea. She was built with a manually operated davit for launching the Y-class inflatable, which was stowed on top of the wheelhouse. This davit was replaced by rails which were put in place across the stern. (By courtesy of Brian Bevan)

A fine photograph of 54ft Arun City of Bradford IV at full speed. She served at the Humber for a decade and achieved an outstanding record of service, being used for some of the most famous rescues in the history of the RNLI. (By courtesy of Syd Rollinson)

The crew of City of Bradford IV on the bow of the lifeboat, from left to right, Superintendent Coxswain Brian Bevan, David Capes, Second Coxswain Dennis Bailey, Snr, Mechanic Robert White, Michael Storey and Syd Rollinson. (By courtesy of the RNLI)

City of Bradford IV out of the water at Robson's Boatyard, South Shields, undergoing routine maintenance in 1985. (By courtesy of Brian Bevan)

The 52ft Arun Kenneth Thelwall powers along at full speed during her trials, before coming to the Humber. (By courtesy of the RNLI)

Dressed overall, Kenneth Thelwall makes her way to Hull Marina for her naming ceremony on 19 September 1987. (Paul Arro)

Two fine photographs showing the 52ft Arun Kenneth Thelwall on exercise; she served at the Humber from 1987 to 1997. (By courtesy of Brian Bevan)

The relief 52ft Arun Margaret Russell Fraser in Grimsby Docks, passing the two shore facilities, past and present, used by the crew when bad weather forces the lifeboat into the docks. The grey building on the far left was completed in 1994; before this came into use, the Naval Cadet building (on the right) was available for the crew's use. (By courtesy of Brian Bevan)

On the boarding boat leaving Kenneth Thelwall at her moorings, with Coxswain Brian Bevan in the front middle steering, and, from left to right, Assistant Mechanic Les Roberts, and crew members Shaun Sonley, Dave Steenvoorden, and Chris Barnes. (By courtesy of Brian Bevan)

On board Kenneth Thelwall in Grimsby Dock are, from left to right, Mechanic Peter Thorpe, Assistant Mechanic Les Roberts, crew member Shaun Sonley, Second Coxswain Bob White, and Coxswain Brian Bevan. (By courtesy of Brian Bevan)

Relief 52ft Arun Edith Emilie at moorings off the Pilot Jetty in April 1985; the relief boat was on temporary duty from March 1985 to May 1986. The McLachlan boarding boat A-505, moored off the jetty, served from 1977 to 1987, having been built in 1970 as an ILB for Eastney. (Paul Arro)

The impressive sight of 17m Severn-class lifeboat Pride of the Humber at full speed while on trials, prior to coming to Spurn Point. (By courtesy of the RNLI)

17m Severn Pride of the Humber in rough seas. (By courtesy of Brian Bevan)

Escorted by Kenneth Thelwall, Pride of the Humber arrives at Spurn Point for the first time on 8 March 1997. (Paul Arro)

Pride of the Humber arriving at Spurn Point for the first time, 8 March 1997, after a passage north from the RNLI's headquarters at Poole. (Nicholas Leach)

Kenneth Thelwall (on right) and Pride of the Humber arrive at Grimsby for a publicity visit on the day the new 17m Severn arrived on the Humber. (By courtesy of Grimsby Evening Telegraph)

Kenneth Thelwall and Pride of the Humber together at Grimsby Docks with the two boarding boats purpose-built for use at Spurn Point. (By courtesy of Brian Bevan)

17m Severn Pride of the Humber on exercise off Spurn Point, April 2005. (Nicholas Leach)

Relief Severn lifeboat Fraser Flyer approaching the yacht Molly Louise on 12 August 2006. The lifeboat was called to assist the yacht, which had been hit by a freak wave resulting in the death of one sailor and three yachtsmen being washed overboard. The Skegness and Humber lifeboats worked together to undertake a successful rescue operation. (By courtesy of the RNLI)

The relief 17m Severn lifeboat Fraser Flyer, built in 1998, moored off the Pilot Jetty while on temporary duty during summer 2006. (Tony Denton)

Pride of the Humber in attendance at the naming ceremony of the new Atlantic 75 B-778 Joan Mary at Mablethorpe, 22 April 2002. (By courtesy of Grimsby Evening Telegraph)

The lifeboat crew boarding Pride of the Humber off the Pilot Jetty. (Nicholas Leach)

Humber lifeboat crew returning to the Pilot Jetty in the purpose-built boarding boat BB-240, with Coxswain Dave Steenvoorden at the helm. (Nicholas Leach)

Pride of the Humber on exercise off Spurn Point. (Nicholas Leach)

Pride of the Humber at her moorings off Spurn, ready for her next service. (Nicholas Leach)

Superintendent Coxswain Dave Steenvoorden (second from left) represented the RNLI's North operational division at the Ceremony of Dedication of the RNLI's memorial sculpture in Poole, Dorset, on 3 October 2009. (Nigel Millard, by courtesy of the RNLI)

The full-time crew members of the Humber lifeboat on the bridge of Pride of the Humber in May 2010, the 200th anniversary year. They are, left to right, Superintendent Coxswain David Steenvoorden, Mechanic Colin Fisk snr, crew member Colin Fisk jnr, crew member Steve Purvis and Second Coxswain Martyn Hagan. (Nicholas Leach)

City of Bradford IV in Grimsby Docks. (By courtesy of Syd Rollinson)

winds, with very choppy seas and frequent heavy snow showers, while the temperature was well below freezing. At 9.30 p.m. the lifeboatmen using the searchlight spotted the casualty, and through the binoculars the crew could see people on board *Nicholas* waving their arms for help. Coxswain Bevan took the lifeboat to within 400 yards of the casualty and the lifeboat's inflatable Y boat was launched, manned by Peter Jordan, as helm, with Dennis Bailey, Jnr, as crew.

In heavy snow and blinding spray, they got as close as they could by using the dinghy's small outboard engine. Then, on reaching very shallow water, both lifeboatmen jumped overboard and hauled the Y boat a further 100 yards through the water and onto the mud. They walked the last 100 yards to *Nicholas*, each step requiring a considerable effort, as they sank about a foot into the thick, sticky mud. They found that *Nicholas* had an anchor cable wrapped round her propeller and, after discussing the situation over the radio with Coxswain Bevan, it was decided to lay out another anchor from the casualty to secure her and then to bring the two men, both of whom were suffering from the cold, back to the waiting lifeboat. However, the boat's owner had an artificial leg, so the only way to get him to the Y boat was to carry him. With the man on his shoulders and Peter Jordan steadying them and shining the torch ahead, Dennis Bailey, Jnr, set off towards the Y boat. Considerable effort was required to get back to the small inflatable as they continued to sink deep into the mud. Slowly they headed towards the dinghy, although by the time they reached it both lifeboatmen were exhausted. The disabled man was put aboard and, with Dennis Bailey, Jnr, almost up to his waist in mud and freezing water, Peter Jordan restarted the engine and took the disabled man out to the lifeboat, where he was hauled aboard, using the electric winch.

Peter Jordan took the Y boat back to the mud bank, embarked the second survivor and Dennis Bailey, Jnr, and headed back to the lifeboat, where all were hauled aboard and the Y boat was recovered. The two lifeboatmen and the second survivor were covered in mud, soaked to the waist and extremely cold. Coxswain Bevan took the lifeboat into deeper water, with his knowledge of the area proving essential

HRH Duke of Kent with Superintendent Coxswain
Brian Bevan on a visit to Spurn Point, 1979.
(By courtesy of Brian Bevan)

Coxswain Brian Bevan being presented with a
bar to his Bronze medal by Princess Alice in 1981.
(By courtesy of Brian Bevan)

for a safe passage through the dried-out mudbanks which gave, in places, only five feet of water beneath the lifeboat's keel. But they returned safely to Spurn and the survivors were landed at 1.25 a.m. For their courage and great determination during this extremely difficult rescue, lifeboatmen Peter Jordan and Dennis Bailey, Jnr, were each accorded the RNLI's Thanks on Vellum. A Letter of Appreciation signed by the Director of the RNLI, Rear Admiral W. Graham, was also sent to Coxswain Brian Bevan and the other members of the crew for their part in this service.

City of Bradford IV returned to station in May 1981 and was busy throughout the summer, performing numerous medical evacuations, landing sick or injured personnel from fishing vessels, tankers and cargo vessels, while the last service of the year proved to be a particularly fine one. She was called out on the evening of 13 December 1981 in violent seas and a storm force ten south-easterly gale to the coaster *Harry Mitchell*, which had developed a thirty degree list after her cargo shifted. The casualty was nearly five miles north-east of the Humber lightvessel when *City of Bradford IV* put out at 11.18 p.m. The lifeboat had to reduce speed once she had cleared Spurn Point as she battled the extremely heavy seas. As she made her way out to the coaster, the lifeboat had the seas on her beam and was repeatedly knocked onto her side, but Coxswain Brian Bevan was still able to maintain a speed of fourteen knots. The lifeboatmen sighted *Harry Mitchell* at 12.39 a.m., by when the wind was gusting to force eleven. In the heavy, breaking seas and swell, the casualty's master was having great difficulty holding his ship bow on to the wind and sea, with the ship's rudder and propeller often clear of the water.

As the vessel listed thirty degrees to port, huge baulks of timber were hanging over her side, and her port side was at times under water up to the middle of the deck. In order to take the crew off the coaster, Coxswain Bevan asked the master to turn the ship to port and head on a north-westerly course so as to provide a lee for the lifeboat. Although one of the two helicopters that had set off to help arrived, in the appalling conditions, and with the violent motion of the casualty, winching anyone off the ship would have been extremely hazardous. The lifeboatmen therefore prepared to go alongside, with the lifeboat's port bow heavily fendered and three crew positioned on the open foredeck with their life lines fastened to the guard rails, and Assistant Mechanic Peter Thorpe operating the searchlight. The lifeboat's first approach had to be abandoned when a heavy sea hit the stern of the coaster, lifting it clear of the water, exposing the propeller and the rudder. A second attempt also had to be abandoned after a huge wave pushed the lifeboat towards the coaster's stern. But as both vessels bottomed out in a trough, Coxswain Bevan quickly took the lifeboat up to the coaster and one man jumped to safety.

As Coxswain Bevan took the lifeboat in again, another huge wave lifted the lifeboat's stern and the coaster started to fall down the wave and onto the bows of the lifeboat. Coxswain Bevan put the throttles full astern and the lifeboat pulled clear. The three lifeboatmen on the foredeck were very close to being crushed as the side of the coaster scraped the top of the lifeboat's bow pulpit rail. Four more attempts had to be made before a further two survivors were rescued, after which the coaster's master radioed that he and the mate would remain on board to try and get the coaster to the shelter of the Humber. The helicopter then left, the pilot radioing his congratulations to Coxswain Bevan and his crew.

After her captain managed to turn her head to sea, *Harry Mitchell* set course for the Humber and, escorted by the lifeboat, headed slowly south. She entered the river at 5.40 a.m. when, in moderating conditions, a pilot boarded and the three men that had been taken off were returned by the lifeboat to the cargo vessel, after which the lifeboat was released and returned to Spurn for 6 a.m. Following this outstanding rescue, carried out in truly appalling conditions, Superintendent Coxswain Bevan was awarded his second Bronze medal by the RNLI, with Medal Service certificates being presented to Second Coxswain Dennis Bailey, Mechanic Robert S. White, Assistant Mechanic Peter Thorpe and crew members Sydney Rollinson and Jack Essex.

On 17 November 1984 *City of Bradford IV* was involved in an unusual service after the 100-year-old 86ft gaff-rigged ketch *William McCann* went aground at Donna Nook during the night. Her eleven passengers had been lifted off during the night by helicopter, while *City of Bradford IV* stood by. The vessel's eight crew had decided to stay aboard to try to refloat the ketch at high tide. The following day the lifeboat, with Superintendent Coxswain Brian Bevan in command, launched at 12.08 a.m. to help while refloating was attempted. The crew of eight was still aboard, the vessel was making some water in the stern and there was heavy surf. Lifeboat crew using the 18ft 6in McLachlan boarding boat helped connect a tow rope, but unfortunately the ketch's propeller was fouled by the tow rope and the attempt had to be abandoned. The following day the lifeboat and boarding boat were again at the scene and this time a tow

54ft Arun City of Bradford IV at Robson's Boatyard, South Shields, in 1984, undergoing maintenance work. (By courtesy of Brian Bevan)

City of Bradford IV towing in the fishing vessel Rayella, 4 September 1980.
(By courtesy of Brian Bevan)

rope was successfully connected. As *William McCann* began to come off the bank, her stern hit another sand bank and this caused the tow to part. Using the boarding boat the lifeboat crew reconnected the line and the casualty was towed clear. She was making water aft, but a portable pump kept the water level at a manageable level. The ketch was towed to Grimsby and berthed in the Fish Dock at 4.56 p.m. At 5 p.m. the lifeboat left Grimsby for a more routine service to land a sick man from the cargo vessel *Grollen*.

On 29 March 1985 *City of Bradford IV* went for survey at Robson's Boatyard, South Shields, and the relief 52ft Arun *Edith Emilie* arrived for a temporary stint. She remained at Spurn for more than a year, undertaking numerous services during that time. *City of Bradford IV* returned from refit on 22 May 1986 and a few months later was involved in another fine service. Just before 8 a.m. on 30 October 1986 Coxswain Brian Bevan was informed that the 24ft yacht *Rachael* was in difficulties thirty-eight miles north-east of Spurn Point. A nearby drilling rig had sent her standby boat *Hatherleigh* and a helicopter to fix the yacht's exact position, and *Hatherleigh* stood by the yacht until the lifeboat reached her. Both of the yacht's crew were exhausted and one was suffering from acute seasickness, so time was of the essence.

City of Bradford IV slipped her moorings at 8.40 a.m. and headed out into very rough seas and a south-westerly gale, which was forecast to increase to storm force ten. Several times the lifeboat was laid over on her beam ends as she ran before the heavy breaking seas, while the wind was driving the yacht away from the lifeboat. When the lifeboat crew finally reached the casualty, at 12.50 p.m., the yacht was sixty-three miles north-east of Spurn Point. Her skipper asked for one of the lifeboatmen to be transferred across and Jack Essex volunteered to try and get aboard. Coxswain Bevan cautiously manoeuvred the lifeboat towards the yacht and, when they were just 2ft apart, Essex leapt across and got aboard safely.

A long towline was made up, being weighted down in the middle with two heavy fenders, to keep it down in the water. At 1.11 p.m. the line was passed across to the yacht and secured by Jack Essex, who then prepared for the long tow back. The wind by that time was force nine, and was creating very confused seas in the area, but the tow got under way at about four knots with the boats heading directly into the wind and sea, with Coxswain Bevan making for Scarborough. Once in the lee of the land, at 11.40 p.m., the Scarborough lifeboat *Amelia* was launched to assist. By then Jack Essex had spent over ten hours almost continuously at the tiller and hand pump on board the yacht. The Scarborough crew passed sandwiches to the Humber lifeboatmen and took over the tow, enabling *City of Bradford IV* to head southward to Spurn, where she arrived at 2.30 a.m., by when she had been at sea for eighteen hours. In recognition of this long and demanding service, a Framed Letter of Thanks, signed by the RNLI Chairman, His Grace The Duke of Atholl, was presented to Coxswain Bevan and his crew.

By the time of the last notable service undertaken by *City of Bradford IV*, plans were in place to replace her with a new 52ft Arun lifeboat. But she was much in demand during 1986 and 1987 as she completed her last year of service at Spurn. Many of her calls were to evacuate sick or injured crew from the many cargo vessels using the east coast and the ports along the Humber, and while most of these calls proved to be routine, one on 15 January 1987 was somewhat more challenging. The 18,000-ton Greek tanker *Kithnos* was heading north of the Humber lightvessel at 4.18 p.m. when one of her crew was reported to be suffering from a severe nose bleed and required medical treatment.

Humber Coastguard alerted a helicopter from RAF Leconfield to airlift the seaman at first light, but this had to be aborted at 8.18 a.m. because of icing in the sub-zero temperatures and snow showers. The captain of *Kithnos* expressed anxiety at the worsening condition of his crew member and so *City of Bradford IV* was called out. With Superintendent Coxswain Brian Bevan at the helm, she slipped her moorings at 8.36 a.m. to rendezvous with the tanker fourteen miles north-east of Spurn Point. A force eight gale, which had been blowing for three days, had prevented the Humber pilots boarding shipping for

City of Bradford IV and the boarding boat on service to the ketch William McCann on 17 November 1984. (By courtesy of the RNLI)

City of Bradford IV on station at Tobermory in August 1997. After she left Humber, the 54ft Arun went to Thurso, Ballyglass and Tobermory before being sold out of service in October 1998 to a private buyer in the West Midlands. (Nicholas Leach)

the previous forty-eight hours. Nevertheless, a message from the doctor at Hull Royal Infirmary indicated that it was a matter of urgency that the seaman be landed for hospital treatment and, if possible, that he be given morphine. Humber lifeboat was alongside *Kithnos* by 9.25 a.m. and the senior first-aider, Second Coxswain Dennis Bailey Snr, volunteered to try to board the vessel by pilot ladder to administer the morphine and supervise the transfer of the seaman in the lifeboat's Neil Robertson stretcher. With waves breaking over the deck of the tanker, the man was lowered down to the lifeboat and Second Coxswain Bailey rejoined his colleagues aboard the lifeboat by 9.54 a.m. The lifeboat then made for the shelter of Spurn Bight, where the de-iced RAF helicopter was able to lift off the seaman and then take him to Grimsby General Hospital, where he made a full recovery. Following this service, a Framed Letter of Thanks from the Duke of Atholl, chairman of the RNLI, was presented to Superintendent Coxswain Brian Bevan, Second Coxswain Dennis Bailey, Mechanic Robert White, Assistant Mechanic Peter Thorpe and crew members Jack Essex and David Cape. A further letter of appreciation for the part he played was sent by the chairman to Second Coxswain Bailey.

This service was undertaken just after it had been formally announced that a new lifeboat was being built for the Humber, and for the remainder of her time at Spurn *City of Bradford IV* performed a series of largely routine rescues. During her last full month on station, July 1987, a wide variety of craft were helped, including several yachts, a fishing vessel, as well as a couple of sick crew members on board cargo vessels. She departed Spurn in August 1987 and was reallocated to Thurso, where she served from March 1988 to March 1989. Following the year in Scotland, she went to Ballyglass on the west coast of Ireland for ten months until going to Tobermory on Mull in February 1991. She served there until July 1998 and was sold out of service in October 1998.

Kenneth Thelwall

I n December 1986 the RNLI announced that a new lifeboat was being built to replace the ten-year-old _City of Bradford IV_, which had been worked very hard during her years at Spurn. The new 52ft Arun-class lifeboat, which was fitted out at Berthon Boat Company at Lymington at a cost of £500,000, was similar in many respects to the boat she was replacing, but was slightly shorter, at 52ft rather than 54ft, and incorporated all of the standard modifications made to the Arun design during the build programme. The GRP hull had been moulded by Halmatic Ltd, of Havant, as had that of _City of Bradford IV_, but the new boat had slightly more powerful engines – twin 485hp Caterpillar 3408TA diesels – which gave her a speed of about eighteen knots. After fitting out at Berthon between June 1986 and April 1987, self-righting and initial trials began on 21 April 1987 and continued until 12 June 1987. Following a final series of trials from the end of June until 10 July 1987, she was sailed to the RNLI Depot at Poole.

The boat was funded from the legacy of Kenneth Thelwall, of Walkington, East Riding, and named after her donor. At the time that his bequest had been received, it was the largest from which the RNLI had benefited. As well as funding the Humber boat, the legacy provided a 47ft Tyne class, named _Kenneth Thelwall II_, which was completed in 1990 and sent to Ramsgate. The Humber lifeboat was the thirty-seventh Arun to be built, and by the time she was under construction the Arun had proved itself to be a particularly fine design of lifeboat, with the medal-winning services performed by _City of Bradford IV_ showing the boat's abilities in extreme conditions. This had been formally recognised in 1982, when a

52ft Arun Kenneth Thelwall at Berthon Boat Co., Lymington, on 25 May 1997 just before she was handed over to the RNLI. (By courtesy of the RNLI)

Kenneth Thelwall on trials in 1987 shortly after she had been built. (By courtesy of the RNLI)

The 52ft Arun Kenneth Thelwall arrives at Spurn on 13 August 1987. (Grimsby Evening Telegraph)

Kenneth Thelwall moored at the Pilot Jetty on 13 August 1987, the day she first arrived at Spurn Point following a passage from Poole. (Paul Arro)

Design Council Award was presented to the RNLI by HRH Duke of Edinburgh in acknowledgement of the outstanding hull and overall design of the boat, the first lifeboat type to receive such an award.

Kenneth Thelwall was sailed from Poole to her new station by a minimum number of crew, as some were left at Spurn to ensure *City of Bradford IV* remained fully operational. The crew was made up of Divisional Inspector Tom Nutman, Divisional Engineer Eddie Irwin, Superintendent Coxswain Brian Bevan, Mechanic Bob White, crew member Syd Rollinson and relief crew member Dave Hodgson. The boat left Poole on 11 August 1987 and headed up the east coast for her station on a crew training passage. The first leg took the new lifeboat to Ramsgate, where she stayed overnight. She sailed the following morning for Lowestoft for a second overnight stay, and left there the following morning to arrive at the Humber that afternoon. Just as the new lifeboat reached Spurn on 13 August, a Mayday call was received from the yacht *Marique*, which had the three crew on board, and was taking in water six miles south-east of Spurn. She required immediate assistance so Coxswain Brian Bevan immediately set course for the casualty, while Second Coxswain Dennis Bailey, Snr, put to sea in *City of Bradford IV*, manned by the rest of the crew from Spurn.

The new lifeboat was first on scene, reaching the yacht at 1.30 p.m. to find that she had been holed, water was coming on board and her engine and pump were out of action. The owner's wife and daughter were taken aboard the new lifeboat, and then *City of Bradford IV* and the D-class inflatable from Cleethorpes, both of which were waiting to greet the new lifeboat, reached the scene. One of the Humber crew was put aboard the yacht, together with one of the Cleethorpes crew and a portable pump, and the yacht was taken in tow by *City of Bradford IV* to Grimsby, accompanied by the new lifeboat. The yacht was berthed at the port at 4.06 p.m., after which the lifeboats returned to Spurn Point. After the gear had been moved from *City of Bradford IV* to *Kenneth Thelwall*, the new boat was placed on station at 6 p.m.

The new Arun was named and dedicated at a ceremony held at Hull Marina on 19 September 1987. A large crowd welcomed the lifeboat at 2.30 p.m. for a hasty mooring operation, decoration and the

Kenneth Thelwall in Hull Marina for her naming ceremony. (By courtesy of the RNLI)

fitting of the bottle of champagne, and they were entertained by the Filey Fishermen's Choir. A large number of supporters from many parts of the country were in attendance as proceedings were opened by Hull solicitor Hugh Williamson. Christopher Hobson, a Beverley solicitor and executor of the estate of Kenneth Thelwall, handed the boat over to Gilbert Gray QC representing the RNLI's Committee of Management. Tom Nutman, Divisional Inspector East, received the lifeboat into the care of the station. The Rev Frank La Touche, port chaplain to the Mission to Seamen, conducted the service of dedication, which was followed by a vote of thanks by Mrs Sheila Nelson, chairman of Hull ladies' lifeboat guild. Commander Brian Miles, the RNLI's deputy director, paid tribute to the lifeboatmen's wives, and then introduced Mrs Ann Bevan, wife of Superintendent Coxswain Brian Bevan, who named the lifeboat, 'on behalf of all the wives and families'.

Like her predecessors, *Kenneth Thelwall* enjoyed a fine record of service at Spurn Point, serving the Humber for just under a decade and completing almost 400 service launches during that time. Her first year on service was characterised by a series of largely routine services, with launches to several yachts in difficulty in August and September 1987. In 1988 the relief lifeboat *Edith Emilie* was on station during September and October, while *Kenneth Thelwall* went to Robson's Boatyard at South Shields for survey.

On 24 March 1989 the Humber lifeboat crew undertook a fine double service. The first call came at 12.50 p.m. after the 86ft gaff-rigged ketch *William McCann*, with nineteen men on board, got into difficulties south of Withernsea in very bad conditions, extremely rough seas and storm force ten westerly winds gusting to seventy knots. Because of the severe weather, the lifeboat was sheltering in Grimsby Docks, from where the crew could board without facing the extreme of attempting to get to the lifeboat at her moorings at Spurn. *Kenneth Thelwall* left Grimsby Docks just after 1 p.m. and reached the scene at 2.35 p.m., finding the casualty just north of Withernsea. After checking that everyone on board was alright and that the ketch's engine was working, the Bridlington lifeboat, which had also been called out, began escorting the ketch slowly northwards towards Bridlington.

At 3.20 p.m., while *Kenneth Thelwall* was returning to Grimsby, Coxswain Bevan received a call from the Coastguard, reporting the 72ft ketch *Christian Brugge* in difficulties. Five crew were on board the casualty, which was in trouble seventeen miles south-east of Spurn Point. A helicopter located the ketch and stood by until the lifeboat arrived on scene. The ketch was then making about two knots and, with the lifeboat providing an escort, she headed slowly towards Grimsby. The vessels reached port at 12.25 a.m., and the lifeboat remained in the Docks overnight because of the bad weather. A Letter of Thanks, signed by the RNLI's Chief of Operations, Captain George Cooper, was later sent to Coxswain Brian Bevan and his crew, 'for a first class service lasting nearly twelve hours in force ten winds and rough seas'.

Another challenging incident was dealt with on 5 June 1989. During the late afternoon, while listening to the crews of some local fishing boats on the radio, Coxswain Bevan heard concern expressed about the 33ft stern trawler *Emma D* and her crew of two, a husband and wife, which was six hours overdue. Coxswain Bevan contacted one of the local skippers by radio to confirm the details, and then decided to launch the lifeboat to investigate. He notified the Coastguard, as well as the crew of a helicopter which was in the area, and which immediately diverted to help. *Kenneth Thelwall* slipped her moorings at 4.36 p.m. and, together with other vessels, began a search for the missing trawler. At 5.05 p.m. an empty five-gallon fuel drum was found and an oil slick was spotted.

At 5.55 p.m. Coxswain Bevan contacted the skipper of the trawler *Coromandel*, which, together with the trawler *Frances Bojen*, was going up river to port. They were asked to help by making a sonar sweep close to No.56 buoy and, on the first sweep, an object was shown up on the sea bed. The trawlers then strung a wire between them and trawled the area. They were stopped when the wire caught a submerged object, at which point another five-gallon drum floated to the surface. As it was known that *Emma D*

The second Arun to serve at Spurn Point, Kenneth Thelwall, at moorings off the Pilot Jetty with the lighthouse in the background. (By courtesy of Brian Bevan)

(Above) Humber Station. David Smith (left), Superintendent Coxswain Brian Bevan (middle) and Frank Barass (right) after Mr Smith and Mr Barass were rescued after freak storms and 60-knot gales sank their yacht, Jonquil on 31 July 1989. (By courtesy of the RNLI)

(Left) The wooden boarding boat, one of two such craft specially designed for the Humber, under construction at the International Boatbuilding Centre in Lowestoft, 1990. (By courtesy of Brian Bevan)

carried such drums on deck, it appeared that the vessel had foundered. The two trawlers then left the scene, with Coxswain Bevan thanking them for their assistance, and the site of the wreck was marked with a buoy. Further searches for the missing couple were then undertaken by the Humber lifeboat, Cleethorpes inshore lifeboat and the Vigilantes Rescue Boat. Sadly nothing was found and the search was called off after a few hours, with *Kenneth Thelwall* returning to station at 9 p.m. The RNLI's Chief of Operations, Commodore George Cooper, later sent a Letter of Thanks to the skipper of the trawler *Coromandel*, Jens Bojen, for the help given by the two trawlers.

At 5 a.m. on 17 September 1989 *Kenneth Thelwall* put to sea to help two vessels that had collided near the Humber Light Buoy, ten miles east of Spurn Point. The 28,700-ton bulk carrier *Fiona*, which was on fire, and the Liberian oil tanker *Phillips Oklahoma*, which had twenty-five crew and was also on fire, were the vessels involved. Helicopters and other ships had raced to the scene to offer assistance, and *Kenneth Thelwall* reached the area at 5.37 a.m. The tanker was blazing from a ruptured tank on her starboard side, and her accommodation and the starboard bridge wing were engulfed in flames and thick black smoke. Oil, which was escaping from the tanker, was alight on the surface of the sea and stretched for almost half a mile downtide. *Fiona*'s master reported that the blaze on his vessel was under control and the minesweeper HMS *Middleton* was standing by.

On the blazing tanker, however, the situation was more difficult and some men could be seen fighting the fire with hoses, but the majority of the crew had gathered amidships wearing life jackets ready to be evacuated. Three pilot ladders had been lowered over the port side and, as the rig supply vessel *Sterling Tern* went to the starboard side to fight the fire with her water cannon, Coxswain Bevan took the lifeboat towards the ladders on the port side. The tanker's situation appeared to be getting worse, with balls of fire regularly erupting from the vessel, and so the master agreed to evacuate all non-essential crew. The lifeboat took off sixteen, leaving nine on board, and later transferred the rescued men to a car transporter to get warm drinks and food. The lifeboat continued to stand by and, once more fire fighters had been put aboard the tanker, the fire was brought under control. It was put out by 9.45 a.m., and as fire crews continued to damp down the remnants of the blaze, the lifeboat collected the sixteen men from the car transporter and headed for Grimsby, where they were landed at 11.13 a.m.

The Philippine Ambassador in the United Kingdom later wrote to Superintendent Coxswain Brian Bevan in appreciation of the efforts of the Humber crew, 'expressing my deepest gratitude and appreciation to you and your members, for the brave and courageous rescue'. The owners of the tanker also wrote to the RNLI at Poole expressing 'thanks for the prompt assistance rendered by Humber lifeboat, when our motor tanker *Phillips Oklahoma* was involved in a collision and resultant fire, on 17 September last'. A donation to RNLI funds was also made by the owners.

As well as attending to merchant vessels and undertaking medical evacuations, which were relatively frequent demands on the Spurn crew, aircraft have also got into difficulty and, during the afternoon of

Kenneth Thelwall, the second Arun-class lifeboat to serve at the Humber, at speed in the Humber Estuary, with Spurn Point behind, June 1995. (By courtesy of Brian Bevan)

14 August 1990, two RAF Tornado aircraft collided off Spurn Point. So *Kenneth Thelwall* put to sea at 3.30 p.m., with several other vessels and helicopters, to search for survivors. Two airmen were picked up by one of the helicopters, but there was no sign of the other crew men so a search of the area began. Coxswain Bevan was designated on-scene commander and a search with eight other vessels was organised. Although various pieces of wreckage were recovered, sadly no more survivors were found and the search was eventually called off at 8.30 p.m. All the items that had been recovered were transferred to the lifeboat, which took them to Grimsby and then returned to station at 10.40 p.m.

Three days later another Tornado jet crashed into the sea, but this time further out, about eleven miles north-east of Spurn Point. The lifeboat put to sea at 2.09 a.m. and, on arrival at the scene forty-five minutes later, Coxswain Bevan was made on-scene commander. With lifeboats from Bridlington and Skegness searching to the north and south respectively, nine other vessels helped the Humber lifeboat search the immediate crash area, along with two helicopters and a Nimrod aircraft. Despite rough seas and a very strong north-westerly wind, the search continued in the pitch dark. Unfortunately only wreckage was found, and no bodies were recovered. At 11.55 a.m. HMS *Dumbarton* took over as on-scene commander and, with a number of recovered items on board, *Kenneth Thelwall* made for Grimsby, where the wreckage was handed over to police and RAF personnel. The lifeboat returned to station at 2.14 p.m. George Cooper, the RNLI's Chief of Operations, recently promoted to Commodore RNR, later sent a Letter of Appreciation to Superintendent Coxswain Bevan 'for your professional approach to the duties of on-scene commander and directing a thorough search on both occasions'.

Just over a month later, on 19 September 1990, the Humber lifeboatmen were called out to help a vessel in severe weather. Because of the fierce north-westerly gale creating very rough seas at Spurn *Kenneth Thelwall* was sheltering in Grimsby Docks when the call came. Second Coxswain Ian Firman, who was in command of the lifeboat at the time, was informed at 9.38 a.m. that the yacht *Catalyst* may be in need of assistance. The Coastguard had lost radio contact with the yacht's crew, but it was known that the vessel had engine trouble and the crew was unsure of the yacht's position. The lifeboat put out from Grimsby at 9.54 a.m. to search an area near the Protector Buoy, with the Skegness lifeboat and a

Kenneth Thelwall at her moorings off Spurn Point, May 1994. (Nicholas Leach)

Two photographs of Kenneth Thelwall at speed in the Humber Estuary, with the lifeboat house, lighthouse and Pilot Jetty forming the backdrop. (By courtesy of Brian Bevan)

helicopter also involved. In rough seas with frequent violent squalls, the gale steadily increased to storm force ten, a fishery protection vessel reported that they had heard the crew of the yacht on the radio and had obtained a bearing which put the yacht further to the east.

The yacht was located just over three miles south of the Dowsing lightvessel and so Humber lifeboat made for this position. The helicopter found the yacht and stood by until the lifeboat reached the scene, by when the wind had eased slightly, to gale force, but was expected to strengthen again later. The crew of the yacht were told to make for the Humber, but after thirty-five minutes the yacht had made no progress at all. As the wind began to increase in strength again, the yacht was taken in tow by the lifeboat and the two vessels headed slowly towards the river. As the wind increased in strength, the seas grew even heavier and the lifeboatmen had to closely watch the yacht which, at one stage, was thrown onto her side by a huge wave. Slowly, however, the tow continued, with winds of fifty knots encountered off

Kenneth Thelwall at Girvan at the end of a survey at Coastal Marine in August 1996. She was at the yard from early March 1996 with the relief 52ft Arun Margaret Russell Fraser taking her place at the Humber. (Nicholas Leach)

the Humber light float. But the vessels entered the river safely and reached Grimsby, where the lifeboat remained because of the very bad weather.

A very long service was undertaken in January 1994. While *Kenneth Thelwall* and her crew were sheltering in Grimsby Docks on the evening of 26 January, because rough seas and a south-westerly gale made boarding at Spurn impossible, the Coastguard contacted Coxswain Bevan to request lifeboat assistance with the escort of the Russian cargo vessel *Aegviidu*. The vessel's cargo had shifted when she was eighty-seven miles north-east of Spurn Point, heading towards the Humber. The lifeboat left Grimsby at 8.35 p.m. and reached the casualty forty-four miles from Spurn Point, three and a half hours later. In very rough seas, the lifeboat escorted the vessel as far as the Spurn light float, which was reached at 3.45 a.m. A pilot then transferred across from the pilot boat, and he helped the vessel anchor in the river. The lifeboat was released, and she returned to Grimsby Docks at 4.55 a.m.

Less than a month later the lifeboat was involved in another excellent service. On 15 February 1994 the fishing vessel *Eventide*, with a crew of four, got into difficulty sixteen miles north-east of Spurn Point, with broken steering. In an easterly gale, very heavy seas with twenty-five-foot swell and temperatures below freezing, *Kenneth Thelwall* slipped her moorings at 3.20 a.m. and headed out to sea. As she cleared Spurn Point, she met the full force of the storm and, as she crashed down off one huge wave, the motor on the winch used for launching and recovering the inflatable Y boat suddenly started. Coxswain Bevan reduced speed, brought the lifeboat head to sea, and the crew checked the Y boat. The fastenings were secure, but the motor was still running and had to be switched off manually. The lifeboat then proceeded on her way at reduced speed to prevent further pounding, and she reached the casualty at 4.30 a.m.

The easterly gale was gusting to severe gale force and the casualty was lying broadside to the swell. Coxswain Bevan manoeuvred the lifeboat upwind of the heavily rolling fishing vessel and the lifeboat crew passed across a towline. A heavy towline was hauled across and secured and the lifeboat went slowly ahead, although the casualty was shearing violently from side to side, making the passage very difficult. The skipper was asked to put his engine in reverse if the vessel appeared to be about to overrun the lifeboat, and this made the tow slightly easier. During the tow, undertaken at very slow speed in the heavy swell, at times only the fishing vessel's masts were visible to the lifeboatmen. As the lifeboat and her tow reached the Humber Estuary, the danger of the tow rope parting and the following seas driving the fishing vessel ashore became a danger, so shipping in the area was asked to give the lifeboat and casualty a wide berth. The Bull light float was passed at 7 a.m. and the vessels then gained a degree of shelter from Spurn Point. Half an hour later the tow was shortened and the fishing vessel was brought into Grimsby Fish Dock. Temporary repairs were made to the lifeboat's Y boat recovery system and, in heavy snow, the lifeboat returned to station at 10.20 a.m. For this excellent service, a Framed Letter of Thanks signed by the Chairman of the RNLI was later presented to Coxswain Brian Bevan and his crew, Second Coxswain Bob White, Mechanic Peter Thorpe and crew members Les Roberts, Syd Rollinson, David Steenvoorden and Chris Barnes.

On occasions the Humber lifeboat crew have worked with lifeboats from the neighbouring stations of Bridlington and Skegness. One such occasion was in January 1995, when *Kenneth Thelwall* worked with Bridlington lifeboat to help the Cypriot cargo vessel *Aurora-H*. The vessel had lost her rudder in a south-easterly gale and very rough seas on 16 January 1995, and her crew had dropped anchor fourteen miles east of Hornsea. Bridlington lifeboat stood by throughout the night, and at 6.10 a.m. on 17 January *Kenneth Thelwall* put to sea to relieve her. Humber lifeboat reached the scene at 7.30 a.m., after a twenty-one-mile passage in extremely rough conditions, thus allowing the Bridlington lifeboat to

The Spurn peninsula is susceptible to being damaged during extreme weather, and particularly bad storms can make the roadway disappear. In February 1996 severe weather along the east coast affected the Humber lifeboat; conditions were so bad that she could not go to Grimsby to shelter as usual, forcing Coxswain Brian Bevan and his crew to ride out the storm on board at the moorings off Spurn. Exceptionally high tides during this storm breached a 300-yard section of the road (above) and the spit was almost completely breached. Although access was only possible either by foot or four-wheel-drive vehicle after the storm, the spit remained intact. Following a meeting between the RNLI, the Humber Pilots and the Yorkshire Wildlife Trust, who own the peninsula, a plan was drawn up to build a new road, which was constructed from linked concrete sections. These provided the flexibility so they could be moved if necessary should further erosion occur. (By courtesy of Brian Bevan)

During the summer of 1995, the lifeboat house and slipway, which had been built at Spurn in 1923, were demolished. The original slipway remained in place beneath the later slipway (above), but the whole structure was removed (Photos by courtesy of Brian Bevan)

return to station. *Kenneth Thelwall* then stood by throughout the morning and early afternoon until, at 3.45 p.m., a tug arrived from Immingham to help. In very rough seas, with winds gusting to force nine, it took two attempts to get a tow wire across to the cargo vessel. But once the tow was secure, the vessel slipped her anchor and, with the tug, headed slowly south. The lifeboat escorted the vessels for a couple of hours to ensure the tow was proceeding safely. As both vessels were making steady progress, the lifeboat returned to Spurn, albeit at slow speed as the wind had risen to storm force ten. The lifeboat reached her moorings at Spurn at 9.25 p.m. having spent sixteen hours at sea in some of the most difficult conditions.

Pride of the Humber

In August 1993 the RNLI announced that a new 17m Severn-class lifeboat had been allocated to the Humber to replace the ten-year-old *Kenneth Thelwall*. The Severn represented a new generation of faster all-weather lifeboat types that had been designed by the RNLI to replace the Arun and Waveney classes, which had been in service since the 1960s. It was one of two new designs, developed during the 1990s, which were capable of twenty-five knots at full speed and incorporated the latest equipment and technology to make rescue work safer, easier and more efficient. The other design was the smaller 14m Trent. The Severn was deemed ideal for rescue work off the Humber and the fifth boat of the class was allocated to the station. The new lifeboat, self-righting by virtue of the inherent buoyancy in the watertight wheelhouse, was moulded in fibre-reinforced composite at Green Marine's Lymington

17m Severn-class lifeboat Pride of the Humber on trials prior to coming to Spurn Point.
(By courtesy of the Grimsby Evening Telegraph)

boatyard and the hull was fitted out by Halmatic, at Northam in Southampton. Twin Caterpillar 3412 diesel engines, each of 1,200bhp, provided the power to give a top speed of twenty-five knots. The boat had a range of approximately 250 nautical miles and was fitted with the latest navigational aids.

The new lifeboat was principally funded by the Humber Lifeboat Appeal, which was launched in February 1994 in the north-east and ran throughout 1994 and 1995. As a result of fund-raising activities by volunteer supporters, the Appeal raised £1 million towards the cost of the new lifeboat, with further funding coming from a £230,000 legacy from Mrs Mary Elizabeth Self, of Cleethorpes, and the remainder from the bequests of Miss Lucy Chandley and Miss Margery Ivory Hooton, as well as various other legacies. The new lifeboat was named *Pride of the Humber* in recognition of the success of the appeal and the efforts of those involved in raising the funds.

In 1995, after fitting out at Halmatic's yard had been completed, the new lifeboat underwent a series of trials. Although these were completed by January 1996, the lifeboat spent the next nine months undergoing modifications at FBM Marine in Cowes. The new lifeboat was due to arrive in October 1996, but was delayed when remedial work to repair blisters in the fibre-reinforced-concrete outer skin of the hull had to be undertaken and repairs took longer than originally estimated. But after another exhaustive trials and testing programme on the Humber boat and other boats of the class, the issues with the hull had been resolved and the boat could enter service. *Pride of the Humber* completed her proving trials in February 1997 and, ready for service, she was taken to the RNLI's Depot at Poole. With the new lifeboat accepted into service, Superintendent Coxswain Brian Bevan and his crew went to Poole for an intensive two-day training course during the first week of March 1997. The course included practical exercises, as well as classroom work, a night passage and an exercise with a coastguard search and rescue helicopter.

Once crew training had been completed, *Pride of the Humber* left Poole for the passage home, manned by Divisional Inspector Kieran Nash, Divisional Engineer Nick Day, Suptintendent Coxswain Brian Bevan,

Pride of the Humber arriving at Spurn Point on 8 March 1997. (Nicholas Leach)

Kenneth Thelwall and Pride of the Humber moored at the Pilot Jetty, with the Cleethorpes D-class inflatable D-454 Blue Peter VI also welcoming the new lifeboat, 8 March 1997. (Nicholas Leach)

Arrival of Pride of the Humber, 8 March 1997, with (left) the boarding boat being launched, and (right) the new 17m Severn approaching the Pilot Jetty for the first time. (Nicholas Leach)

Having been greeted at Spurn Point, Pride of the Humber sets off for Grimsby for a publicity event after her arrival on 8 March 1997. (Nicholas Leach)

The boarding boats BB-239 and BB-240 with Kenneth Thelwall (on left) and Pride of the Humber moored together at Hull. (By courtesy of Brian Bevan)

After going to Spurn Point, Pride of the Humber is escorted into Grimsby by Kenneth Thelwall during the day of her arrival on 8 March 1997. (Tony Denton)

Second Coxswain Bob White, Mechanic Peter Thorpe, Second Mechanic Les Roberts, and crew members Dave Steenvoorden, Chris Barnes and Nick Thorpe. As these were the full-time crew from Spurn, a relief crew was sent to man the station while they were away. The first leg of the passage saw the boat head east and stop at Ramsgate overnight. The next leg was across the Channel to Belgium to make a courtesy visit to the Zeebrugge Lifeboat and Pilot Station. By coincidence, the morning of the boat's arrival coincided with the anniversary of the *Herald of Free Enterprise* tragedy, and the Humber crew were made very welcome during the memorial events in the Belgian port. After an overnight stay at Zeebrugge, the lifeboat crossed the North Sea to Lowestoft for a final overnight stop. *Pride of the Humber* left Lowestoft the next morning and sailed north to Spurn, where she arrived on Saturday 8 March 1997 to be escorted alongside the Pilot Jetty by *Kenneth Thelwall* and the Cleethorpes inshore lifeboat D-454. The lifeboatmen's families welcomed the crew and looked over the new lifeboat, which was then taken across to Grimsby Docks to be shown to those who had been involved in the fund-raising appeal.

More than 1,000 guests and supporters were present at Hull Marina for the naming ceremony of the new lifeboat on 24 September 1997, which was blessed with brilliant sunshine. With the lifeboat moored in the marina and the lifeboat crew and families in attendance, Tom Martin, Vice Chairman of the Humber Lifeboat Appeal, opened proceedings. Iain Bryce, Chairman of the Appeal, formally handed over the boat to David Acland, Chairman of the RNLI, who in turn passed her into the care of the Humber station. Divisional Inspector Kieran Nash accepted the boat on behalf of the station, and then, 'the crowd roared its approval as Kieran announced that he would check with Superintendent Coxswain Brian Bevan and crew if they would care to accept the boat, and they replied that they would!' The service of dedication was conducted by Canon John Waller, Vicar of Holy Trinity Church, assisted by David Saltiel, Padre to the Royal Mission for Deep Sea Fishermen, Rev Duncan Harris, of the Mission to Seamen, and Bishop O'Brien, Bishop of Middlesbrough. At the end of the formalities, Mrs Christine Goodall, RNLI Regional Manager, proposed a vote of thanks, before HRH The Duke of Kent, President of the RNLI, stepped forward to name the new lifeboat *Pride of the Humber*. The Duke then went for a short trip on the boat with other invited guests.

Throughout the summer prior to her naming ceremony, *Pride of the Humber* had been involved in a good number of services. Indeed, on 9 March 1997, the day after she had been placed on station, the new lifeboat was called upon. She launched at 2 p.m. to the fishing vessel *Marmik*, of Ramsgate, which

(Above) The scene at Hull Marina on 24 September 1997 during the naming ceremony of Pride of the Humber. (By courtesy of Brian Bevan)

(Right) On board Pride of the Humber at the end of her naming ceremony are, from left to right, Bob White, Peter Thorpe and Brian Bevan. (Cliff Crone)

With the Duke of Kent alongside him on the flying bridge, Superintendent Coxswain Brian Bevan takes Pride of the Humber out of the marina at the end of her naming ceremony for a short trip in the river. (Cliff Crone)

Pride of the Humber returns to Hull Marina with the invited guests after a short trip at the end of her naming ceremony. (Cliff Crone)

was disabled after its propeller had been fouled. With one man on board, the vessel was just over four miles from Spurn and had gone aground on the Clee Sands, so the Cleethorpes inshore lifeboat was also launched to assist. But the casualty was too large for the ILB to tow, so the new lifeboat was called to help. Once the lifeboat was on scene, Second Coxswain Bob White was transferred across to the casualty and, at 2.15 p.m., a towline was passed to the lifeboat, which then brought the casualty into Grimsby Docks just over half an hour later.

Another relatively straightforward service was carried out by *Pride of the Humber* on 24 April 1997. When the call came, the lifeboat was sheltering in Grimsby Docks because near-gale-force westerly winds made boarding her at Spurn too dangerous. The Coastguard informed Coxswain Brian Bevan that the 24ft fishing vessel *Valentine*, of Hull, which had been working out of Easington, was in difficulty a mile off Kilnsea with a broken gearbox. The lifeboat left Grimsby at 12.25 p.m., and reached the casualty, which was manned by three crew, forty minutes later. A towline was connected to the casualty, which was taken to Easington, at which point the lifeboat's inflatable Y boat was launched and, manned by two lifeboatmen, helped to beach the boat safely.

The first life-saving service by *Pride of the Humber* took place on 3 May 1997. Humber Coastguard requested an immediate launch after a Mayday had been received at 5.08 p.m. from the rigid inflatable *Reef Rash II*, which had five divers on board and was in difficulty east of the Spurn lightvessel in choppy seas and a force five south-easterly wind. The lifeboat slipped her moorings within five minutes of the call, and was on scene just over a quarter of an hour later. The casualty had come off a large wave, which had caused part of the sponson to come away from the hull, and she was taking on water. One person had gone over the side to try to effect a repair, but water continued to fill the boat. Once on scene the lifeboat took off the five occupants and their gear, and a tow was rigged. With the boat then lighter in the water, she towed well and the water drained away. A mile off Cleethorpes two of the crew were put back on

(Above) Pride of the Humber at moorings off the Pilot Jetty, September 1998, in her original livery with the operational number, 17-05, on her superstructure. (Nicholas Leach)

(Left) Brian Bevan on board Pride of the Humber. Brian served as Superintendent Coxswain for more than twenty-five years, until November 2001, commanded four different lifeboats, and achieved an outstanding record of service. (RNLI)

the casualty and they managed to restart the engines. Cleethorpes inshore lifeboat was also launched to assist, and escorted the casualty to the beach. One of the Humber crew went ashore in the ILB, while two of the casualty's crew were taken into the Royal Dock Basin at Grimsby. *Pride of the Humber* left Grimsby at 7.15 p.m. and within half an hour was back at Spurn ready for service.

Two days later, *Pride of the Humber* was called out again. She left Spurn at 10.20 p.m. and headed into rough seas, a near gale force northerly wind, with sleet and snow showers to go to the coaster *Carmel*, which had engine and electrical problems twenty-five miles east of the Humber estuary, and was in need of assistance. At 11.25 p.m. the lifeboat reached the coaster, which had three crew on board, and a towline was rigged. In the rough seas, however, this parted, and the prevailing conditions made the situation very difficult for the lifeboat crew. However, the tow was reconnected and this time it held, so the lifeboat was able to head slowly towards the Humber, towing the coaster to an anchorage where she waited for a tug. The casualty was taken into Grimsby Docks on the next tide, and the lifeboat returned to station.

On 31 January 1999 a fine service was undertaken in conjunction with the Cleethorpes inshore lifeboat. *Pride of the Humber* was asked to provide back up for the ILB, which had launched after a woman had been reported cut off by the tide at Donna Nook, about seven miles south of Cleethorpes. Humber lifeboat slipped moorings at 5.56 p.m. and reached the search area fifteen minutes later. The tide was ebbing, which made the area, notorious for its sandbanks and gulleys, even more treacherous than usual. The woman had last been seen at about 5.20 p.m. by her partner, who had waded ashore, chest deep in water, with his son on his shoulders, and raised the alarm. Coastguard mobiles and search parties were combing the shore and Cleethorpes ILB and RAF Sea King Helicopter Rescue 128 were on scene searching out to sea. With just ten feet of water under the keel, the lifeboat was in a difficult position, and was just about to make for deeper water at 6.22 p.m. when one of the three crew on the upper steering position manning the searchlights heard a cry for help.

The lifeboat was immediately turned towards the shore and two crew went onto the bows to listen for further cries. The casualty was heard again calling out, but could not be seen in the darkness. Attempts were made to direct the helicopter in the direction of the shouting, but the helicopter crew could not see anything. The lifeboat crew fired a parachute flare to illuminate the area, and then the casualty was spotted about 200 yards away, struggling and in considerable distress, having been in the water for over an hour. The lifeboat went in to recover her, and at 6.28 p.m. was alongside the casualty, with ten feet of water still under the keel. The crew pulled the woman on board, and the lifeboat was taken into deeper water while the woman, who was totally disorientated and suffering from shock and hypothermia, was taken inside the cabin and wrapped in blankets. Helicopter R128 evacuated the survivor from the lifeboat and took her to Grimsby hospital, after which the lifeboat left the area to escort Cleethorpes ILB back to station. By 7.30 p.m. *Pride of the Humber* was back on station and being refuelled.

In 2001 Superintendent Coxswain Brian Bevan retired from the post after more than twenty-five years, during which time he had become one of the most famous lifeboatmen in the RNLI's history. He was replaced by Bob White, who served as Superintendent Coxswain from November 2001 to May 2003.

Pride of the Humber powers her way through the North Sea. (By courtesy of Brian Bevan)

David Steenvoorden at the wheel of Pride of the Humber as she leaves Grimsby Docks. Dave was appointed Superintendent Coxswain at Spurn in April 2004, having been full-time crew at the station since 1990. Between 1987 and 1990, he was a volunteer on the inshore lifeboat at Cleethorpes and was awarded the RNLI's Bronze medal in recognition of his courage, leadership and fine seamanship when the ILB rescued five canoeists and their canoes in difficulties in the Humber Estuary on 30 July 1989. The ILB then went on to assist the yacht Serenus in the same service, in a north-westerly storm and confused seas. He was awarded a collective framed chairman's Letter of Appreciation for a service on 30 July 1989 when twenty-nine people were rescued and four rafts saved during a charity raft race, with two other boats, when the wind suddenly increased to force seven. (Nicholas Leach)

Bob joined the Humber crew in 1980 after a year as a full-time mechanic with the RNLI, and in 1990 was appointed as Second Coxswain at Spurn. He remained in that post until he succeeded Brian Bevan as Superintendent Coxswain, retiring from the service when he reached the mandatory retirement age of fifty-five. His replacement as Coxswain in 2003 was Ian Firman, who had been Coxswain at Aldeburgh, and had also served on Scarborough lifeboat as well as having spent a short time on the Humber crew.

The last service with Bob White as Coxswain took place on 16 May 2003 when *Pride of the Humber* launched to the yacht *Katanne*, which had fouled her propeller. While the lifeboat was setting out, however, she was diverted to help the pilot boat *Humber Alert*, which was on fire with two crew on board. The fire had been put out by the time the lifeboat arrived and another pilot boat, *Rover*, had taken *Humber Alert* in tow. The lifeboat was tasked to evacuate Karl White, Bob's son who was crew on the pilot boat, as he had been overcome by fumes, and landed him at Spurn Point, where an ambulance was waiting to take him to hospital. The lifeboat then returned to the pilot launch and towed that back to Spurn. Once that had been secured, the lifeboat went back to help the yacht, the original casualty. The lifeboat crew assisted in clearing its propellers, enabling the yacht to continue on its way.

On 26 February 2004 Humber lifeboat crew joined forces with their Cleethorpes counterparts again to save the lives of two fishermen on a drifting fishing vessel, the 11.5m beam trawler *Dollard*, which was in trouble just over four miles south-east of Spurn Point. Another fishing vessel, *Morning Star*, had spotted

The boarding boat storage arrangement on the Pilot Jetty (above), with the rigid-hulled boarding boat beneath the davit. After the boat has been launched to take the crew to the lifeboat, it is placed on the mooring (below) used by the lifeboat. (Nicholas Leach)

When weather conditions in the Humber are too bad for boarding the lifeboat at Spurn Point, the boat is brought across to shelter at a berth at Grimsby, and this small accommodation block, installed in 1994 at the docks, is used by the crew, providing bunks, kitchen and toilet facilities. The crew (below) on duty at Grimsby in September 2004 were, from left to right, Martyn Hagan, Colin Fisk, Bryan White, Dave Steenvoorden and David Lane. (Nicholas Leach)

Pride of the Humber leaving the berth at Grimsby (above) used when the weather at Spurn Point prohibits the crew safely boarding the lifeboat, and (below) on exercise in the river off the Docks, September 2004. (Nicholas Leach)

the casualty, informed the Humber Coastguard it was in trouble, and made three unsuccessful attempts to attach a tow. Cleethorpes station was alerted and the ILB launched at 4.08 p.m. in very poor visibility, with snow showers, surf and high winds, with four rather than three crew members on board. Meanwhile the Humber crew, under Acting Superintendent Coxswain Dave Steenvoorden, boarded *Pride of the Humber* in difficult conditions at Spurn, and at 4.12 p.m. set off into the force eight winds and heavy snow.

Pride of the Humber reached *Morning Star* at 4.21 p.m., and saw *Dollard* well inside the surf line, over half a mile away. It was difficult to see the casualty because of the snow, wind and spray, and the swell was steeper in the shallows, up to three metres and breaking. *Dollard* had touched the bottom once or twice and was continually being struck by breaking waves. Her crew had an anchor down, but it was on a very short cable and was dragging, and the vessel was heading towards the shore. Soon after 4.30 p.m. the Cleethorpes ILB arrived on scene with helmsman Gary Barlow having to constantly manoeuvre the lifeboat to cope with the unpredictable wave patterns, and the whole crew remaining vigilant to avoid being caught out by a wave which could capsize the inflatable.

As the fishermen would not leave their boat an attempt was made to establish a tow and bring the casualty clear of the surf. However, the D class could not tow the large vessel and *Pride of the Humber* was half a mile away, with the echo sounder at times reading just a metre and a half of water under the keel. Two crew were put aboard *Dollard* to help with the tow, but transferring them was difficult as *Dollard* was being buffeted, with her bows being lifted by large breaking waves. Showing superb seamanship, helmsman Barlow manoeuvred the ILB alongside and crew members Tony Salters and Ian Sanderson clambered aboard. *Morning Star*, whose draught was considerably less than that of *Pride of the Humber*, agreed to help establish a tow, so the ILB collected a long mooring rope from the Severn. But after the

On 4 April 2006 HRH Duke of Kent visited lifeboat stations from Skegness to Bridlington. At the Humber, Superintendent Coxswain Dave Steenvoorden met the Duke, who was taken on board Pride of the Humber accompanied by RNLI Chief Executive Andrew Fremantle. (Dave Keegan, by courtesy of the RNLI)

The seven houses at Spurn Point for the full-time lifeboat crew, with the Superintendent Coxswain's house on the right. The houses, built in the mid-1970s, were modernised and improved in 2008 and represent an important element of the Humber station. (Nicholas Leach)

rope had been thrown across to the ILB, *Morning Star* decided it was too dangerous to help and moved away. At this point a series of waves hit *Dollard*, pushing her even closer to the shore, so the crew on the ILB had to handle the tow. Meanwhile *Pride of the Humber* had edged towards the casualty as the lifeboat crew had spotted a deeper channel, which enabled the lifeboat to get within eighty metres of the casualty. At times the echo sounder was reading zero, but the lifeboat did not touch bottom.

Because the ILB would not be able to take the heavy tow rope through the surf, a mooring rope was prepared as a temporary measure to at least get *Dollard* out of the surf. Helmsman Barlow again executed a skilful manoeuvre to get close to the Severn for the line to be thrown, and then made an approach to the starboard bow of the casualty, dragging the rope behind. The line was passed across to *Dollard* and secured by one of the Cleethorpes crew. On board *Dollard*, the lifeboatmen cut the anchor cable and helped the skipper raise the trawl beams, with some of the nets entangled in the propeller. Once the towline had been secured between casualty and lifeboat, the ILB stood by while the Humber lifeboat slowly started to pull the casualty clear. Superintendant Coxswain Steenvoorden cautiously pulled *Dollard* at just two knots through the surf and into an area of deeper water. With the light fading and in waves up to four metres high, the Severn safely cleared the surf at 5.30 p.m. The temporary tow had been enough, but at this point it was replaced by a heavier rope. As the ILB had finished their part in the rescue, and with the two Cleethorpes crew members staying on board *Dollard*, Helmsman Barlow set off back to Cleethorpes. Those on board *Dollard* had an uncomfortable passage with wind against tide making the seas very steep as they headed to Grimsby Dock, where *Pride of the Humber* and her tow arrived at 7.50 p.m.

For this difficult rescue, Gary Barlow was awarded the Silver medal for his courage, leadership and skill, and the three crew members received Bronze medals. Dave Steenvoorden was accorded the Thanks Inscribed on Vellum for his leadership and skill and the rest of the Humber crew received Medal Service certificates. RNLI Operations Director Michael Vlasto commented, 'Crews from both the inshore and all weather lifeboats worked together, putting all their training into practice, to ensure no-one was lost to the sea that night – they all deserve our praise and their individual awards.'

Pride of the Humber on exercise off Spurn Point in the River Humber with Cleethorpes D-class inshore lifeboat D-618 Blue Peter VI. (Nicholas Leach)

At the time of this service, Dave Steenvoorden was Acting Superintendent Coxswain, but on 7 April 2004 his appointment was made permanent. Almost immediately after being told he had been appointed, he was out on service after the yacht *Duet* got into trouble at the entrance to the Humber. The relief lifeboat *The Will* was being refuelled at the time, and as soon as this had been completed and the boat securely moored, the lifeboat crew set off in *Pride of the Humber* at 6.40 p.m. Arriving on scene, the lifeboat crew found the yacht under storm sail and making heavy weather of the conditions. The skipper was asked to drop his sail so that the lifeboat could come alongside to take off the sick crew. Once the transfer had been safely completed, one of the lifeboat crew went aboard to assist with rigging a tow while the sick crew member was given seasickness tablets on the lifeboat. The casualty was then slowly and carefully towed to Grimsby, with the lifeboat crew contending with the challenging conditions. On arriving at Grimsby Fish Dock, the yacht's crew were passed to the care of Cleethorpes Coastguard, and the lifeboat returned to station and was ready for service at 11.45 p.m.

Another challenging service was carried out on 11 January 2005 after the fishing vessel *Sorrento* got into difficulty with mechanical problems. In a south-westerly force nine gale, with rough seas, the vessel was in some danger, so Superintendent Coxswain Dave Steenvoorden decided to launch. *Pride of the Humber* put out at 2.43 p.m., and due to the severity of the weather the boarding boat was put back onto her cradle as it would have been in danger of capsizing if left on the moorings. The lifeboat made best speed to *Sorrento*, going at full speed but, at times, surfing down large seas. The lifeboat arrived on scene at 5.07 p.m. by when it was dark and the crew faced the force nine gale with five-metre seas. *Sorrento*, steaming under low power, was making very slow progress and her skipper asked if the lifeboat could tow them as he expected the engine to fail. Under the instructions of Superintendent Coxswain Steenvoorden, the lifeboat crew rigged the tow and made ready for the transfer of the line. It took seven attempts to get the line across, as both boats were moving violently in the heavy seas, and the strong wind hindered the transfer of the heaving line. But when the tow had finally been made fast, the lifeboat

The Humber crew outside the crew facility, left to right (seated), Colin Fisk and his son Taylor, Steve Purvis, Martyn Hagan and Dan Atkinson. Standing are, left to right, Brian White and Dave Steenvoorden. (By courtesy of the RNLI)

(Below) Mechanic David Lane in the engine room of Pride of the Humber. (Nicholas Leach)

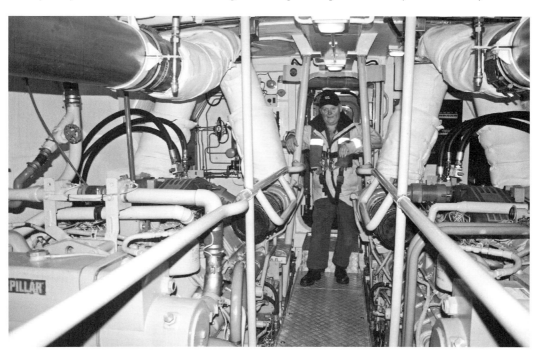

set course for Grimsby, although progress was very slow due to the weather and the size of *Sorrento*. The wind was force eight to nine, but it eased to force seven with the sea conditions also improving, and the speed of the tow was increased to almost five knots. The wind strengthened to force eight a couple of hours later, but the tow continued unaffected and the vessels eventually arrived at Grimsby at 6.35 a.m. on 12 January. *Sorrento* was berthed safely but, due to the conditions at Spurn, the lifeboat was refuelled in Grimsby and stayed there until 5.45 p.m. when the weather had eased, allowing her to return to station.

On 23 February 2006, while the crew was aboard the lifeboat carrying out planned maintenance, Humber Coastguard requested an immediate launch after receiving a Mayday from the standby vessel *Putford Trader*, which was at the Rough Gas Field and reported an explosion and fire on board the 47/3B gas rig. The lifeboat slipped her moorings at 10.48 a.m., and three RAF rescue helicopters were scrambled at the same time. The lifeboat reached the gas rig within an hour and found two of the helicopters already on scene with an evacuation underway. One of the rig's emergency lifeboats had been launched and was being towed by *Putford Trader*'s daughter boat. The Coastguard asked the lifeboat crew to act as a safety boat while the helicopters evacuated persons off the rig. The helicopters took twenty-four persons off, leaving twenty-five essential personnel aboard. Two people were taken to Hull Royal Infirmary, while the remainder were landed at Humberside Airport by the helicopters. The fire was extinguished by 12.30 p.m., and the lifeboat remained on scene until the damage had been fully assessed. At 2.12 p.m. the situation had been brought under control so the lifeboat was stood down. The lifeboat was requested to take the rig's lifeboat under tow as the rig's recovery system had been damaged, so she took the tow off *Putford Trader*, which was then able to remain at the gas field. During the service crewman Chris Allen sustained a cut to his head after banging it on the wheelhouse door; the wound was cleaned and bandaged.

A very difficult service was undertaken on 12 August 2006 during which the lifeboat crew had to contend with rough seas and force eight to nine winds. The incident began after the rig support vessel *Putford Provider* reported that the yacht *Molly Louise*, with four people on board, was in difficulty in a northerly gale, Superintendent Coxswain Dave Steenvoorden decided to put to sea immediately, but boarding the relief lifeboat *Fraser Flyer*, which was on station at Spurn, was difficult in the challenging

A dramatic photograph of the Humber's relief lifeboat Fraser Flyer towing the yacht Molly Louise on 12 August 2006, with the RAF rescue helicopter on scene, seen from on board the Skegness lifeboats. (By courtesy of the RNLI)

Pride of the Humber sets off from Spurn Point, with the lighthouse and Pilot Jetty in the background. (Nicholas Leach)

conditions. Once the crew was on board, the lifeboat's moorings were slipped and she headed towards the casualty. The passage to the scene was made more difficult because the port engine was overheating, and it eventually had to be stopped, with the lifeboat continuing on one engine.

The yacht, which was approximately twenty-eight miles east of the station, had put out a Mayday call, and RAF Rescue Helicopter 128 had been tasked to help as the situation had become so serious. On board *Putford Provider,* the crew could see the yacht, which had no sail and was beam on to the three-metre seas. By about 5 p.m. the helicopter was on scene and trying to call the yacht, but as no response was received and nobody could be seen on board, *Putford Provider* went alongside and a crew member called the yacht with a loud hailer. At around 5.26 p.m. *Putford Provider* reported that only one person was on the yacht, as his three companions had been washed overboard when the yacht was knocked down. Meanwhile, Skegness lifeboat *Lincolnshire Poacher* had launched, putting out at 5.35 p.m., as the Humber lifeboat's port engine continued to cause problems and the boat could only make about fourteen knots.

At 5.36 p.m. the helicopter reported that three people had been seen in the water, and with the Humber lifeboat now on scene, went to pick up the casualties, while the lifeboat slowly approached the yacht. In the northerly force eight to nine winds, with short five to seven-metre-steep seas, *Putford Provider* was positioned to give the lifeboat a lee as she was manoeuvred into position to transfer two crew, a difficult task using just one engine. But, after two attempts, the lifeboat got alongside long enough for crew member Bryan White to get onto the yacht; after a further two approaches, Dan Atkinson also got across. Conditions were very difficult and at one point the yacht was knocked over by a very large sea, so a speedy transfer of the remaining yachtsman to the lifeboat was essential. It took several attempts to get the man across to the lifeboat. During the transfer, an unexpectedly large wave hit the lifeboat, pushing her over onto the yacht, and when the yacht fell away Martyn Hagan and Pete Price had to cling onto the survivor to prevent him falling into the sea. Although he was initially in danger of being trapped, the lifeboat crew hastily hauled him over the rail to safety. He had a suspected broken wrist and was very confused, but was tended to inside the lifeboat's survivor cabin.

Once the survivor was safely aboard the lifeboat, a tow could be rigged, so a line was passed across to the yacht and secured at the first attempt. But a large wave picked up the yacht and turned it through 180 degrees and on top of the towline, which went under the keel. The line had to be slipped, recovered and, after two more attempts, it was secured again, during which time the yacht was knocked over twice more. By this time Skegness lifeboat had reached the scene and stood by during the next phase of the rescue. The survivor on the lifeboat was then winched into the helicopter so that he could be taken to hospital. After the winching, the tow to Grimsby began, with the Skegness lifeboat escorting the two vessels into the river. The tow was very slow due to the severe winds, force seven to nine, and the casualty and lifeboat eventually reached the port at 1.10 a.m. the following morning.

The two lifeboat crew on the yacht took it into the dock under its own power and, once they were back on board, the lifeboat returned to station. Following this rescue, the Thanks of the Institution Inscribed on Vellum was accorded to Superintendent Coxswain David Steenvoorden, and Assistant Mechanic Daniel Atkinson received a Framed Letter of Thanks signed by the Chairman for his part in the rescue.

On 20 May 2007 the lifeboat was involved in a long service after Humber Coastguard requested assistance for the fishing vessel *Abbie Lee*, which was having fuel problems. The lifeboat slipped moorings at 9.16 a.m. and set course for the vessel. During the passage the lifeboat encountered severe weather conditions and the crew were strapped into their seats. Once on scene, the crew found the fishing vessel was making about two knots and the skipper had requested a tow because the engine was cutting out when he increased the power, so a towline was quickly passed across and course was set for Grimsby. The tow went without incident, even though the heavy seas made conditions difficult for both

The fishing vessel Abbie Lee being taken in tow by Pride of the Humber on 20 May 2007. (By courtesy of Dave Steenvoorden)

The view from Pride of the Humber of the 47/3B gas rig, at the Rough Gas Field, which caught fire on 21 February 2006. (By courtesy of Dave Steenvoorden)

the lifeboat crew and those on board the fishing vessel. The tow was slipped at Grimsby Docks where the vessel went through the lock under her own power. As the weather conditions at Spurn Point were poor, the lifeboat was refuelled in Grimsby before returning to station.

An incident involving all the rescue services took place on 23 July 2009, when the former fishing boat *Corsair* got into difficulty and began taking on water at the entrance to Grimsby Dock. *Pride of the Humber* launched at 9.45 a.m., with Cleethorpes inshore lifeboat, Rescue Helicopter 128 and two pilot boats also proceeding to the scene. While en route to *Corsair*, the lifeboat crew readied the salvage pump for immediate use, while Cleethorpes ILB transferred a crewman aboard. *Corsair* was refused

Humber lifeboat crew outside Holy Trinity Church in Hull in April 2010 for the anniversary church service marking 200 years of life-saving at Spurn Point, with notable personnel in attendance. Back row, left to right, Steve Purvis, Greg Hanks, Matthew Ainley (relief crew), Calum Reed, Karl Steenvoorden (holding flag), Charlie Jackson (relief crew), Andy Hall (relief crew), Thomas Ward (relief crew), and Colin Fisk, Jnr; at the front are Martyn Hagan, Dave Steenvoorden and Colin Fisk snr. (Steve Medcalf)

entry to Grimsby Fish Dock in case she sank in the lock and blocked it. Humber lifeboat arrived at 10.05 a.m. and the salvage pump and crewman Steve Purvis were transferred to the casualty. Within minutes the pump had stopped any further rise in the water level, and Rescue Helicopter 128 dropped another pump onto *Corsair*, together with a winchman. Lifeboatman M. Holley went aboard to assist with the pumps, which reduced the water level significantly, but as it could not be seen where the water was coming in, it was decided to run *Corsair* aground at Cleethorpes so that the extent of the damage could be ascertained. Rescue 128 was released at 11.15 a.m., and Cleethorpes ILB took most of the people off *Corsair* and transferred them aboard *Pride of the Humber*, leaving only crewman Purvis, a lifeboatman from Cleethorpes, and the vessel's skipper aboard. *Corsair* was then run up onto the beach and secured.

After *Corsair* had been pumped dry, plank damage could be seen in various places, mostly above the waterline. With the vessel safe, the two lifeboatmen and the vessel's skipper were taken off by Cleethorpes ILB. The Harbour Master agreed to refloat *Corsair* on the incoming tide and place the vessel in the Fish Dock. At 3.15 p.m. crewman Purvis, two of the Cleethorpes crew and the skipper went back aboard *Corsair*. As fuel had overflowed into the vessel's engine room, the bilge pumps were shut down and the lifeboat towed *Corsair* to Grimsby. At 3.55 p.m. the towline was attached, and at about two to three knots the vessel was taken to Grimsby Fish Dock, arriving at 5.30 p.m. Twenty minutes later *Corsair* was alongside in the dock, the pumps had been recovered and the helicopter pump handed to the Coastguard unit, after which the lifeboat returned to station.

In 2010 the Humber lifeboat station celebrated its bicentenary, marking two centuries of life-saving off Spurn Point and the Humber Estuary, and a number of events were organised to commemorate the historic landmark. During its long and illustrious history, the lifeboat station at the Humber has become one of the most famous in the country thanks in part to its unique status as the only all-weather lifeboat manned by a full-time crew. The exploits of the lifeboatmen, particularly during the twentieth century, have also raised the station's profile considerably, while today's full-time lifeboat crew continue the tradition of saving those in peril on the sea. Between 1911, when the RNLI took over the station, and 31 December 2009 the Humber lifeboats have launched 2,268 times on service, saving 790 lives.

The impressive sight of Pride of the Humber leaving Spurn Point on exercise. (Nicholas Leach)

Appendices

A · LIFEBOAT SUMMARY

Years on station (record)	Dimensions Type (oars)	Cost ON	Year built Builder	Name Donor
1810 – 1823	North Country (10)	£200 —	1810 Greathead, Sth. Shields	[Not named] Hull Trinity House
1824 – 1852	30'2" x 10' North Country (10)	£190 —	1824 Thomas Mason, Hull	[Not named] Hull Trinity House
1852 – 1881 (1854–81: 97/77)	30' x 9'3" Self-righter (10)	£112 —	1852 Hallett, Hull	[Not named] Hull Trinity House
1881 – 1901 (49/224)	32'6" x 9'8" Non-SR (10)	£195 —	1881 John Ed. Cooper, Hull	Mew (?) Hull Trinity House
1901 – 1903 (0/0)	38'1" x 9'1" Self-righter (12)	£424 206	1890 D. Livie & Sons, Dundee	Manchester Unity (loaned by RNLI) Independent Order of Odd Fellows
1903 – 1913 (1911-13: 10/9)	34'6" x 9'10" Non-SR (10)	£700 631	1903 Earles SB&E Co., Hull	[Not named] Hull Trinity House / 1911- RNLI
1913 – 1919 (34/32)	38' x 10' Liverpool (10)	£1,054 516	1903 Thames IW, Blackwall	Charles Deere James [Reserve 9] Mrs S. C. Guthrie, Tunbridge Wells
1919 – 1923 (33/25)	40' x 11' Watson (M)	£7,156 651	1918 Summers & Payne/ completed by Saunders	Samuel Oakes Legacy of Mrs Elizabeth M. Laing, Barnes
1923 – 1929 (36/37) and 1930 – 1932	45' x 12'6" Watson (M)	£12,780 680	1923 J. S. White, Cowes	City of Bradford I City of Bradford Lifeboat Fund
1929 – 1954 (228/305)	45'6" x 12'6" Watson (M)	£8,662 709	1929 S. E. Saunders, Cowes	City of Bradford II City of Bradford Lifeboat Fund
1954 – 1977 (351/107)	46'9" x 12'9" Watson (M)	£29,593 911	1954 J. S. White, Cowes	City of Bradford III City of Bradford Lifeboat Fund
1968 – 1969 (1/0)	46' x 12'9" Watson (M)	£10,145 828	1939 J. S. White, Cowes	The Princess Royal (Civ. Service No.7) Civil Service Lifeboat Fund
1977 – 1987 (416/106)	54' x 17' Arun (M)	£163,453 1052	1976 Halmatic Ltd, Havant	City of Bradford IV City of Bradford Lord Mayor's Appeal
1987 – 1997 (383/68)	52' x 17' Arun (M)	£574,433 1123	1987 Hull by Halmatic Ltd/ Berthon Bt Co. fit out	Kenneth Thelwall Legacy of Kenneth Thelwall, Walkington, Yorks
1997–	17m x 5.5m Severn (M)	£1,400,000 1216	1995/6 Hull by Green Marine/ Halmatic Ltd fit out	Pride of the Humber Humber Lifeboat Appeal and various bequests and legacies

(M) indicates motor lifeboat

B · RNLI MOTOR LIFEBOATS

Samuel Oakes

Official Number	651
On station	11 Nov 1919 – Nov 1923
Record	33 launches, 25 lives saved
Dimensions	40ft x 11ft x 5ft 6in
Type	Watson motor
Engines	Single 40hp Tylor C.2 four-cylinder petrol
Weight	10 tons 4 cwt
Built	Summers & Payne; completed by S. E. Saunders, Cowes; yard no.S16
Donor	Legacy of Mrs Elizabeth Mary Laing, Barnes
Cost	£7,155 10s 5d
Disposal	After service at Weymouth 1924-29 and Shoreham Harbour 1929-33, sold out of service in January 1933 and renamed *Esmee* and later *Grey Gull*; she was burnt out at Rochester in the 1980s

City of Bradford II

Official Number	709
On station	13 Feb 1929 – Nov 1953
Record	228 launches, 305 lives saved
Dimensions	45ft 6in x 12ft 6in x 6ft 3in
Type	Watson motor
Engines	Twin 40bhp Weyburn CE.4 petrol, maximum speed 8.07 knots
Weight	18 tons 10 cwt
Built	S. E. Saunders, Cowes; yard no.W1662
Donor	Legacy of James M. Howson of Harrogate and funds raised by City of Bradford and the Airedale and Wharfedale Districts.
Cost	£8,662 17s 9d
Disposal	Served at Amble 1954-57 and in the Reserve Fleet until sold Dec 1968: became a pleasure boat named *Frieda* based in Northern Ireland; subsequently reverted to her lifeboat name

City of Bradford III

Official Number	911
On station	Jan 1954 – May 1977
Record	351 launches, 107 lives saved
Dimensions	46ft 9in x 12ft 9in
Type	Watson motor
Engines	Twin 40hp Ferry VE.4 RNLI design four-cylinder petrol; re-engined 1968 with twin 70hp Parsons Barracuda II diesels
Weight	21 tons 15 cwt
Built	J. S. White, Cowes; yard no.W5432
Donor	City of Bradford Lifeboat Fund
Cost	£29,593
Disposal	Served at Lytham St Annes from 1978 to 1985 until sold out of service in July 1985; kept in Cornwall as a pleasure boat retaining her lifeboat name, until moving to South Wales in 2009 and then Salcombe in 2010

City of Bradford IV

Official Number	1052 (54-07)
On station	Mar 1977 – Aug 1987
Record	416 launches, 106 lives saved
Dimensions	52ft x 17ft
Type	Arun
Engines	Twin 460hp Caterpillar D343TA six-cylinder diesels
Weight	32 tons 8 cwt
Built	Halmatic Ltd, Havant; yard no.WR4908
Donor	City of Bradford Appeal, Sheffield Lifeboat Fund and the International Transport Workers Federation
Cost	£163,453
Disposal	Served at Thurso, Ballyglass and Tobermory until sold out of service on 22 Oct 1998 to become a pleasure boat under the names *Lady Arun*, *Theocrat*, *Restless* and *Solidian*

Kenneth Thelwall

Official Number	1123 (52-37)
On station	Aug 1987 – Mar 1997
Record	383 launches, 68 lives saved
Dimensions	52ft x 17ft
Type	Arun
Engines	Twin 485hp Caterpillar 3408TA diesels
Weight	30.66 tonnes
Built	Halmatic Ltd, Havant; fitted out by Berthon Boat Co., Lymington; yard no.1014
Donor	Legacy of Mr Kenneth Thelwall, Walkington, Yorkshire.
Cost	£574,434
Disposal	Transferred to the Relief Fleet, stationed at Holyhead 1998-2003, and then sold out of service in July 2005 to China Rescue & Salvage Bureau; shipped to China, where she was renamed *Huaying 399* for service at Wenzhou, Zhejiang

Pride of the Humber

Official Number	1216 (17-05)
On station	8 Mar 1997 –
Dimensions	17m x 5.5m x 3.3m
Type	Severn
Engines	Twin 1,200hp Caterpillar 3412 diesels, each of 2300rpm
Wieght	41 tonnes
Built	Green Marine, Lymington; fitted out by Halmatic Ltd; yard no.MR 3861
Donor	Humber Lifeboat Appeal 1994 and 1995; fund-raising of North East region volunteers; and bequests of Miss Lucy Chandley, Miss Margery Ivory Hootor, Mrs Mary Self of Cleethorpes, as well as various other legacies
Cost	£1,464,125

lifeboat of 1903

1912	Jan 6	Steam trawler Agatha, of Grimsby, saved 9
1913	Jan 13	Steam trawler Cancer, of Grimsby, stood by and gave help
	19	Barge Cambria, of London, saved vessel

Charles Deere James lifeboat

1913	Dec 8	*Motor fishing boat Pat, of Grimsby, saved vessel
1914	Feb 7	Steamship Balvenie, of Glasgow, stood by
	Mar 25	Brigantine Jean Anderson, of Hull, assisted to save vessel and 6
	Sep 9	*Sloop Chesterfield, of Lynn, saved 3
	Oct 29	Schooner Union, of Portsmouth, stood by
	Dec 23	Steamship Elantsobe, of Bilbao, assisted to save
1915	Feb 15	Steamship CT.8, rendered assistance, stood by
	27	Schooner William and Alice, of Hull, saved 4
	Dec 3	Steamship Fieldig, of Brevik, rendered assistance
	6	Steamship Lady Ann, of Sunderland, stood by
	7	Steamship Lady Ann, of Sunderland, assisted to save vessel
	9-10	Steamship Florence, of Stockholm, saved 8
	10-20	Steamship Minsk, of Copenhagen, assisted to save mined and abandoned vessel
1916	Jan 10	Steamship Parklands, of West Hartlepool, rendered assistance and stood by
	Dec 28	Steamship Laxton, of Goole, landed 7
1917	Feb 21	Steam trawler Wigan, of Fleetwood, rendered assistance
1918	Jan 28	Steam trawler Crystal, of Hull, assisted to save trawler
	July 5	*Smack Amy King, of Grimsby, landed 1
	17	*Seaplane, saved 2
	Oct 6	Schooner Amy, of Newcastle, assisted to save vessel and 5

*Boarding boat service

Samuel Oakes lifeboat

1919	Dec 16	Steam trawler Prince Victor, of Grimsby, rendered assistance and stood by
1920	Jan 8	Barque Paul, of Pori, stood by and assisted to save
	May 4	Steam trawler Ronso, of Grimsby, stood by
	18	Ketch Wellington, of London, saved vessel and 3
	19	Ketch Wellington, of London, broken adrift, saved vessel
		Ketch Wellington, of London, reboarded crew
	June 12*	Tug Robert Forest, of Grimsby, saved 2
	Nov 19	Bull lightvessel, rendered assistance
	Dec 3	3-masted schooner Julia Maria, of Riga, assisted vessel and stood by
1921	April 8	Sloop Liberty, of Hull, saved vessel
	Sep 30	Sloop Paradise, of Barton, rendered assistance
	Dec 23	Steam trawler Xania, of Grimsby, saved vessel
		Steam trawler Pomana, of Hull, saved vessel
1922	June 16	Steam trawler Gozo, of Hull, stood by, rendered assistance
	21	Steam trawler Serapion, of Grimsby, rendered assistance
	28	Steam trawler Darracq, of Grimsby, stood by
	July 7	Rowing boat, saved 3
	Dec 6	Schooner Hosanna, of Thurso, saved 5
		Schooner Hosanna, of Thurso, saved vessel
	19	Steam trawler Earl Granard, of Grimsby, stood by

City of Bradford lifeboat

1923	Aug 29	Sloop Spring, of Hull, saved vessel and 3
	Sep 25	Steam trawler Portsmouth, of Grimsby, saved vessel and 9
1924	July 6	Boat, of Haile Fort, stood by
	Oct 16	Steamship Harlech, of London, landed 14 from trawler Elf King, of Grimsby
1925	Nov 25	Steamship Whinstone, of Preston, saved 6
	Dec 27*	Steam trawler Editor, of Grimsby, assisted to save
1926	Feb 9	Steam trawler Dinorah, of Grimsby, saved 11
	14	Steamship Tabora, of Cardiff, stood by
	Mar 23	Steam trawler Salmonby, of Boston, saved 2

	Apr 7	Boat, saved abandoned boat
	Aug 14	Racing yacht Piccolo, of Owston Ferry, saved yacht and 4
	Oct 9	Dredger Kite, of Newcastle, saved 4
1927	Feb 17	Steam trawler Pomona, of Hull, stood by
	May 8	Steam trawler Rigoletto, of Grimsby, stood by
	Nov 8	Steam trawler Bessie, of Grimsby, rendered assistance and landed an injured man
	22	Schooner Ornen, of Svendborg, assisted to save vessel and 7
1928	Mar 16	Steam trawler Night Hawk, of Grimsby, rendered assistance
	June 6	Steam trawler Abelia, of Grimsby, stood by
1930	Nov 1	Steam trawler Kingston Olivine, of Hull, rendered assistance
1931	Mar 7	Steamship Tern, of London, stood by and landed 2
	Dec 1	Steam trawler St Irene, of hull, stood by
1932	Jan 27	lifeboat boarding dinghy, towed in dinghy and landed 2
1933	July 9	Yacht Alice, of Oslo, saved yacht and landed 3

City of Bradford II lifeboat

1929	Sep 19	Motor boat Curlew, of Whitby, saved boat and 2
	Oct 15	Steam trawler Barle, of Grimsby, stood by
	Nov 26	Steam trawler Sea Lion, of Grimsby, stood by
	Dec 18	Steam trawler Bengal, of Grimsby, stood by
1930	Aug 23	Auxiliary sloop Dakar, of Hull, saved vessel and 2
1931	May 29	Fishing boat Ella, of Ockero, in tow of trawler, escorted
	June 14	Fishing boat Felix, of Hull, escorted
1932	Sep 18	Yacht Thrush, of Hull, saved yacht and 3
1933	Jan 13	Steam trawler Teanio, of Hull, rendered assistance
	14	Steamship Arantzaya, of Bilbao, rendered assistance
	Apr 1	Steam trawler Lord Harewood, of Grimsby, rendered assistance
	Oct 13	Steam trawler Kirby, of Grimsby, assisted to save vessel and 12
	Dec 15	Steam trawler Thanet, of Hull, rendered assistance
1934	Mar 2	Steamship The Monarch, of Glasgow, stood by
	Apr 5	Steamship Lancashire, of Sunderland, landed 10
		Steamship Lancashire, of Sunderland, stood by and reboarded crew and passengers
	May 17	Steam trawler Salacon, of Grimsby, rendered assistance and stood by
	21	Rowing boat Ivy, of Tunstall, saved boat and 2
	Sep 8	Fishing vessel Nordstjernen, of Fredrikshavn, rendered assistance
	19	Motor launch Sunbeam, of Cleethorpes, saved launch and 14
	Oct 3	Steam drifter Silver Prince, of Lowestoft, gave assistance
	Nov 24	Steam trawler Chrysea, of Grimsby, stood by
1935	Jan 22	Steam trawler Havardour Isfirdingur, of Isafjordur, rendered assistance
	Oct 12	Bull Fort, took a sick man to Grimsby
	19	Steamship Magrix, of Hull, stood by
(BB)	Nov 13	Middle Gas Float, secured drifting float
	14	Middle Gas Float, towed float to safe mooring
	25	Steamship Groveland, of Raa, stood by, gave help
1936	Feb 17	Motor barge River Witham, of Hull, stood by
	23	Steam trawler Algorma, of Grimsby, stood by
	Mar 11	Motor vessel Mary Birch, of Hull, stood by and escorted
	May 31	Fishing boat The Lily, of Grimsby, rendered assistance
	Aug 18	Steam trawler Runswick Bay, of Hull, rendered assistance
	Nov 12	Fishing vessel Aud Schou, of Frederickhavn, saved vessel
	23	Steamship Everolanda, of Riga, landed sick woman
1937	Feb 21	Steam trawler Rose of England, of Grimsby, saved 5
	Apr 6	Steam trawler Sir John Lister, of Hull, rendered assistance
	May 11	Bull lightvessel, investigated report of collision
	Aug 27	Steam trawler Scarron, of Grimsby, stood by and landed an injured man

	30	Fishing vessel Sophie, of Fredens Hafen, rendered assistance
Aug	31	Motor Yacht Sea Hawk, of Nottingham, saved yacht and 2
Oct	3	Steamship Ais Georgis, of Piraeus, assisted to save vessel and 21
	20	Bull Fort, landed a sick man
	21	Steam trawler Kings's Grey, of Hull, rendered assistance
Dec	13	Bull lightvessel, stood by and rendered assistance
	17	Steam Trawler Almandine, of Hull, rendered assistance
		Humber lightvessel, landed an injured man
1938 Feb	12	Steamship Deerwood, of London, stood by and rendered assistance
	14	Steamship King Edgar, of London, stood by
Mar	20	Motor vessel Confid, of Rotterdam, stood by and rendered assistance
May	27	Fishing boat Young Dick, of Hull, rendered assistance, saved boat and 1

J. W. Archer reserve lifeboat

| 1938 Aug | 7 | Steam trawler Capricornus, of Grimsby, stood by |
| | 29 | Steamship Salerno, of Hull, rendered assistance |

City of Bradford II lifeboat

1939	Jan 3	Steam trawler Spaniard, of Hull, rendered assistance
	20	Motor vessel Peterborough Trader, of Wisbech, stood by
Feb	14	Steam trawler Hausa, of Hull, stood by
July	23	Sailing boat Pinta, of Hull, rendered assistance
Aug	22	Steam trawler Cape Palliser, of Hull, rendered assistance
Sep	22	Steam trawler Kopenes, of Grimsby, stood by
Oct	10	Steam trawler Saltaire, of Grimsby, saved 9
		Steam trawler Saltaire, of Grimsby, (2nd service), saved 7
	17	Steam trawler Dane, of Hull, rendered assistance
Nov	3	Steamship Canada, of Copenhagen, saved 14
	11	Steamship Dryburgh, of Leith, saved 16
	12	Steamship Fireglow, of London, saved vessel
		Steamship Deerpool, of West Hartlepool, saved (including 4 from a tug) 34
	14	Boats of Steamship Georgios, of Piraeus, saved 22
	24	Steamship Mangalore, of Liverpool, saved 58
1940	Jan 11	Steamship Pitwines, of London, gave help
Feb	2	Steam trawler Barbados, of Grimsby, gave help
	3	Steamship Kildale, of Whitby, saved 9
	5	Steam trawler Barbados, of Grimsby, saved 11
	6	Steam trawler Barbados, of Grimsby, stood by
	7	Steam trawler Barbados, of Grimsby, stood by
	12	Steam trawler Gurth, of Grimsby, saved 9
	14	Steamship Castor, of Bergen, stood by
Mar	8	Steam trawler Vindelicia, of Grimsby, gave help
Oct	14	Trinity House vessel Reculver, of London, took out a doctor and saved 4
	29	British aircraft, picked up a body
Nov	25	HM Motor launch III, took out a doctor
	29	HM Trawler Recordo, took an injured man to Grimsby
1941	Jan 15	Steam trawler Stalker, of Grimsby, landed 11 from minesweeper Lady Stanley
	22	HM Tug St Syrus, from Minesweeper Fitzgerald, and picked up a body
Feb	27	Steamship Venus, of Rotterdam, gave help
		Balloon vessel Thora, saved 8
Apr	18	Steam trawler Donalda, of Grimsby, stood by
May	7	British aircraft, picked up 2 bodies
1942	Mar 3	Boat, saved boat and 3
1943	Jan 6	Phillips Defence Unit 3, saved 5
	7	HM Trawler Almandine, saved 19
	11	Steamship Anna, of Nieuport, saved 8
		Steamship Anna, of Nieuport, (second launch), stood by
Apr	26	Balloon Ship Thorp, saved 1
Aug	1	Steamship Lee S. Overman, of Wilmington, stood by
Nov	9	Steamship Broughty, of Dundee, gave help
1944	Apr 22	Steam trawler Chandos, of Grimsby, assisted to save vessel
Oct	14	Fishing vessel J. N. Fibiger, of Hirtshals, gave help
Dec	24	HM LC (G)110, escorted craft

1946	Jan 18	Humber lightvessel, landed an injured man
Sep	12	Yacht Lilian, saved yacht and 2
Nov	16	Humber lightvessel, landed an injured man
1947	Feb 21	Motor vessel Vrede, of Rotterdam, attempted to refloat
Aug	16	Steamship Lady Anstruther, of Glasgow, landed 15
Dec	17	Fishing vessel Ebor Jewel, gave help

Milburn reserve lifeboat

| 1948 June 13 | Motor cruiser Alisdair, of London, gave help |
| July | 7 | Motor yacht Dawn Patrol, of Brough, gave help |

City of Bradford II lifeboat

1948	Aug 9	Motor launch Phillip Rex, of Hull, saved vessel
1949	Jan 28	Motor vessel Northgate, of hull, gave help
July	31	Rubber dinghy, saved dinghy and 3
1950	July 6	Fishing vessel Kutter, of Denmark, landed Captain and injured man, and reboarded Captain
1951	Jan 6	Steam trawler Siluria, of Grimsby, stood by
	14	Humber lightvessel, landed a sick man
Aug	8	Steamship Afterglow, of London, landed inj. man

Edward Z. Dresden reserve lifeboat

| 1952 | Jan 21 | Boat of steamship Don, of Goole, gave help |
| Apr | 1 | Barge Zuversicht, of Hamburg, gave help |

City of Bradford II lifeboat

1952 May 27	Tug Scotsman, of hull, landed an injured man from HM Tug Mediator
June	3	Motor boat Ivy Dale, of London, gave help
1953	Feb 13	Steamship Monkton Combe, of Bristol, landed an injured man and reboarded him
		Steamship Sirius, of Stockholm, put doctor on board
Mar	1	Humber lightvessel, landed a sick man
Aug	16	Humber lightvessel, landed an injured man
Oct	10	Bull Fort, landed an injured man
	21	Steamship Nestos, of Piraeus, gave help

City of Bradford III lifeboat

1954	May 5	Humber lightvessel, landed a sick man
Nov	14	Steamship Caronte, of Rouen, took out a doctor
1955	Mar 13	Steamship Hadiotis, of Syre, landed a sick man
May	31	Yacht Kayak, of Beverley, gave help
Aug	15	Steamship Atlantic Star, of Panama, took out doctor
Oct	23	Outer Dowsing lightvessel, landed an injured man
	24	Auxiliary barge Pudge, of London, gave help
	25	Auxiliary barge Pudge, of London, gave help
1956	Jan 8	Motor vessel Stevonia, of Goole, stood by
May	31	Trawler Havkvern, of Bergen, landed an injured man
1957	May 15	Motor boat Daphne, gave help
Nov	19	Steam Trawler Remexo, of Grimsby, transferred 8 to HMS Wave and stood by
		Steam Trawler Loch Park, of Grimsby, stood by
1958	Jan 16	RAF Aircraft, recovered wreckage
Apr	8	Bull lightvessel, landed a body
June	6	Rowing boat, saved boat and 1
	24	Motor yacht Swordfish, gave help
Nov	24	Humber lightvessel, landed an injured man
1959	Jan 1	Fishing boat Excelsior, of Hull, saved boat and 2
Mar	8	Admiralty vessel DGV.400, took out a doctor and landed 1
July	24	Fishing boat Meggies, of Grimsby, in tow of fishing boat My Gratitude, of Grimsby, escorted
	26	Cabin cruiser Cormorant, of hull, gave help
	30	Cabin cruiser Ethnein, saved cruiser and 3
Aug	3	Yacht Sea Rover, of South Shields, gave help
	21	Yacht Witez II, stood by
	25	Yacht Laertes, of Grimsby, gave help
1960	May 15	Canoe, landed 2 children from motor vessel Tolsta
June	20	Motor vessel Gloxinia, of North Shields, landed a sick man, thereby saving 1
July	14	Yacht Sthoreen, saved yacht and 1
Aug	13	Fishing boat Tove, saved boat and 2
Sep	20	Yacht Toad, saved yacht and 2
Oct	22	Motor vessel Humbergate, of Goole, gave help
	23	Motor vessel Humbergate, of Goole, gave help

The yacht Daphne aground at Spurn Point, 15 May 1957. (Robertson Buchan Collection)

	20	Dowsing lightvessel, landed a sick man
	Aug 18	Yacht Italdo, saved yacht and 3
	Oct 8	Steamship Baron Berwick, of Ardrossan, landed a sick man
	15	Ex-Naal Pinnace, saved craft and 1
	Nov 5	Sick man on board motor vessel Fokke De Jong, of Workum, landed a sick man
	12	Motor boat Foreland, saved boat and 2
1964	Jan 4	Steamship Dorrefs, of Monrovia, landed a sick man
	July 13	Steamship Aggi, of Haugesund, took out a doctor
	Aug 1	Cabin cruiser Altonia, saved cruiser and 3
	26	Dowsing lightvessel, landed a sick man
	29	Trawler Delft, of Ijmuiden, landed an injured man
	Sep 6	Cabin cruiser Aquila, gave help
		Motor vessel Stelianos, of Piraeus, stood by
	9	Motor vessel Aethon, of Piraeus, landed a sick woman and her husband
	Oct 4	RNLB The Cuttle, of the Reserve Fleet, gave help
	6	RNLB The Cuttle, of the Reserve Fleet, saved lifeboat
		Injured man on board motor vessel Thorpe Grange, of London, landed an injured man
	14	Motor vessel Jushnij Bug (USSR), landed sick woman
	Nov 6	Motor vessel Artigas, of Beirut, landed injured man
	28	Motor vessel Royal Gate, stood by

Inshore Rescue Boat

1964	May 28	2 missing boys, unsuccessful search
	Aug 23	Yacht Veronique, escorted yacht
		Yacht Dolphin, gave help

City of Bradford III lifeboat

1965	Jan 2	Launch from Pilot Cutter, saved boat and 2
	May 13	Humber lightvessel, took out Police Officers
	Aug 19	Steamship Smolensk, of Riga, took out a doctor
	20	Steamship Smolensk, of Riga, landed 3 men (1 injured, 1 sick and an interpreter)
	24	Steamship Aegaion, of Piraeus, landed a sick man
	30	Fishing boat Pandora, of Grimsby, saved boat and 3
	Sep 1	Steamship Areti, of Beirut, landed a sick man
	25	Yacht Dowssabel, of Scarborough, in tow of motor vessel Reef Bank, of Grimsby, stood by
	29	Steamship Areti, of Beirut, landed a sick man
	Oct 18	Trawler St Joachim, of Boulogne, landed injured man
	31	Fishing boat Fair Adventure, of Folkestone, escorted
	Dec 27	Oil rig Sea Gem, stood by
	30	Oil rig Sea Gem, gave help
1966	Jan 29	Dowsing lightvessel, landed a sick man
	Feb 10	Fishing boat Northlands, saved boat and 3
	Apr 30	Auster Aircraft, recovered wreckage
	May 5	Motor vessel Dryburgh, of Leith, landed a sick man
	Sep 13	Cabin cruiser Petan, gave help
	Oct 19	Dowsing lightvessel, landed a sick man
1967	Feb 6	Dowsing lightvessel, landed a sick man
	Apr 20	Cabin cruiser Stella Peacock, gave help
	26	Dowsing lightvessel, landed an injured man
	30	Trawler Sunningdale, of Grimsby, gave help, esc'td
	June 3	Trawler Henri Altazin, of Boulogne, landed sick man
	July 8	Yacht Venture, saved yacht and 2
	Aug 5	Motor vessel Tynewood, of Middlesborough, took out a doctor and landed a body

Edward and Isabella Irwin reserve lifeboat

1967	Aug 23	Small motor boat, stood by
	27	Steamship Knossos, of Piraeus, landed a sick man
	Oct 7	Fishing boat Sea Venture, saved boat and 4
	31	Trawler Waddington, of Grimsby, took out a doctor
	Nov 27	Tanker Peking, of Odessa, landed sick man, saving 1
1968	Jan 11	Trawler Ross Genet, of Grimsby, gave help
	24	Men stranded on Haile Sand Fort, landed 2
	Feb 18	Motor boat, saved boat and 2
	Mar 6	Trawler Ross Hawk, of Grimsby, stood by
	Apr 11	Humber lightvessel, landed a sick man
	28	Motor vessel Svea, of Halso, took out a doctor

	30	Trawler Boston Pegasus, of Lowestoft, landed injured man
	Nov 1	Army tender Pendonna, saved tender and 2
1961	Feb 20	Humber lightvessel, landed an injured man
	May 5	Bull lightvessel, landed an injured man
	Aug 12	Fishing boat Royal Charter, gave help
	13	Fishing boat Royal Charter, gave help
	19	Yacht Alycone, gave help
	Sep 11	Dinghy, stood by
	Nov 20	Steamship Fulham VIII, of London, landed 5 and a body, crew of trawler Jules Degne, of Ostend

City of Bradford II reserve lifeboat

1962	Jan 18	Steamship Bencruchan, of Leith, took out a doctor
	Feb 16	Yacht Star Song, of Colchester, saved 2
	23	Bull lightvessel, landed a sick man

City of Bradford III lifeboat

1962	May 12	Trawler Monbretia, of Grimsby, saved trawler
	23	Yacht Valhalla, in tow of fishing boat Peggy III, of Grimsby, escorted
	June 14	Cabin cruiser Mary II, of Cleethorpes, recovered derelict cruiser
	July 19	Fishing boat Dorothy, of Grimsby, saved boat and 6
	Aug 17	Rubber raft from survey vessel Vigia, landed 2 and raft from trawler Scampton
	Sep 16	Yacht Kathene, saved yacht and 2
	21	Drifter Tea Rose, of Fraserburgh, landed a sick man
	Dec 15	Barge Will Everard, of London, saved (and a dog) 3
1963	Jan 7	Dowsing lightvessel, landed an injured man
	12	Boats of pilot vessel J. H. Fisher, of Hull, gave help
	16	Trawler North King, of Monrovia, landed a sick man
	Apr 30	Trawler Dorothy, of Grimsby, gave help
	May 17	Steamship Grane Fors, of Panama, landed sick man

May 11   Motor vessel Aquarius, of Katwijk-aan-Zee, landed a sick man

City of Bradford III lifeboat

1968 May 17   Trawler Guidesman, of London, stood by
      June 12   Boat of motor vessel Delphic Eagle, of Monrovia, saved boat and 3
          13   Motor vessel Delphic Eagle, of Monrovia, landed a sick man, saving 1
      Aug 11   Fishing boat Nimrod, gave help

Princess Royale (Civil Service No.7) lifeboat

1968 Oct 13   Tender Reise (attending dredger Queen of Holland), saved 5

City of Bradford III lifeboat

1968 Nov 24   Motor vessel Morava, of Rijeka, landed a sick man
          30   Trawler Saxon Onward, of Grimsby, took out a doctor
      Dec 28   Spurn lightvessel, landed a sick man
1969   Jan 3   Ore carrier Anaris, of Stockholm, landed a sick man
      Feb 6   Motor vessel Hoofinch, of Hull, landed an injured man
      Apr 3   Motor vessel Cormain, landed an injured man
          6   Motor vessel Huntress, saved boat and 4
          8   Injured man on board motor vessel Hudson Light, of London, landed injured man
         13   Fishing boat Elaine, saved boat and 4
         20   Motor vessel Themistocles, of Piraeus, landed a sick man
      May 1   Motor vessel Njandoma, took out a doctor
      June 23   Cabin cruiser Jaymac, in tow of tug Headman, of Hull, stood by and escorted
      Aug 4   Motor boat Thunderbolt, saved boat and 4
          5   Motor boat Etna II, saved 1
         30   Motor vessel Vamos, of Harlingen, gave help
      Sep 3   Cabin cruiser Lady Pat, gave help
          4   Tanker Anco Star, of Alesund, landed an injured woman
      Oct 16   Ore carrier Switzerland, of Panama, landed a sick woman, thereby saving 1
         25   Motor vessel Angelic Wings, of Piraeus, landed a sick man, thereby saving 1
      Dec 20   Trawler Lofoten, of Grimsby, gave help
         21   Trawler Lofoten, of Grimsby, stood by
1970 Feb 16   Converted ship's boat Blue Bird II, saved boat and 3
         21   Motor vessel Salat, of Bordeaux, took out a doctor
      Apr 11   Sick man on board motor vessel Ribblehead, of Middlesborough, landed sick man
      May 11   Trawler Hoger Hill, took out a doctor and escorted
      Aug 22   Motor tanker Ethali, of Monrovia, landed an injured amn
      Sep 22   Motor vessel Tor Scandia, of London, landed a sick man
      Oct 7   Motor vessel Edenmore, of London, landed a sick man
         26   Motor vessel Marioulio V, of Piraeus, landed a sick man
      Dec 8   Motor vessel Jark, of Oslo, gave help and landed 10
         23   Motor vessel Narwal, of Kalmar, landed a sick man
1971   Jan 22   Motor vessel APJ Akash, of Bombay, landed a sick man
      June 20   Auxiliary sloop Kagnar, of Hull, escorted
         28   Catamaran Shidajo, saved catamaran and 2
      Aug 3   Persons stranded on disused fort, saved 5
          8   Motor boat, saved boat and 8
         18   Auxiliary ketch Day Dream, saved 4
      Sep 26   Injured child on board motor vessel Karin Winkler, of Bremen, landed an injured child
         27   Injured man on board motor vessel Marianne, of Hamburg, landed an injured man
      Nov 5   Trawler Saxon Progress, of Grimsby, took out a doctor and gave help
         17   Steamship Brimsdown, of London, took out a doctor, landed a sick man
1972   Jan 12   Trawler Streymoy, of Grimsby, saved trawler and 2
         24   Trawler Anita Ann, of Grimsby, gave help
      Mar 5   Motor vessel Servus, of Stockholm, took a doctor to an injured man
      Dec 25   Motor vessel Scottish Wasa, of Bristol, landed injured man
1973   Jan 24   Motor vessel Providentia, landed sick man
         28   Bulk carrier Marly II, of Antwerp, landed sick man, thereby saving a life

      Feb 6   Trinity House vessel Mermaid, of London, landed an injured man
      Apr 18   Catamaran Iro Tiki, saved craft and 3
      Sep 12   3 people cut off by the tide, gave help
         27   Motor vessel Longstone, of Newcastle, landed a sick man
         29   Fishing vessel Marineol, landed a sick man and escorted
      Oct 21   Yacht Shadder, stood by
         28   Motor schooner Venture, gave help
      Nov 24   Trawler Kingston Pearl, of Hull, landed an injured man
1974   Jan 11   Ship's lifeboat, recovered wreckage
         26   Motor barge Goldilocks, saved barge and 2
      Feb 7   Trinity House pilot launch Prickett, escorted
      Mar 4   Trawler Scampron, of Grimsby, took out a doctor re suspected death
      Apr 21   Motor vessel Colston, of Bristol, gave help re sick man
      June 6   Cabin cruiser Ragna, saved cruiser and 4
      July 28   Outboard motor dinghy, saved boat and 1
      Sep 3   Motor vessel Norderstedt, of Magadiscio, escorted
      Dec 17   Pilot cutter William Fenton, of Hull, landed 14
1975   Jan 16   Motor vessel Baltic Variant, of London, landed injured man
      Feb 27   Motor vessel Hermes, landed a sick man
      Mar 13   Cabin cruiser Otaki, gave help
         29   Catamaran Coronis, saved craft
      May 26   Yacht White Roma, gave help
               Yacht Huckleberry Friend, stood by
         30   Fishing boat Anina, gave help
      June 21   Tug Sea Bristolian, of Bristol, and 2 trawlers, stood by
               Yacht Autumn Rose, escorted
         29   Yacht Yorkshire Pud, gave help
      Aug 10   Cabin cruiser Gay Lady II, gave help
               Yacht Bobtail, gave help
         19   Yacht Chebamblo, gave help
      Sep 14   Yacht Lady Nancy, saved yacht
         19   Trawler Juhel, landed an injured man
      Oct 2   Trawler Rynmond III, landed an injured man
         12   Fishing boat Grenaa Star, saved boat and 4
         20   Humber lightvessel, landed a sick man
      Nov 21   Trawler Gladeto, of Grimsby, stood by
      Dec 14   Motor boat Michelle, saved boat and 3
1976   Jan 4   Fishing boat Ella Grethe, saved boat and 1
         19   Motor vessel Canton, landed a sick man
         22   Fishing boat Maxwell, gave help re sick man
      Apr 1   Tug Torque, in collision with fishing vessel Linda-Marie, landed 5
         21   Motor vessel Fryser, gave help to injured man
      June 17   Fishing boat Paul Anthony, of Grimsby, gave help
               Spurn lightvessel, gave help
      Aug 12   Cabin cruiser Violet, gave help
      Sep 12   Rig supply vessel Spearfish, of Lowestoft, escorted
         20   Motor boat Lindum Lady, gave help
      Oct 1   Trawler Marbi, took a doctor to 2 injured men
         10   Dinghy, tender to rig supply Fastnet Shore, of London, gave help
      Nov 14   Fishing boat Exceed, gave help
      Dec 16   Motor boat Robert R. Richardson, stood by
         20   Boat, saved boat and 2
1977   Jan 2   Tanker Anchorman, of London, landed a sick man
         12   Fishing boat Sea Triumph, recovered wreckage
         17   Motor vessel Saaremaa, of Tallin, landed a sick man
      Mar 11   Motor vessel Joselyne, landed 2 injured men

City of Bradford IV lifeboat

1977 May 28   Trawler Sioux, of Grimsby, landed a body
               Trawler Sioux, of Grimsby, took out doctor to see survivor on board oil rig standby vessel Margaret Christina, of Lowestoft
         29   Motor vessel Jutta, landed an injured man

City of Bradford III relief lifeboat

1977 Apr 12   Motor vessel Isparta, landed 6 sick persons
         17   Humber lightvessel, landed a sick man

City of Bradford IV lifeboat

1977 May 10   Dowsing lightvessel, landed a sick man
     June 2   Motor vessel Gemstone, of Monrovia, landed a sick man
         5   Cabin cruiser Marcheesa, landed a sick woman, saving 1
           Cabin cruiser Leopard II, escorted
       14   Cabin cruiser Osprey, escorted
       22   Trawler Bermuda, of Lowestoft, saved vessel and 7
       26   Cabin cruiser Alf One, gave help
           Cabin cruiser Crystal Wave, gave help
           Rubber dinghy, landed 6
     July 14   Chemical tanker Bow Alecto, of Bergen, gave help
       18   Yacht Foreshoreman, gave help
     Aug 15   Trawler Wellspring, landed an injured man
       25   Fishing boat Shearbill, of Grimsby, landed 4
     Sep 20   Motor vessel Semlow, took out a doctor to a sick person
     Oct 14   Cabin cruiser Sea Swallow, gave help
       23   Converted barge Medal, saved craft and 8
     Nov 14   Motor vessel Halco Holwerda, of Heerenveen, landed 1
1978   Jan 3   Fishing boat Lead Us, saved boat and 1
       10   Fishing boat Burton Pidsea, gave help
       28   Motor vessel Septimus, of Copenhagen, stood by
     Mar 9   Motor vessel Beeding, of London, took out a doctor to an injured man
       11   Trawler Boston Halifax, of Lowestoft, stood by
       17   Motor vessel Lune Fisher, of Barrow, escorted
       26   Motor vessel Floreat, gave help
     Apr 1   Pilot launch Captain Newlove, of Hull, gave help
         2   Humber lightvessel, took out doctor and landed a sick man
       16   Motor vessel Fordonna, landed a sick man
     May 7   Trawler Vikingborg, took out a doctor and landed an injured man
         8   Chemical Tanker Post Entente, landed 2 sick men
       14   Gas tanker Nicole, of Helsingborg, took out a doctor and landed a sick man
       24   Fishing coble Serene, gave help
     June 16   Fishing boat Courage, gave help

John Gellatly Hyndman relief lifeboat

1978 July 19   Fishing boat Willemina, gave help
     Aug 1   Motor vessel Walchand, landed a sick man
         3   Fishing boat Seacat, gave help
         8   Cabin cruiser Mary Ann, gave help
           Trawler Carl Borum, landed an injured man

City of Bradford IV lifeboat

1978 Aug 12   Cabin cruiser Sea Urchin, gave help
       27   Cabin cruiser Rangi I, gave help
       28   Fishing boat Leanda, took out a doctor and landed an injured man
     Sep 2   Motor vessel Breitenburg, of Stade, saved 6
       13   Barge Hebelift 3, stood by
       16   Cabin cruiser Langer, escorted
       24   Chemical tanker Cullen Bay, gave help
     Oct 2   Fishing boat Cullen Bay, gave help
         4   Yacht Valida, saved yacht and 1
       14   Trawler Cap Des Palmes, landed a sick man
       27   Motor vessel Lindo, of Stockholm, landed sick man
     Nov 19   Motor boat, gave help
       25   Motor vessel Ileoluki, took out a doctor
     Dec 2   Motor vessel Novaya Zemlya, of Klaipeda, landed sick man
         7   Motor vessel Woolacombe, landed an injured man
         8   Motor vessel Jette Wonsild, of Copenhagen, landed an injured man
       18   Fishing boat Falke, gave help
       24   Ex-ship's lifeboat Lucky Robin, gave help
       30   Motor vessel Diana V, of Rotterdam, saved 6
1979   Jan 1   Sick man on chemical tanker Asperity, landed a sick man
       11   Cargo vessel Philippa, stood by vessel
       19   Cargo vessel Oude Maas, escorted vessel
     Feb 14   Cargo vessel Revi, saved 2
       15   Cargo vessel Savinesti, escorted vessel
       25   Cabin cruiser K.9, escorted boat
     Mar 6   Fishing cobles, escorted boats

           Sick man on board cargo vessel Angela Helen, landed a sick man
       20   2 injured men on board tanker Fernhurst, landed 2 injured men
     Apr 1   Motor fishing vessel Tino, gave help
         4   Sick man on trawler Tom Grant, landed a sick man
       13   Injured man on board cargo vessel Coran-W, took out doctor and landed an injured man, saving 1
       15   Fishing coble Serene, gave help
       28   Sick man on Margaret Simone, landed a sick man
     May 13   Ship's lifeboat, gave help
       21   Motor fishing vessel Kirsty Jane, gave help
       23   Injured man on board ore carrier Dinos M, landed an injured man
       27   Sick man on cargo vessel Veritas, landed a sick man
       28   Injured woman on board cargo vessel Punta Sugar, landed a sick woman
     June 2   Injured man on board motor fishing vessel Fingel, landed an injured man
         5   Sick man on tanker Luminetta, landed a sick man
       13   Injured man on board cargo vessel Sormovskiy–7, landed an injured man
       17   Sick man on tanker Cielo Rosso, landed a sick man
       25   Cabin cruiser, gave help

T. G. B. relief lifeboat

1979 July 6   Motor fishing vessel Irma Marcell, gave help

City of Bradford IV lifeboat

1979 July 24   Aircraft, recovered wreckage
     Aug 14   Yacht Vanity Fair, saved boat and 4
       25   Sick man on board oil chemical tanker Unicorn Ladd, landed a sick man
       28   Motor fishing vessel Christine H, gave help
           Motor fishing vessel Christine H, stood by
       29   Motor fishing vessel Christine H, gave help
     Sep 13   Motor fishing vessel Lead Us, gave help
       20   Dredger Skarthi, escorted vessel
       29   Cabin cruiser Perpatrian, saved boat and 1
     Oct 11   Injured man on board cargo vessel Roebuck, landed an injured man
       16   Motor fishing vessel Agnes C II, gave help
       22   Motor fishing vessel Zanto, gave help
       27   Sick man on board trawler Golfbreker, took out doctor and landed an injured man
     Nov 29   Motor fishing vessel Sarah Thinnesen, gave help
1980   Jan 20   Injured man on board diving support vessel Duplus, landed an injured man
           Sick man on cargo vessel Sky Venture, landed a sick man
       26   Tug Kathleen, gave help
     Feb 4   Sick man on tanker Fuyoh Maru, landed a sick man
         5   Injured man on board trawler Shamrock, landed an injured man
       12   Sick woman on bulk carrier Libra, landed sick woman
       13   Sick man on tanker Annuity, landed a sick man
     Mar 3   Survivors of sunken fishing vessel Olympic on board motor fishing vessel Pansy, landed 3
       20   Motor boat Arctic Tern, saved boat
       21   Injured man on tanker Cielo Rosso, landed an injured man
     Apr 13   Fishing vessel Lena Sorenson, gave help
       24   Fishing vessel Sylvana Susanna, gave help
     May 15   Motor launch Danny Boy, saved boat and 2
       26   Sick woman on board passenger/cargo vessel Norland, took out doctor
     June 5   Injured man on board motor fishing vessel Kevan, took out doctor and landed an injured man
       29   Yacht Wind Ability, gave help
       30   Cargo vessel Arran Firth, escorted vessel
     July 1   Yacht Storm Vogel, gave help
           Sick man on board cargo vessel Bona Fe, landed sick man
       12   Motor fishing vessel Betty, gave help
       19   Injured boy on board cabin cruiser Dolphin, landed an injured boy

	20	Yacht Milonquera, gave help
	22	Sick man on bulk carrier Ivi, landed a sick man
Aug 5		Sick man on cargo vessel Anntoro, landed a sick man
	19	Injured man on board cargo vessel Wendy Weston, landed an injured man
	26	Injured man on board trawler Kamina, landed injured man
	31	Yacht Endeavour, saved boat and 3
Sep 3		Injured man on board rig standby safety vessel Aruba, landed an injured man
	4	Motor fishing vessel Jilannon, in tow of motor fishing vessel Craigievar, gave help
		Motor fishing vessel Rayella, gave help
	7	Motor fishing vessel Patricia, gave help
Oct 7		Sick man on trawler Louise Evrard, landed a sick man
	8	Sick man on cargo vessel Security, landed a sick man
	20	Fishing vessel Bevnic, gave help

Edith Emilie relief lifeboat

1980 Oct 24		Sick man on cargo vessel Goplana, landed a sick man
		Cabin cruiser Shawandzee, gave help
	25	Fishing boat Osprey, gave help
	29	Sick man on board Spurn lightvessel, landed a body
Dec 3		Sick man on coaster Day In, landed a sick man
	4	Fishing vessel Melissa Louise, saved boat and 1
	5	Sick man on trawler Barbados, landed a sick man
	6	Motor boat, saved 2
1981 Jan 9		Aircraft, of USA, gave help
	10	Cargo vessel Alice PG, escorted vessel
		Divers on service to crashed aircraft, stood by
	18	Fishing vessel Iris Dean, gave help
	24	Injured man on board cargo vessel Playa De Ezaro, landed an injured man
Feb 3		Fishing vessel Inger-Lene, escorted vessel
	17	Sick man on board bulk carrier Aquarius, took out doctor and landed a sick man
	19	Sick man on tanker Northern Star, landed a sick man
Mar 7		Oil rig standby vessel Benella, gave help
	29	Sick man on board oil rig supply vessel Suffolk Blazer, landed a sick man
Apr 25		Cargo vessel Lisbet Coast, escorted vessel
	27	Sick man on bulk carrier Ermis, landed a sick man

City of Bradford IV lifeboat

1981 June 6		Yacht Timsah II, gave help
	20	Yacht Westerly, gave help
	26	Dredger s'Gravenhage, stood by vessel
July 13		Sick man on board fishing vessel Marilyn Olesen, landed a sick man
	14	Fishing vessel M Aaen, gave help
	15	Cabin cruiser Our Redundancy, gave help
	21	Cabin cruiser Larina II, gave help
	25	Injured man on board fishing vessel Maxwell, landed an injured man
Aug 1		Sick man on fishing vessel Dorny, landed a sick man
	2	Injured man on board fishing vessel Busen Junior, landed an injured man
	3	Injured man on board tanker Polarisman, landed an injured man
	6	Injured man on board LPG carrier Hestia, landed an injured man
	7	Sick man on tanker La Cumbre, landed a body
	18	Fishing vessel Lindenborg, stood by vessel
	24	Injured boy on board trawler Christopher, landed an injured boy
	25	Fishing vessel Tuborg, gave help
	28	Injured man on board fishing vessel Lochearn, took out doctor and landed an injured man
	31	Injured man on board tanker Mare Iratum, landed an injured man
Sep 20		Yacht Sally-O-Mally, escorted boat
	22	Sick man on trawler Shannon, landed a sick man
	27	Motor boat Lisa-Ann, gave help
	30	Yacht Moji-Too, saved boat and (also a dog) 2

Oct 12		Fishing vessel Zegan, saved vessel and 2
	14	Sick man on board tanker Veleka, landed a sick man
Oct 15		Injured man on board diving support ship Oil Endeavour, landed an injured man
	22	Sick man on cargo vessel Eildon, landed sick man
	23	Fishing boat Morning After, gave help
	24	Injured man on board trawler Trendsetter, landed an injured man
Nov 7		Injured man on board survey vessel Siesella, landed an injured man
	19	Sick man on bulk carrier Paralos, landed a sick man
Dec 5		Sick man on coaster Coran W, landed a sick man
	8	Motor fishing vessel Frances, gave help
		Injured man on board motor vessel Ruciane, landed an injured man
	9	Motor boat, gave help
	13	Cargo vessel Harry Mitchell, saved 3
1982 Jan 12		Sick man on cargo vessel Ivan Bolotnikov, landed sick man
	17	Fishing vessel Primula, gave help
	28	Injured man on board bulk carrier Gemini Friendship, landed an injured man
	29	Sick man on board oil pollution recovery vessel Fasgadair, landed a sick man
Feb 4		Sick man on cargo vessel Cotinga, landed a sick man
	6	Injured man on board cargo vessel Wegro, landed an injured man
	20	Motor boat Ranger, landed 5
	28	Speedboat Lightening, saved boat and 1
Mar 14		Sick man on board tanker Katina, landed a sick man
	29	Injured man on board cargo vessel Family Fortini, landed an injured man
Apr 6		Sick man on board cargo vessel Kingsnorth Fisher, landed a sick man
	23	Yacht Maid of Iona, gave help
	25	2 injured men on board tanker Poseidon, took out doctor and landed 2 injured men
	30	Sick man on cargo vessel Selbydyke, landed a sick man
June 2		Yacht Arctic Saga, gave help
	6	Cabin cruiser Ariguani, saved 5
	7	Sick man on board tanker In Safra, landed a sick man
	29	Trawler Tanganes, gave help
July 4		Sick man on cargo vessel Salaj, landed a sick man
	26	Injured man on board bulk carrier London Viscount, landed an injured man
Aug 8		Dinghy, gave help
	20	Injured man on board tanker Sprague Arcturus, landed an injured man
	25	Rubber dinghy, saved dinghy and 5
	31	Motor yacht Midnight Moon, gave help

Edith Emilie relief lifeboat

1982 Sep 2		Motor boat, saved boat and 2
	3	Cabin cruiser Trocadero, saved vessel and 2
	8	Sick man on fishing vessel Talona, landed a sick man
	12	Injured man on board trawler Jechrisa Marie, took out doctor and landed an injured man
	19	Fishing vessel Glenray, gave help
Oct 2		Yacht Vandar, gave help

City of Bradford VI lifeboat

1982 Oct 20		Injured man on board tanker Oilman, landed injured man
Nov 1		Trawler Pickering, saved vessel and 6
	3	Trawler St Amant, gave help
	9	Fishing vessel Galilean, gave help
Dec 1		Fishing vessel Moontan, gave help
	4	Fishing vessel Danbrit, gave help
1983 Jan 12		Converted ship's lifeboat Hi-Fi, saved vessel and 2
	22	Motor boat, gave help
Mar 13		Injured man on board trawler Margaret Jane, landed an injured man
	15	Fishing vessel First Chance, gave help
		Cabin cruiser Joraca, gave help
Apr 17		Rubber dinghy Sea Rider I, gave help

26 Sick man on cargo vessel Santo Pioneer, landed a sick man
Sick man on bulk carrier Lok Palak, landed a sick man
Apr 27 Injured man on board trawler Jean Scott, landed an injured man
May 13 Sick man on board tanker Stolt Eagle, landed sick man
29 Rubber dinghy Searider I, saved boat and landed 7
June 1 Yacht Rebecca, escorted boat
Yachts Olga and Oeding, gave help
15 Fishing vessel White Bank, escorted vessel
16 Injured man on board trawler Pernille Vibeke, landed an injured man
19 Fishing coble Friendship, gave help
July 13 Trawler Angele Emiel, gave help
27 Injured man on board crane barge McDermott Derrick Barge 101, landed an injured man
31 Trawler Leason, gave help
Aug 4 Fishing vessel Falkenborg, gave help
7 Yacht Falke, gave help
14 Yacht Fifine, gave help
22 Injured man on board fishing vessel Coeur De Lion, landed an injured man
Sep 10 Cabin cruiser Nameless One, saved boat and 7
11 Yacht Ocean Venture, saved boat and 4
Motor vessel Mairi Everard, escorted vessel
16 Fishing vessel Kristina Anne, gave help
19 Injured man on trawler Donia, landed an injured man

Wavy Line relief lifeboat

1983 Sep 24 Yacht Lillian Rose, gave help
27 Sick man on fishing vessel Cineraria, landed a sick man

City of Bradford IV lifeboat

1983 Oct 15 Fishing vessel Janet Jensen, stood by vessel
22 Sick man on board tanker Kimolos, landed a sick man
27 Motor boat Darlea, gave help
31 Injured man on board trawler Laurids Skomager, landed an injured man
Nov 10 Injured man on trawler Vicky, landed injured man
20 Motor boat Emma Louise, gave help
24 Motor vessel Jens Peters, stood by vessel
Dec 1 Injured man on board bulk carrier Sumburgh Head, took out doctor and landed an injured man
4 Fishing coble Sincerity, gave help
8 Fishing vessel Lillian, landed 5 and saved vessel
1984 Jan 7 Injured skipper on motor fishing vessel Christine H, took out relief skipper and landed injured man
9 Injured man on trawler Neptunus, landed an injured man

Ralph and Bonella Farrant relief lifeboat

1984 Jan 28 Trawler Angele Emiel, gave help
Feb 13 Sick man on board cargo vessel Birthe Dancoast, landed a sick man
15 Injured man on board bulk carrier Bulknes, landed an injured man
16 Fishing vessel Vera Irene, stood by vessel
Mar 8 Motor boat Osprey, gave help
21 Sick man on board tug Euroman, landed a sick man
Apr 9 Motor fishing vessel Nicol Simone, gave help
16 Sick man on board cargo vessel Bergstraum, stood by
22 Sick man on board trawler Darwin, landed sick man
28 Sick girl on board liquefied gas carrier Niels Henrik Abel, landed a sick girl
May 4 Fishing boat Calypso, gave help
9 Cabin cruiser Rackana, gave help
10 2 injured men on board cargo vessel Grobin, took out doctor and landed 2 injured men
12 Fishing coble Sea Lover, stood by boat
18 Fishing vessel Madalia, gave help
22 Yacht Bec-Fi, saved boat and 4
24 Sick man on cargo vessel Birling, landed sick man
30 Yacht Leyte, gave help
31 Yacht Firebird, gave help
Yacht Silver Dawn, gave help

June 10 Injured man from yacht El-Cid on board pilot boat, took out doctor and landed an injured man
11 Sick man on cargo vessel Mingary, landed a sick man
17 Cabin cruiser Moravia, gave help
25 Sick man on board tanker Niagara, landed a sick man

City of Bradford IV lifeboat

1984 July 12 Injured man on board trawler Solveig Holm, landed an injured man
15 Yacht Dunlin, saved boat and 2
19 Sick man on board cargo vessel Northumbria Lass, landed an injured man
22 Motor boat Maaike, gave help
28 Fishing boat Anthony Smith, gave help
Aug 2 Yacht Karelia, gave help
5 Motor yacht Nado, saved boat and 2
Motor yacht Zwalker, saved boat and landed 3
18 Sick man on board cargo vessel Ilka, landed a sick man
27 Injured man on board tanker John M, landed injured man
28 Motor fishing vessel Lady Jane, gave help
29 Yacht Hermes, saved boat and 3
30 Cabin cruisers Paim and Enchantress, gave help
Sep 2 Catamaran Felinity II, gave help
18 Motor cruiser Minden Rose, gave help
21 Fishing boat Solanjul, gave help
25 Fishing vessel Dover Star, landed 3
26 Injured man on board fishing vessel Mark Nielsen, landed an injured man
Trawler St Leger, saved vessel
Oct 7 Sick man on board cargo vessel Ali Baba, took out doctor
10 Sick man on board cargo vessel Tor Neerlandia, landed an injured man
28 Motor cruiser T. W. Pickett, escorted boat
31 Sick woman on board cargo vessel Vishva Siddhi, landed 2 injured persons
Nov 6 Sick man on board tanker Sealift Arabian Sea, landed a sick man
8 2 injured men on board cargo vessel Raffelberg, landed 2 injured men
9 Fishing boat Sybil, gave help
14 Injured man on board trawler Ross Tiger, landed an injured man
17 Yacht William McCann, stood by boat
18 Yacht William McCann, stood by boat
19 Yacht William McCann, gave help
Sick man on board cargo vessel Grollen, landed a sick man
20 Helicopter, recovered wreckage
25 Dinghy, escorted boat
Dec 6 Trawler Angele Emiel, gave help
7 Sick man on cargo vessel Raffelberg, landed a sick man
10 Cabin cruiser Ceffylmor II, gave help
24 Converted ship's lifeboat Janet, gave help
29 Sick man on board cargo vessel Celebrity, landed sick man
1985 Jan 20 Injured man on board tanker Georgios Vergottis, landed an injured man
31 Fishing boat, escorted boat
Feb 10 Cargo vessels Arcturus and Jan Meeder, gave help
11 Injured man on board rig supply ship Stirling Tern, landed an injured man
15 Motor fishing vessel Christine H, gave help
20 Dinghy, gave help
Mar 25 Injured man on board cargo vessel St Michael, took out doctor and landed an injured man
27 Injured man on board rig supply ship Stirling Puck, landed an injured man

Edith Emilie relief lifeboat

1985 Mar 31 Rubber dinghy Searider II, gave help
Motor boat Emma Louise, gave help
Apr 8 Yacht Lone Snow Goose, gave help
10 Injured man on board trawler Tino, took out doctor and landed an injured man
23 Yacht Damian, gave help

May 5   Yacht Dana, escorted boat
     14   Yacht Ocean Mix, gave help
     15   Sick man on board cargo vessel Bell Comet, landed a
          sick man
     27   Yacht Lady II, gave help
June 19   Cabin cruiser Neeron, gave help
July 12   Fishing vessel Trudella, gave help
     15   Cargo vessel Sota Eduardo, stood by and landed 10
          Motor boat Nicolee, gave help
     21   Cabin cruiser Osprey, gave help
     27   Yacht Roanna, saved boat and 2
Aug 29   Injured man on board fishing vessel Sarah H, landed an
          injured man
Sep 12   Injured man on board tanker Nicholas M, landed an
          injured man
     16   Sick man on board cargo vessel Coburg, landed a sick man
     18   Fishing vessel Betty A, gave help
     26   Fishing boats Challenge, Heike and Sincerity, gave help
     29   Cabin cruiser Freedom, gave help
Oct 15   Yacht Frangipani, gave help
     29   Sick man on board yacht Marksman, landed a sick man
Nov 1   Yacht Callisto, saved boat and 2
      9   Motor cruiser Alpha Diver, saved boat and 2
     11   Injured man on board cargo vessel Dawn, landed an
          injured man
     24   Cabin cruiser Dominic, gave help
Dec 5   Fishing vessel Effort, gave help
     15   Injured man on board dredger/sand carrier Bow Prince,
          landed an injured man
1986 Jan 6   Injured man on board tanker Phillips Oklahoma, landed an
              injured man
     11   Injured man on board rig supply ship Stirling Merlin,
          landed an injured man
     26   Fishing boat 1, gave help
Feb 25   Sick man on board tug Lady Sarah, landed a sick man
     26   Cargo vessel Alliance, stood by vessel
     27   Cargo vessel Alliance, stood by vessel
Mar 8   Sick man on board cargo vessel Semi II, landed a sick man
     12   Sick man on supply ship Spurn Haven, took out doctor
     20   Fishing vessel Sonia Jane, gave help
Apr 3   Fishing vessel Sea Venture, gave help
      7   Survivors of Dutch fishing vessel Hanny, on bd rig supply
          ship Stirling Osprey, landed 7
May 4   Fishing boat Effort, gave help
      7   Motor launch John Creighton, gave help
     15   Yacht Skua 4, gave help
     18   Fishing boat Seacat, gave help
          Fishing boat Seacat, landed 2 (and a dog)

City of Bradford IV lifeboat
1986 May 31 Sick man on board Humber lightvessel, landed a sick man
June 22   Fishing vessel Guide Us, gave help
     23   Sea Cadet training vessel Apollo, gave help
          Injured man on board liquefied gas carrier Helen, landed
          an injured man
July 9   Injured man on board tanker Celtic Trader, landed an
          injured man
     13   Sick man on board fishing vessel Grampian Craig, landed
          a sick man
     25   Cabin cruiser Tug of Mutton, gave help
     26   Motor boat Erica Paula, saved boat and 1
     31   Yacht Lady Hilda, gave help
Aug 2   Yacht Zarophe, saved boat and 3
Sep 7   Yacht Tally Ho, gave help
     21   Yacht Craimar, gave help
     25   Fishing vessel Our Tracy, gave help
Oct 3   Motor boat, gave help
      4   Injured man on board fishing vessel Gladness, landed an
          injured man
     11   Fishing boat Moonlight, gave help
          Fishing boat Effort, gave help
     26   Cargo vessel Treasure, gave help
     30   Yacht Rachael, saved boat and 2

Nov 13   Fishing vessel Talamar, saved boat and 3
     29   Motor boat Victoria, gave help
Dec 13   Fishing boat Anrum, gave help
     17   Motor boat, landed a body
1987 Jan 15 Sick man on board Greek cargo vessel Kithnos, saved 1
     24   Injured person on Spurn Point, gave help
Feb 2   Injured man on board French seismic survey vessel
          Odyssee, landed an injured man
     16   Injured man on board fishing vessel Marilyn Olesen, of
          Grimsby, landed an injured man
     22   Fishing boat Central Lady, craft brought in – gave help
Mar 2   Cabin cruiser Rackana, saved boat and 2
     15   Cabin cruiser, craft brought in – gave help
     16   Injured man on board tanker Mobil Navigator, landed an
          injured man
     17   Fishing boat Catherine Clare, craft brought in – gave help
     25   Tug/diving ship Spurn Haven, landed an injured man
     27   Dutch dredger Orion, landed an injured man
Apr 4   Motor fishing vessel Euroclynden, craft brought in
     14   Cargo vessel Skradin, of Yugoslavia, landed 1
     24   Motor fishing vessel Emmanuel, of Grimsby, craft brought
          in – gave help
May 1   Motor fishing vessel Emmanuel, of Grimsby, craft brought
          in – gave help
      2   Motor yacht Detura, saved vessel and landed 3
     12   Sick woman on board Swedish cargo vessel, landed a
          sick woman
          Spanish tanker Toluena, landed an injured man
     18   Fishing boat Our Tracy, of Grimsby, craft brought in
     22   Rig supply vessel Maersk Battler, landed an injured man
     26   Fishing coble Sincerity, craft brought in – gave help
June 23   Fishing coble Sincerity, craft brought in – gave help
     26   Fishing boat, craft brought in – gave help
July 1   Motor fishing vessel Emmanuel, craft brought in
      6   Sick man on board Dowsing lightvessel, landed a sick man
      9   Belgian motor yacht Terepo, gave help
     10   Sick man on board Norwegian tanker Saltstraum, landed a
          sick man
     12   Fishing boat, craft brought in – gave help
     18   Yacht, craft brought in – gave help
     31   Yacht Selkie, gave help
Aug 13   Yacht Marique, saved boat and 1

Kenneth Thelwall lifeboat
1987 Aug 13 Yacht Marique, saved 2
     20   Cabin cruiser Crestwood, gave help
     22   Fishing vessel Mercury, of Buckie, gave help
     24   Yacht Song-of-the-Sea, gave help
          Yacht Normane, landed 2
     30   Yacht Pieris, gave help
     31   Yacht Normane, landed 2
Sep 14   Yacht Perigny, of Whitby, saved boat and 4
     26   Yacht Chenoa, gave help
Oct 10   Cabin cruiser Aleeanco, gave help
     11   Sick man on board cargo vessel Maria H, of West
          Germany, landed a sick man
Dec 1   Coble Heike, escorted boat
      5   Motor boat Andross, gave help
1988 Jan 7   Injured man on board cargo vessel Outokumpu, of
              Finland, landed an injured man
Feb 8   Fishing vessel Christine H, of Grimsby, escorted vessel
     19   Fishing vessel Argosy, gave help
          Fishing vessel Mystery, gave help
Mar 11   Cabin cruiser Maid of Kent, escorted boat
Apr 6   Cargo vessel Berglift, saved 6
     16   Yacht Harlequin, stood by boat
     21   Fishing vessel Martin Norman, gave help
     27   Injured man on board cargo vessel Vinga, of Sweden,
          landed an injured man
May 7   Wreckage in sea, recovered wreckage
     30   Cabin cruiser Edinasivall, escorted boat
June 3   Yacht Mister Shifter, gave help
      9   Trimaran Triple Star, gave help

	June 11	Injured man on board cabin cruiser Barbara Jean, landed an injured man

June 11   Injured man on board cabin cruiser Barbara Jean, landed an injured man
          Cabin cruiser Barbara Jean, gave help
23   Cargo vessel Irving Forest, of Bermuda, in collision with gas drilling rig Glomar Labrador I, gave help
26   Coble Sincerity, gave help
27   Sick man on board cargo vessel Osmussaar, of Russia, landed a sick man
July 2   Fishing vessel Lynn-E, gave help
23   Motor cruiser Themsen, gave help
Aug 2   Cabin cruiser Cygnet, gave help
3   Yacht Fleetwing, of Grimsby, gave help
12   Yacht Cygnet, gave help
          Yacht Thee Runa, gave help
27   Yacht Step in Time, of Grimsby, gave help
28   Sick man on board fishing vessel Zeetrapper, of Belgium, landed a sick man
29   Fishing vessel T-Westdeip, of Belgium, gave help

Edith Emilie relief lifeboat

1988 Sep 12   Yacht Karen Kelly, saved boat and 2
26   Injured man on board fishing vessel Karen, of Grimsby, landed an injured man
Oct 2   Mine in sea, took out naval mine disposal unit
9   Motor boat Seamoon, of Grimsby, gave help

Kenneth Thelwall lifeboat

1988 Oct 16   Injured man on board cabin cruiser Jarvit, of Grimsby, landed an injured man
19   Yacht Humbug, saved boat and landed 3
21   Fishing vessel June Rose of Leith, gave help
Nov 6   Cabin cruiser Maimonde, gave help
8   Injured man on board tanker Vakis Tsakiroglou, of Cyprus, landed an injured man
17   Diving support vessel Shoreline Engineer, gave help
24   Sick man on board cargo vessel Adelaide, of Cyprus, landed a sick man
25   Sick man on board tanker Northgate, of Douglas, landed a sick man
Dec 16   Sick man on board tanker Authenticity, of London, landed a sick man
1989 Feb 21   Injured man on board cargo vessel Sormovs Kiy-6, of USSR, landed an injured man
Mar 24   Yacht Christian Brugge, escorted boat
30   Fishing vessel Sarah Visholm, of Grimsby, landed 6 and saved 2 liferafts
Apr 3   Fishing vessel Galatea C, of Hull, gave help
5   Rig Standby safety vessel Dawn Gem, of Aberdeen, stood by vessel
7   Fishing coble Dawn, of Hull, gave help
10   Yacht Pennard, gave help
11   Fishing vessel Charlotte Frank, of Denmark, gave help
20   Fishing vessel Nicky Demus, of Grimsby, gave help
May 2   Fishing coble Dawn, of Grimsby, gave help
3   Fishing vessel Kronborg, of Hull, gave help
6   Injured man on board MOD salvage vessel Salmoor, landed an injured man
15   Injured man on board cargo vessel Skipper Most, of Denmark, landed an injured man
16   Injured man on board tanker British Trent, of Bermuda, landed an injured man
18   Fishing vessel Caroline Sue, gave help
              Injured man on board fishing vessel Skalafjall, landed an injured man
19   Fishing vessel Marilyn E. G., saved boat and 2
24   Yacht Everlark, escorted boat
June 1   Yacht Journeyman, gave help
4   Yacht Sanchia, gave help
6   Fishing vessel Emma D, gave help
July 2   Fishing vessel Morning Glory, gave help
4   Tanker Coral Essberger, stood by
6   Cabin cruiser Fairway, gave help
16   House boat Radiant Sun, gave help

July 30   Yacht Jon Quil, saved 2
          Yacht Fast Frame, saved boat and 5
          Yacht War Cry, stood by boat
Aug 8   Body in seas, landed a body
          Body in seas, landed a body
14   Yacht Kada, gave help
22   Fishing vessel Albar, gave help
25   Cabin cruiser Rekardoom, gave help
          Injured man on board bulk carrier Torgnes, landed an injured man
Sep 9   Yacht Christianus Quintus, saved boat and 2
12   2 sick persons on board yacht Blue Bird, landed 2 sick persons
17   Tanker Phillips Oklahoma, in collision with ore/bulk/oil carrier Fiona, landed 16
27   Fishing vessel Harvester, gave help
30   Fishing vessel Margaret G, gave help
          Motor cruiser Iona, gave help
Oct 6   Fishing vessel Flamborough Light, gave help
10   Fishing vessel Sea Spray, gave help
19   Dowsing Light Float, landed 4
27   Yacht Jobina, gave help
29   Liquefied gas carrier Lissy Schulte, gave help
30   Fishing vessel Juno, gave help
31   Cabin cruiser White Rose, gave help
Nov 1   Refrigerated cargo vessel Sigurd Jarl, stood by vessel
7   Diving vessel Kernovs, gave help
25   Cabin cruiser Lady Mary Christina, escorted boat
1990 Jan 12   Sick man on board research vessel Geco Beta, landed a sick man
Feb 11   Yacht Jinty, gave help

Newsbuoy relief lifeboat

1990 Feb 26   Sick man on board rig standby safety vessel Putford Guardian, landed a sick man
              Fishing vessel Eventide, gave help
27   Sick man on tanker Shell Seafarer, landed a sick man
Mar 6   Yacht Southern Cross, gave help
              Fishing vessel Fiona Jane, gave help

Kenneth Thelwall lifeboat

1990 Apr 9   Cargo vessel Domna Maria, landed an injured man
15   Motor cruiser Pansy, saved boat and 2
21   Fishing boat Portunus, gave help
23   Sick man on board cargo vessel Sovietskaya Yakutiya, landed a sick man
May 17   Sick man on board bulk carrier Cerro Bolivar, landed a sick man
18   Injured man on board fishing vessel Samantha, landed an injured man
21   Cabin cruiser Lady Violet, gave help
29   Motor cruiser Byron, gave help
              Fishing vessel Mariness, gave help
30   Injured man on board fishing vessel Katrina Thomsen, landed an injured man
June 10   Fishing coble Fair Katie, gave help
11   Fishing boat Susan Mary II, gave help
12   Yacht Sakr-el-Bahr, gave help
23   Motor boat Undaunted, gave help
24   Sick man on board tanker Rochen I, landed a sick man
July 1   Sick man on board tanker Nordstraum, landed sick man
3   Fishing boat Jolynn, gave help
18   Injured man on board trawler Port Blanc, landed an injured man
23   Fishing vessel Fleur-de-France, took out police officers
27   Fishing vessel Caroline Due, gave help
30   Fishing vessel Judeann, gave help
31   Injured man on board tabker Fortune, landed injured man
Aug 3   Motor cruiser Emily G, gave help
5   Injured man on board cargo vessel Gerhard Prahm, landed an injured man
6   Sick man on cargo vessel Gerhard Prahm, landed sick man
14   2 aircraft, recovered wreckage

Aug 17	Aircraft, recovered wreckage
20	Yacht Faenoe, saved boat and 2
Sep 8	Sick man on board research vessel Seismariner, landed a sick man
13	Sick man on board RMAS salvage vessel Goosander, took out doctor and landed a sick man
19	Yacht Catalyst, saved boat and 4
24	Fishing boat Susan Mary II, gave help
Oct 1	Fishing vessel Albar, gave help
9	Cabin cruiser Santa Caterina, gave help
	Yacht Dorothy Ann, gave help
13	Injured man on board tanker Argentum, landed an injured man
14	Fishing vessel Lady Jean, gave help
15	Yacht Nilkant, gave help
21	Yacht Opua, gave help
26	Injured man on board cargo vessel Nautila, landed an injured man
Nov 1	Cargo vessel Emerald, stood by
6	Fishing vessel Mystery, gave help
23	Fishing boat Ednas, gave help
Dec 7	Sick man on board cargo vessel Burevestinik Revolyutsii, landed a sick man
14	Fishing boat Lady Jean, stood by
Dec 3	Fishing vessel Marilyn, saved vessel and 1
1991 Jan 27	Sick man on board tanker Seapride II, landed a sick man
Feb 6	Injured man on board fishing vessel Searcher, landed an injured man

Ralph and Bonella Farrant relief lifeboat

1991 Mar 24	Injured man on board liquefied gas carrier Helen, landed an injured man
29	Injured man on board fishing vessel Karen, landed an injured man
Apr 30	Yacht Katie of Rhu, stood by
May 15	Yacht Frangipani, gave help
17	Sick man on board tug Varnebank, landed a sick man
18	Sick man on board cargo vessel Brabo, landed a sick man
27	Yacht Miel, gave help

Kenneth Thelwall lifeboat

1991 June 15	Fishing boat Free Bird, gave help
	Yacht Pamela Anne, gave help
21	Motor cruiser in tow of fishing vessel Botney Cut, gave help
29	Fishing vessel Excalibur, gave help
July 27	Yacht Jade Gate, gave help
Aug 26	Motor boat, gave help
	Fishing vessel Boy Steven, gave help
30	Fishing vessel Mardyck, gave help
Sep 1	Cabin cruiser Lapwing, gave help
5	Sick man on board survey ship Stm Vega, took out doctor and landed a sick man
12	Sick man on board liquefied gas carrier Derwent, landed a sick man
25	Man brought ashore from dredger Barent Zanen for compassionate reasons
26	General cargo vessel Brummi, escorted vessel
Oct 6	Injured man on board cargo vessel Sovietskiy Moryatk, landed an injured man
9	Yacht Alert, gave help
	Sick man on board tanker Muran, landed a sick man
16	Injured man on board liquefied gas carrier Marianne Kosan, landed an injured man
24	Fishing vessel Silverwood, gave help
27	Yacht Josie, gave help
Nov 6	Fishing vessel Elo, landed 4
18	Cargo vessel Gimo Trader, took out fire personnel
Dec 16	Injured man on board cargo vessel Peter S, landed an injured man
1992 Jan 12	Fishing vessel Frances E, gave help
Feb 7	Fishing vessel Chance, gave help
17	Motor cruiser Peto Swift, gave help
Mar 3	Fishing vessel Steelman, gave help

Mar 12	Fishing vessel Karen, escorted vessel
17	Sick man on fishing vessel Burghley, landed a sick man
May 5	Yacht Avocet, gave help
9	2 canoes, landed 2 and saved 2 canoes
29	Motor cruiser Heatherdown, gave help
30	Injured man on board fishing vessel Arctic Corsair, landed an injured man
	lifeboat to Ro-Ro cargo vessel Tor Anglia, saved boat
	Motor boat Carne Flyer, gave help
31	Cabin cruiser Ocean Star, gave help
June 3	Fishing boat Daz I, gave help
5	Yacht Josine, escorted boat
6	Tug Lady Moira, landed 2
12	Yacht Opua, gave help
July 2	Yacht Gurine, gave help
3	Mine, took out mine disposal personnel
4	Yacht Redcroft, gave help
	Yacht Square Pegg, escorted boat
	Yacht Pandion, gave help
25	Fishing boat Scarthoe, saved boat and 4
30	Injured man on board tanker Alexandros, landed an injured man
Aug 5	Sick woman on board tanker Seaservice, took out doctor and landed a sick man
15	Fishing vessel Susan Mary II, gave help
19	Sick man on bulk carrier Kapitan Boev, landed a sick man
21	Fishing vessel Jolynn, gave help
	Cabin cruiser Bulvan Buccaneer, gave help
	Cabin cruisers Misty Moon and Sea Jay, escorted boats
22	Fishing vessel Susan Mary II, gave help
Sep 6	Fishing vessel Boy Tom, gave help
9	Fishing vessel Susan Mary II, saved boat and 2
11	Trimaran Lady Torrida, gave help
13	Yacht Jason, escorted boat
19	Motor cruiser Seafarer II, gave help
Oct 4	Injured man on board tanker Stolt Margit Terkol, landed an injured man
5	Sick man on board tug/supply ship Boa Eskil, landed a sick man
9	Yacht Fifine, saved boat and 2
18	Yacht Zelia B, gave help
Nov 8	Fishing vessel Susan Mary II, gave help
21	Injured man on board tanker Lisbet, landed injured man
Dec 10	Fishing vessel Marmik, gave help
19	Motor launch, escorted boat
24	Body in seas, landed a body
27	Fishing vessel Wash Princess, gave help
1993 Feb 5	Sick man on board tanker Dutch Faith, landed a sick man
7	Injured man on board Standby Safety Pollution Control vessel Toisa Sentinal, landed an injured man
20	Sick man on board rig standby safety vessel Black Watch, landed a sick man

Edith Emile relief lifeboat

1993 Mar 11	Fishing boat Daz-I, gave help

Kenneth Thelwall lifeboat

1993 Apr 19	Sick man on board tanker Willy, took out medical auxiliary thereby saving a life
22	Injured man on board tanker Fina Belgica, landed an injured man
23	Fishing vessel Scrounger, gave help
24	Cargo vessel Ilean, stood by

Ralph and Bonella Farrant relief lifeboat

1993 May 31	Yacht Stella Maris, saved boat and 4
June 13	Injured man on board fishing vessel Lairlochie, landed an injured man
19	Fishing vessel Susan Mary II, gave help
July 19	Yacht Sunseeker, gave help
21	Fishing vessel Maribel, gave help
24	Motor boat Rosanna III, gave help
Aug 5	Yacht Morven, escorted
17	Yacht Umiak, gave help

Aug 19	Fishing vessel Fin-Ar-Bed, escorted Yacht Sky, gave help
21	Yacht Burnford, gave help
Sep 19	Yacht Penn Player, gave help
25	Yacht Seaward, gave help

Kenneth Thelwall lifeboat

1993	Oct 8	Cargo vessel Sava Star, stood by vessel
	9	Yacht Millstream, gave help
	20	Fishing vessel Carole Anne, gave help
	28	Sick man on cargo vessel Diamond, landed a sick man
	Nov 1	Fishing vessel Chance, gave help
	27	Cabin cruiser Linda Ann with boat Frans-Hal in tow, gave help
1994	Jan 26	Cargo vessel Aegviidu, escorted vessel
	Feb 15	Fishing vessel Eventide, saved 4
	16	Fishing vessel Wash Princess, 2 persons and craft brought in
	20	Sick man on board research vessel Patrick E. Haggerty, landed a sick man
	27	Fishing vessel Dirkje, saved vessel and 6
	Mar 1	Injured man on board fishing vessel Undaunted, landed an injured man
	Apr 29	Sick man on cargo vessel Baltiyskiy 69, landed a sick man
	May 2	Yacht Milon Guera, escorted boat
	6	Yacht Papillon, 4 persons and craft brought in
	7	Injured man on board vehicles carrier Autostrada, landed an injured man
	11	Fishing vessel Sara Maria, 5 persons and craft brought in
	29	Motor cruiser Joken, 3 persons and a dog and craft brought in
	31	Fishing boat Valentine, 3 persons and craft brought in
	June 6	Fishing vessel Ca Ne Fait Rien, 2 persons and craft brought in
	15	Fishing vessel Trefusis, 5 persons and craft brought in
	15	Fishing vessel Lirasa K, 2 persons and craft brought in
	20	Fishing vessel Susan Mary II, 2 persons and craft brought in
	22	Injured man on board dredger sand carrier Sand Wader, landed an injured man
	July 5	Yacht Enif, 2 persons and craft brought in
	11	Sick woman on survey vessel Henny, landed a sick woman
	15	Fishing vessel Susan Mary II, gave help
	20	Fishing vessel Ca Ne Fait Rien, 2 persons and craft brought in
	24	Yacht Eipo, 2 persons and craft brought in
	24	Fishing vessel Wardley, gave help
	29	Fishing vessel Sally Anne, 2 persons and craft brought in
	Aug 11	Yacht Jalesco, 3 lives and boat saved
	16	Fishing vessel Ca Ne Fait Rien, 2 persons and craft brought in
	21	Divers, saved 2
	26	Cabin cruiser Scots Mist, saved band 3
	Sep 4	Sick man on board cargo vessel Koporye, 1 person brought in
	Oct 13	Fishing vessel Antares II, 2 persons and craft brought in
	14	Fishing vessel St Remy, 5 persons and craft brought in
	Nov 3	Injured man on fishing vessel Eos, injured man brought in
	17	Sick man on board bulk carrier Ironbridge, 1 person brought in
	17	Fishing vessel Carole Anne, 3 persons and craft brought in
	23	Injured man on cargo vessel Tuvana, landed injured man
1995	Jan 17	Cargo vessel Aurora-H, stood by vessel
	Feb 5	Fishing vessel Ca Ne Fait Rien, 1 person and craft brought in
	Mar 10	Aircraft, recovered wreckage
	14	Injured man on board tanker United Trader, injured man brought in
	Apr 1	Sail training yacht James Cook, landed 16 and craft brought in
	12	Fishing vessel Boy Darren, 2 persons and craft brought in
	28	Yacht Curlew, 1 person and craft brought in

	May 13	Yacht Curlew, gave help
	21	Cabin cruiser Hogwash, 2 persons and craft brought in
	June 9	Yacht Vagabund, escorted boat
	9	Injured man on board fishing vessel Eventide, landed an injured man
	9	Rig standby safety vessel St Elizabeth, stood by vessel
	July 3	Fishing vessel Ca Ne Fait Rien, 2 persons and craft brought in
	11	Fishing vessel Boy Darren, 2 persons and craft brought in – saved by another lifeboat
	11	Fishing vessel Boy Darren, 2 persons & craft brought in
	12	Yacht Hunters Moon, 1 person and craft brought in
	12	Tug Wyke, stood by
	16	Injured woman on board fishing vessel Sparkling Line, injured person brought in
	28	Fishing boat Sally Ann, 3 persons and craft brought in
	Aug 2	Fishing vessel Wandering Star, 3 persons and craft brought in
	Sep 19	Fishing vessel Galwad-Y-Mor of Lymington, 4 persons landed and craft brought in
	22	Injured man on board liquefied gas tanker Deltagas, injured man brought in
	22	Fishing vessel Coastal Surveyor, 4 persons and craft brought in
	24	Injured man on board tanker Puppy P, injured man brought in
	26	Fishing vessel Helen Claire, 4 persons and craft brought in
	29	Injured man on board fishing vessel Euroclydon, injured man brought in
	30	Fishing vessel Lirasa K, 2 persons and craft brought in
	30	Fishing vessel Sarah Thinnesen, escorted vessel
	30	Fishing vessel Susan Mary II, 4 persons and craft brought in
	Oct 12	Fishing vessel Boy Darren, 2 persons and craft brought in
	21	Fishing vessel Ca Na Fait Rien, 2 persons and craft brought in
	21	Fishing vessel Esther, 2 persons and craft brought in
	22	Yacht Chorus Line, saved boat and 3
	26	Yacht Pilgrim, landed 1 and craft brought in
	Nov 6	Fishing vessel Astrid, landed 2 and craft brought in
	29	Fishing vessel Three Fevers III, landed 4 and saved vessel
	Dec 1	Fishing vessel Fleur De Lys, escorted vessel
	3	Fishing vessel Jean Rene, escorted vessel
	8	Fishing vessel Ca Ne Fait Rien, 2 persons and craft brought in
	29	Cargo vessel Fast Ken, escorted vessel
1996	Jan 16	Fishing vessel Noordpool, escorted craft
	19	Injured man on board cargo vessel Carolina, injured man brought in
	Feb 1	Fishing vessel Ca Na Fait Rien, 2 persons and craft brought in
	2	Fishing vessel Lirasa K, 2 persons and craft brought in
		Fishing vessel Ca Na Fait Rien, 2 persons and craft brought in
	7	Injured man on board cargo vessel Al Mubarakiah, injured man brought in
	18	Injured man on board fishing vessel Iysha, injured man brought in
	19	Cargo vessel Linda Marijke, stood by craft
	20	Fish factory vessel Komandarm Shcherbakov, stood by
	29	Injured man on board tanker Pascale Knutsen, landed an injured man

Margaret Russell Fraser relief lifeboat

1996	Mar 6	Fishing vessel La Belle Ilienne, 3 persons and craft brought in
	28	Fishing vessel Esther, 2 persons and craft brought in
	Apr 24	Fishing vessel Boy Darren, 3 persons and craft brought in
	May 10	Sick man on board cabin cruiser The Three Sisters, landed a sick man
		Cabin cruiser The Three Sisters, escorted craft
	May 13	Fishing vessel Ca Ne Fait Rien, 2 persons and craft brought in

	19	Yacht Kass-A-Nova, 3 persons and craft brought in - saved by another lifeboat
	24	Yacht Spindle, 1 person and craft brought in
	26	Injured man on board fishing vessel Still Waters, landed an injured man
June	1	Fishing vessel Ca Ne Fait Rien, 2 persons and craft brought in
	5	Injured man on board fishing vessel Monika B, injured man brought in
	8	Sick man on board tanker Doris 1, sick man brought in
	11	Sick man on cargo vessel Frisnes, sick man brought in
	13	Cargo vessel Anders Rousing, escorted craft
	16	Yacht Tanga Tika II, 3 persons and craft brought in
	16	Cabin cruiser Sea Hound of Hamble, 2 persons and craft brought in
	25	Fishing vessel Celtic Mor, recovered wreckage
	30	Yacht Corrinth, landed 1 and craft brought in
July	15	Cabin cruiser Odin, 4 persons and craft brought in
	16	Yacht Hydaway, landed 2 and craft brought in
	24	Yacht Breock, 3 persons and craft brought in – saved by another lifeboat
		Fishing vessel Sorrento, saved craft and 5
		Yacht Sunlight, saved craft and 2
Aug	4	Sick man on board tanker Argironissos, landed a sick man
	6	Motor cruiser Granby, 1 person and craft brought in
	7	Catamaran Sebowisha, landed 2 and craft brought in

Kenneth Thelwall lifeboat

1996	Aug 31	Yacht Icenic, 5 persons and craft brought in
	Sep 1	Yacht Icenic, 5 persons and craft brought in
	15	Cabin cruiser Angella II, 2 persons and craft brought in
	27	Cabin cruiser Blazalong, 2 persons and craft brought in
Oct	1	Yacht Agapanthus, 1 person and craft brought in
		Fishing vessel Monika B, escorted craft
	12	Naval divers vessel, escorted craft
	17	Motor cruiser Cascade, landed 3 and craft brought in
Nov	12	Fishing vessel Noordpool, saved craft and 5
	22	Sick man on tanker Caroline Wonsild, landed a sick man
	30	Fishing vessel Galwad-Y-Mor, of Lymington, 5 persons and craft brought in
Dec	19	Motor cruiser Golden Tarka, 2 persons and craft brought in – saved by another lifeboat
	27	Sick man on board ore/bulk oil carrier Bear G, sick man brought in

Pride of the Humber lifeboat

1997	Mar 9	Fishing vessel Marmic, 1 person and craft brought in
	21	Injured man on board tanker Gold Crest, landed an injured man
Apr	24	Fishing vessel Lirisa K, 3 people and craft brought in
	25	Cabin cruiser Vontu, 3 people and craft brought in
May	3	Diver support craft Reef Rash II, saved craft and 5
	5	Fishing vessel Jacinta, 1 person and craft brought in
		Cargo vessel Carmel, saved craft and 3
	10	Yacht Jaro, gave help
	17	Diver support craft, 8 people and craft brought in

Kenneth Thelwall relief lifeboat

1997	May 21	Sick man on board Cargo vessel Gidrostroitel A.P. Aleksandrov, sick man brought in
June	8	2 sick men on board Gemini Girl, 2 sick men brought in
	14	De-commissioned minesweeper Waterwitch, saved craft
	17	Yacht Reynardt, 2 people and craft brought in
	26	Yacht Freewind, saved craft and 2
July	6	Yacht Lady C, 2 people and craft brought in
	18	Yacht Ayesha, assisted to save 3 and craft
	25	Fishing vessel Sarah Thinnesen, gave help

Pride of the Humber lifeboat

1997	Aug 3	Diver support craft Venture, 6 people and craft brought in
	Aug 4	Injured man on board bulk carrier Yamato, injured man brought in

	17	Injured woman on board motor cruiser John H. Vincent, injured woman brought in
	30	Fishing vessel Alison, saved craft and 2
		Yacht Gwenili, 4 people and craft brought in
Sept	08	Yacht Boojum, 1 person and craft brought in
	22	Speed boat Acmi Ski, saved 3
Oct	18	Yacht Katina, 4 people and craft brought in
	23	Yacht Gilly, 1 person and craft brought in
	26	Fishing vessel La Belle Ilienne, 3 people and craft brought in
Nov	11	Injured man on board tanker Powerventure L, injured man brought in
1998	Jan 9	Motor boat, 1 person and craft brought in
	18	Cleethorpes ILB D-454, gave help
Feb	4	Survey vessel Andrews One, gave help
	7	Injured man on board dredger Sand Kite, injured man brought in
	17	Fishing vessel Chrissie H, 4 people and craft brought in
	22	Cabin cruiser Sabre Empress, gave help
	23	Cabin cruiser Sabre Empress, 2 people and craft brought in
Mar	11	Sick man on board cargo vessel Amur 2518, sick man brought in
	26	Sick man on board cargo vessel Frej, sick man brought in
Apr	12	Motor boat The Lark, 2 people and craft brought in
	21	Fishing vessel Gille Brighde, 2 people and craft brought in
May	2	Yacht Dercie, 2 people and craft brought in
July	28	Inflatable dinghy Bulldog, 3 people and craft brought in
	28	Injured man on dredger Sand Kite, injured man brought in
	29	Fishing vessel Boy Darren, 3 people and craft brought in
Aug	2	Cabin cruiser Alma, saved craft and 2
	7	Motor cruiser Chrisrae, 4 people and craft brought in
	12	Yacht Taphin, 2 people and craft brought in
	17	Catamaran Janus, landed 3 and craft brought in
	23	Yacht Tyke, saved craft and 1
	27	RAF air sea rescue craft Spitfire, saved craft and 6
	31	Yacht Gemini of Hamble, 3 people and craft brought in
Sep	5	Catamaran Kitty, 2 people and craft brought in
	06	Cabin cruiser Fontana Candida, gave help
	16	Yacht Kirstina, escorted craft
	23	Cabin cruiser Kirkvik, gave help
	24	Sick man on board tanker Solt Petrel, sick man brought in
Oct	4	Yacht Starchick, escorted craft
	12	Fishing vessel Trefusis, escorted craft
Nov	11	Injured man on board fishing vessel Lundy Gannet, landed an injured man
1999	Jan 7	Fishing vessel Boy Neil, saved craft and 2
	31	Woman in danger of drowning off Donna Nook, assisted to save 1
Feb	27	Fishing vessel Galwad-Y-Mor, 4 people and craft brought in
Mar	5	Yacht Anah, 3 people and craft brought in
	10	Fishing vessel Provider, gave help
	31	Fishing vessel Dollard, 4 people and craft brought in

Fraser Flyer relief lifeboat

1999	Apr 11	Fishing vessel La-Belle-Ilienne, gave help
	27	Sick man on board tanker Catherine Knutsen, sick man brought in
May	4	Inflatable dinghy Seasport, 3 people and craft brought in
	20	Fishing vessel Boy Darren, 4 people and craft brought in

Pride of the Humber lifeboat

1999	June 8	Fishing vessel Dollard, 3 people and craft brought in
	20	Yacht Tismewat, escorted boat
July	24	Fishing vessel Diana, gave help
	30	Yacht Domingo, 1 person and craft brought in
Aug	12	Fishing vessel Rachel S, landed 2 and craft brought in
	17	Barge Wylam, landed 7 and craft brought in
	19	Sick man on Rig Supply vessel Putford Achilles, landed 1
	27	Fishing vessel Gweek Dawn, 2 people and craft brought in
Sept	8	Fishing vessel Boy Darren, 3 people and craft brought in
	27	Dive support vessel Faithful, 2 people and craft brought in

	Nov 10	Fishing vessel Sarah Visholm, 4 people and craft brought in
	15	Fishing vessel Jennalea, 2 people and craft brought in
	22	Fishing vessel Kerloch, landed 5 and craft saved
2000	Jan 4	Fishing Vessel Seasport, 2 people and craft brought in
	16	Fishing vessel Doreen Rosa C, 6 people & craft brought in
	Mar 26	Fishing vessel La Belle Ilenne, 3 people and craft brought in, saved by another lifeboat
	Apr 4	Injured man aboard HMS Bicester, landed 1
	May 3	Fishing vessel Zuider Krus, 4 people and craft brought in
	June 10	Conveyed injured man from bulk carrier Chrismer to the mainland, 1 person brought in
	28	Fishing vessel Black Jack, 2 people and craft brought in
	July 9	Fishing vessel Boy Darren, 4 people and craft brought in
	10	Yacht Honey Bell, escorted craft
	Aug 1	Barge Deighton, 2 people and craft brought in
	31	Yacht Starlight Special 002, gave help
	Sep 16	Fishing vessel Quaker, escorted craft
	24	Pleasure boat Lady Moweena, 3 people and craft brought in
	Oct 9	Fishing vessel Niamh Aine, escorted craft
	27	Injured man aboard motor vessel Nordic Marita, stood by
	Nov 18	Catamaran Snow Leopard, escorted craft
2001	Jan 31	Fishing vessel Boy Darren, landed 3 and craft brought in
	Feb 22	Cabin cruiser Sea Tigress, escorted craft
	Mar 14	Sick person on board merchant vessel Odin, gave help
	Apr 5	Fishing vessel Boy Darren, landed 3 and craft brought in
	8	Fishing vessel Leah Brook, 3 people and and craft brought in
	17	Fishing vessel Kerloch, landed 6 and and craft brought in
	May 3	Fishing vessel Our Roseanne, 2 people and and craft brought in
	5	Yacht Independence, gave help
	12	Cabin cruiser Bluebell, 1 person and craft brought in
	14	Yacht Tiger Lilly, landed 2 and craft brought in
	23	Recovery of human body from the sea, landed a body
	28	Yacht Shamsuddin, 2 people and craft brought in
	30	Fishing vessel Stormy-C, 4 people and craft brought in
	June 5	Fishing vessel Turpin, 3 people and craft brought in
	7	Yacht Souriante, landed 2 and craft brought in
	15	Yacht Markab, landed 2 and craft brought in
	16	Injured man on cargo vessel Elisia, 1 man brought in
	20	Sick seaman on board the ex-Admiralty tender and workboat Dorloch, landed 1
	July 11	Yacht Surprise Royale, landed 4 and craft brought in
	18	Yacht Virgil, 2 people and craft brought in
	22	Ex-ship's lifeboat Kindie, 2 people and craft brought in
	23	Ex-ship's lifeboat Kindie, 2 people and craft brought in
	31	Fishing vessel Crusader, 4 people and craft brought in
	31	Cruiser Winifred Gray, escorted craft
	Aug 1	Cruiser September Song, 6 people and craft brought in
	16	Yacht Freebooter, landed 2 and craft brought in
	24	Fishing vessel Galwad-Y-Mor, escorted craft
	27	Pleasure cruiser Delta Moon, 3 people and craft brought in
	28	Fishing vessel Turpin, 2 people and craft brought in
	Sept 6	Yacht Sula, 2 people and craft brought in
	7	Fishing vessel Euroclydon, saved craft and 6
	23	Yacht Wendy, 1 person and craft brought in
	Oct 2	Powerboat Little Rea, landed 2 and craft brought in
	13	Tug Anglian Earl with fishing vessel Sarah Visholm II in tow, gave help
		Injured man on board merchant vessel Som, landed 1
	17	Trawler Zuiderzee, 4 people and craft brought in
	Nov 3	Fishing vessel Diana, 6 people and craft brought in
	16	Injured crewman on board tanker Presnya, landed 1
2002	Jan 10	Injured person from the coaster Alissa, landed 1
	15	Sick person aboard merchant vessel Sophia, evacuated to hospital by helicopter, gave help
	Mar 1	Injured man on board fishing vessel Golden Reaper, 1 person brought in

Duchess of Kent relief lifeboat

2000	Mar 23	Cabin cruiser Una, escorted craft

	Apr 30	Yacht Carina, landed 3 and craft brought in

Pride of the Humber lifeboat

2000	May 3	Sick woman on board ferry Pride of Hull, landed 1 and 1 person brought in
	6	Pleasure cruiser Monica III, 3 persons and craft brought in
	8	Fishing vessel Marbella, escorted craft
	13	Yacht Sheman, 2 people and craft brought in
	21	Yacht Ayton Serenade, 2 people and craft brought in
	26	People overboard from jet ski, stood by
	27	Fishing vessel Megan Elizabeth, 3 people and craft brought in
	June 2	Fishing vessel Eager Noon, 2 people and craft brought in
	6	Injured man on board fishing vessel Kerloch, 1 person brought in
	8	Fishing vessel Isabelle Kathleen, 3 people and craft brought in
	16	Cabin cruiser Rogues Roost, escorted craft
	28	Dutch yacht Lapislazuli, landed 4 and craft brought in
	30	Fishing vessel Innovator, 5 people and craft brought in
		Angling vessel Impulsive, escorted craft
	July 15	Fishing vessel Destiny, 3 people and craft brought in
	29	Sick man on board Ro-Ro ferry Stenna Searider, landed 1
		Pleasure cruiser Malabar Princess, escorted craft
	31	Yacht Brim, 2 people and craft brought in
		Dutch yacht Lamantijn, 2 people and craft brought in
	Aug 9	Yacht Dragon, gave help
	17	Motor cruiser Gilly Jo, escorted craft
		Powerboat Salinia, 5 people and craft brought in
	24	Fishing vessel Dorian Rosa C, escorted craft
	25	Yacht Magnum, escorted craft
		Cabin cruiser After The Storm, 2 people and craft brought in

Duke of Atholl relief lifeboat

2002	Sept 10	Yacht Tamara, 3 people and craft brought in
	22	Cabin cruiser Rebecca, 2 people and craft brought in
	25	Fishing vessel Misty Blue, landed 3 and craft brought in
	Oct 1	Yacht Aliki, 3 people and craft brought in
	2	Injured man on board fishing vessel Crusader, landed 1
	30	Fishing vessel Misty Blue, 3 people and craft brought in
		Fishing vessel Constant Friend, escorted casualty

Pride of the Humber lifeboat

2002	Nov 16	Fishing vessel La-Belle-Ilienne, 2 people and craft brought in
	Dec 12	Fishing vessel Dorian Rosa C, 7 people and craft brought in
	15	Fishing vessel Galwad-Y-Mor, landed 6 and craft brought in
	22	Sick woman on board ferry Pride of Rotterdam, landed 1
2003	Feb 16	Fishing vessel Dorian Rosa C, 5 people and craft brought in
	22	Sick seaman on board tanker Castillo de Butron, 5 people and craft brought in
	25	Fishing vessel Mary Louise IV, 2 people and craft brought in
	Mar 25	Injured man on board tanker Bro Traveller, landed 1
	26	Fishing vessel Diana, 5 people and craft brought in
	29	Sick man on board support ship Putford Shore, landed 1
	Apr 27	Fishing vessel Our Roseanne, 2 people and craft brought in
	May 16	Pilot launch Alert, landed 1, saved craft and 1
		Yacht Katanne, gave help

The Will relief lifeboat

2003	May 28	Yacht Rambling Rose, 1 person and craft brought in
	29	Yacht Lorinja, 2 people and craft brought in
	31	Yacht Ocean Spirit, 1 person and craft brought in
	June 1	Motor cruiser April Star, gave help
	6	Fishing vessel Diana, 6 people brought in

Pride of the Humber lifeboat

2003	June 19	Trawler Peter Marlene, gave help
	22	Yacht Take 5, escorted craft

23	Dive support craft John Morton, 5 people and craft brought in	
July 3	Fishing vessel Kerloch, 4 people and craft brought in	
4	Cabin cruiser Hambledon, 5 people and craft brought in	
12	Injured man on ferry Pride of Rotterdam, landed 1	
15	Injured man on board pilot boat Humber A, landed 1	
30	Fishing vessel Aleyna, 2 people and craft brought in	
Aug 4	Yacht Mudlark, 2 people and craft brought in	
5	Fishing vessel Boy Darren, 4 people and craft brought in	
10	Fishing vessel Gitte Liza, escorted craft	
12	Fishing vessel Euroclydon, 7 people and craft brought in	
17	Yacht Bombadilla, 2 people and craft brought in	
26	Sick man on board fishing vessel Dollard, landed 1	
29	Fishing vessel Dorian Rosa C, 5 people and craft brought in	
Sept 11	Fishing vessel Talene IV, gave help	
13	Pleasure boat Asklepios, 4 people and craft brought in	
15	Fishing vessel Kerlock, 7 people and craft brought in	
29	Injured person on board oil/gas support vessel Putford Trader, 1 person brought in	
Oct 10	Powerboat Nord Caperen, 3 people and craft brought in	
13	Fishing vessel Eventide, landed 4 and saved craft	
Nov 13	Injured person on board gas standby vessel Putford Trader, 1 person brought in	
15	Sick person on board gas standby vessel Putford Ajax, 1 person brought in	
Dec 21	Jet ski, stood by	
2004 Jan 20	Sick man on board tanker Samamina, landed 1	
23	Tug Thom Heron, stood by	
Feb 14	Conveyed sick man from gas standby vessel Putford Trader to the mainland, landed 1	
27	Fishing vessel Dollard, assisted to save craft and 2	
Mar 13	Fishing vessel Shepherds Lad, 5 persons and craft brought in	
Apr 2	Evacuate an injured person from the Humber Sentinel, 1 person brought in	
7	Yacht Duet, 2 persons and craft brought in	

The Will relief lifeboat

2004 Apr 14	Fishing vessel Ipomoea, 2 persons and craft brought in	

Pride of the Humber lifeboat

2004 Apr 16	Barge Classic Lass, 2 persons and craft brought in	
21	Fishing vessel Dollard, 3 persons and craft brought in	
24	Fishing vessel Our Roseanne, 2 persons and craft brought in	
May 14	2 dogs, gave help – retrieved dogs from sea	
16	Fishing vessel Black Jack, 4 persons and craft brought in	
19	Tender to commercial vessel Bro Sincero, 4 people and craft brought in	
20	Powered boat Norna, 2 persons and craft brought in	
22	Powered boat Mischief, 2 persons and craft brought in	
29	Fishing vessel Isle Venture, 2 persons and craft brought in	
June 6	Fishing vessel Lisanne, 3 persons and craft brought in	
8	Fishing vessel Seonti A, 3 persons and craft brought in	
11	Fishing vessel Lisanne, 3 persons and craft brought in	
20	Yacht Wild Horizon, 4 persons and craft brought in	
26	Yacht Suroma, gave help – towed to deeper water	
	Yacht Suroma, landed 2 and craft brought in	
29	Powered boat Juniper, saved craft and 1	
30	Powered boat Tiziana, 2 persons and craft brought in	
July 2	Fishing vessel Seont, 5 persons and craft brought in	
3	Yacht Blazer, landed 2 and craft brought in	
22	Barge Normanton, 2 persons and craft brought in	
23	Fishing vessel Morning Star MORE HERE	
25	Angling vessel Leahbrooke	
31	Powered boat Carolina Moon	
Aug 6	Yacht Solace, 1 person and craft brought in	
8	Person cut off by the tide, gave help – transferred person	
	Swimmer, gave help – advised swimmer and stood by	
	Powered boat Cornish Maiden, 3 persons and craft brought in	
17	Yacht Wendy, landed 1 and craft brought in	
18	Yacht Sakr El Bahr, 4 persons, 2 dogs and craft brought in	

19	Yacht Chalis, 3 persons and craft brought in	
22	Yacht First Light, 5 persons and craft brought in	
24	Yacht Miel, 2 persons and craft brought in	
Sep 9	Sick man on board tanker Bro Transporter, landed 1	

The Will relief lifeboat

2004 Oct 5	Sick man on board tanker Wear Fisher, landed 1	
17	Fishing vessel Amadeus, 8 persons & craft brought in	
30	Injured man on board fishing vessel Twilight, landed 1	

William Gordon Burr relief lifeboat

2004 Nov 4	Fishing vessel Boy Darren, 4 persons and craft brought in	
8	Fishing vessel Euroclyden, 5 persons and craft brought in	

The Will relief lifeboat

2004 Nov 26	Yacht Broad Blue, assisted to save craft and 2	
Dec 2	Fishing vessel Shepherds Lad, 4 persons and craft brought in	
28	Powered boat Madeline, landed 4 and craft brought in	
2005 Jan 12	Fishing vessel Sorrento, saved boat and 3	
23	Merchant vessels Tor Dania and Ameniaty, stood by	
Feb 7	Power boat Castle Tee Jay, 2 people and craft brought in	

Edward Duke of Windsor relief lifeboat

2005 Feb 21	Fishing vessel Holly J, 4 people and craft brought in	

Pride of the Humber lifeboat

2005 Mar 18	Fishing vessel Gratitude, gave help – transferred pump	
31	Fishing vessel Bridgend, 2 people and craft brought in	
Apr 9	Yacht Nikki, gave help	
28	Fishing vessel Zuiderzee, 4 people and craft brought in	
29	Fishing vessel Harvester, gave help – passed tow to Bridlington lifeboat	
30	Powered boat Enterprise, 2 people and craft brought in	
May 2	Yacht Viking, gave help – completed tow	
3	Injured crewman on board bulk carrier Grafton, landed 1	
11	Injured crewman on merchant vessel Neptune, landed 1	
21	Injured crewman on board bulk carrier Carso, landed 1	
28	Take up role of surface search co-ordinator searching for a missing person in the water	
31	Powered boat Fleetwind, escorted craft	
June 1	Yacht Florence II, craft brought in	
7	Commercial craft CSK Tribute, landed a body	

William Gordon Burr relief lifeboat

2005 June 18	Yacht Spindrift, 2 people and craft brought in	
21	Sick person on board ferry Pride of York, landed 1	

Pride of the Humber lifeboat

2005 July 6	Fishing vessel Boy Darren, 3 people and craft brought in	
	Fishing vessel Shepherds Lad, 4 people and craft brought in	
19	Yacht Galatea, 1 person and craft brought in	
22	Fishing vessel Dorian Rosa C, escorted craft	
	Fishing vessel Seonta, gave help – completed tow	
25	Sick man on board tug Kingcraig, landed a sick person	
26	Yacht Shuna, gave help – took out fuel and supplies	
31	Powered boat Escourt, escorted craft	
Aug 1	Fishing vessel Dream Catcher, 2 persons and craft brought in	
6	Yacht Gemini Girl, gave help – escorted to safety	
17	Yacht Cabriole, 1 person and craft brought in	
20	Sick crew member on fishing vessel Amadeus, landed 1	
22	Yacht Theodora, landed 2 and craft brought in	
26	Powered boat Ballyheo Dream, landed 2	
27	Powered boat Moravia, 2 persons and craft brought in	
31	Injured person on dredger Filippo Brunelleschi, landed 1	
	Powered boat Violet, escorted into Grimsby	
Sep 2	Yacht Batis, 3 persons and craft brought in	

Osier relief lifeboat

2005 Sep 12	Yacht Suroma, landed 1	
	Yacht Suroma, 1 person and craft brought in	
13	Yacht Harmony, gave help	

Pride of the Humber lifeboat

2005	Oct 9	Powered boat Eleanor, 1 person and craft brought in
	Nov 8	Assist in the search for a windsurfer
	10	Yacht Special-K, 1 person and craft brought in
	13	vessel Pelanic II, 2 persons and craft brought in
	15	Fishing vessel Our Roseanne, 2 persons and craft brought to Grimsby
	26	Tanker Navion Britannia, gave help – supplied medications
	Dec 4	Fishing vessel Pandion, 2 persons and craft brought in
	21	Injured man on board tanker Alcedo, landed 1
2006	Jan 30	Fishing vessel Zuider Zee with a fouled propeller, 5 persons and craft brought in
	Feb 5	Fishing vessel Shepherds Lad, 4 and craft brought in
	16	Explosion and fire aboard gas storage rig 47/3B, stood by Gas storage rig lifeboat, craft brought in
	Mar 28	Fishing vessel Kingfisher II, 2 persons and craft brought in
	Apr 3	Man overboard from canoe, saved 1
	11	Powered boat Calypso, escorted craft
	17	Yacht Olive's Rival, 3 persons and craft brought in
	21	Fishing vessel Our Roseanne, 2 persons and craft brought in
	29	Injured fisherman on board Danish vessel Ioner, landed 1
	May 3	Yacht Mercilla, 2 persons and craft brought in
	11	Fishing vessel Drifter, 2 persons and craft brought in
	23	Injured person on pilot launch Humber Neptune, landed 1
	June 7	Merchant vessels Skagern and Samskip Courier, gave help

Fraser Flyer (Civil Service No.43) lifeboat

| 2006 | June 22 | Fishing vessel Shepherds Lad, 4 persons and craft brought in |

Pride of the Humber lifeboat

2006	July 11	Powered boat Don't Delay, 2 persons and craft brought in
	23	Yacht Moonrover, escorted craft
	26	Fishing vessel Boy Darren with a fouled propeller, 4 persons and craft brought in
	29	Yacht Miss Enigma, landed 2 and craft brought in
	30	Yacht Penrover, 4 persons and craft brought in

Fraser Flyer (Civil Service No.43) lifeboat

| 2006 | Aug 5 | Injured person on board rig safety vessel Putford Trader, person brought in |
| | 7 | Powered boat Lora Lee J, 2 persons and craft brought in |

Pride of the Humber lifeboat

| 2006 | Aug 10 | Cabin cruiser Billy Blue, escorted craft |

Edward Duke of Windsor relief lifeboat

| 2006 | Aug 12 | Yacht Molly Louise, saved craft and 1 |
| | 15 | Fishing vessel Flourish, 4 persons and craft brought in |

Pride of the Humber lifeboat

| 2006 | Aug 20 | relief lifeboat Fraser Flyer, gave help |

Edward Duke of Windsor relief lifeboat

2006	Aug 24	Barge De-Hoop III, 4 persons and craft brought in
	25	Barge De-Hoop III, gave help
	27	Yacht At Last with a fouled propeller, 2 persons and craft brought in

The Will relief lifeboat

| 2006 | Aug 30 | Fishing vessel Galwad-Y-Mor, 6 persons and craft brought in |
| | Sep 11 | Fishing vessel Quest, gave help – took over tow from Skegness lifeboat |

Pride of the Humber lifeboat

2006	Sep 16	Cabin cruiser Apache Princess, escorted craft
	Oct 3	Fishing vessel Our Roseanne, 3 persons and craft brought in
	Oct 27	Fishing vessel Good Intent, 4 persons and craft brought in
	Nov 4	Fishing vessel Our Roseanne, landed 3 and craft brought in
	24	Sick person on board ferry Pride of Hull, landed 1

	Dec 11	Sick person on board cargo vessel Bloemgracht, landed 1
	23	Merchant vessel Leonis, gave help
2007	Jan 6	Injured man on Norwegian fishing vessel Ordinant, landed 1
	18	Merchant vessel Sodade, stood by
	Feb 15	Injured man on fishing vessel Stena Searider, landed 1

William Gordon Burr relief lifeboat

| 2007 | Feb 17 | Powered boat Chloe Anne, 4 persons and craft brought in |

Fraser Flyer (Civil Service No.43) lifeboat

2007	Mar 20	Cargo vessel Humber Way, escorted craft
	23	Fishing vessel Shepherds Lad, 5 persons and craft brought in
	24	Yacht Magix, assisted to save craft and 2
	26	Fishing vessel Our Roseanne, 2 persons and craft brought in

Pride of the Humber lifeboat

2007	Apr 6	Pleasure boat Robo-Cat, 2 persons and craft brought in
		Converted trawler Corsair, 3 persons and craft brought in
	14	Yacht Bianca D, landed 3 and craft brought in
	16	Standby the vessel Cherry Sand, gave help
	May 8	Powered boat Protect Me III, 3 persons and craft brought in
	17	Yacht Spirit of Brough, escorted craft
	24	French fishing vessel Saint Josse IV, landed 1
	28	Fishing vessel Abbie Lee, landed 3 and craft brought in
	June 12	Tug Mono Girl, 2 persons and craft brought in
	16	Yacht Lorna Doon, 2 persons and craft brought in

Fraser Flyer (Civil Service No.43) lifeboat

2007	28	Fishing vessel Sweet Waters, 5 persons and craft brought in
	July 1	Inflatable dinghy, 7 persons and craft brought in
	3	Fishing vessel Misty Blue aground off Spurn Point Fishing vessel Misty Blue, refloat and escort back to beach
	23	Yacht Moonbeam of Benfleet, 1 person brought in
	24	Yacht Popstar, 1 person and craft brought in
	26	Yacht Cardiff Clipper, 16 persons and craft brought in
	Aug 8	Yacht Rana, 1 person and craft brought in
	17	Fishing vessel Independence, 2 persons and craft brought in
	25	Yacht Grandee, 3 persons and craft brought in
	26	Buoy tender, landed 1
		Motor cruiser Opus, 2 persons and craft brought in
		Motor cruiser Wonder Hall, gave help – completed tow
	27	Yacht Penn Player, saved craft and landed 3
	Sep 2	Powered boat Julie Ann, 3 persons and craft brought in
	16	Yacht Avilion, 2 persons and craft brought in

Pride of the Humber lifeboat

2007	Sep 23	Gas rig supply vessel Viking Islay, stood by
	26	Yacht Giramondo, saved craft and 1
	Oct 30	Powered boat Lorilei, 1 person and craft brought in
	Nov 1	Sick person on ferry Pride of Hull, landed a sick person
	Dec 17	Fishing vessel Seiont A, gave help – took over tow from Wells lifeboat
	28	Fishing vessel Rachael S, 3 persons and craft brought in
2008	Jan 16	Lifeboat from tanker Clipper Beaune, stood by
	Feb 2	Safety boat Titan, gave help – took over tow from Skegness lifeboat
	Mar 2	Injured person on board tanker SS Fillpine, landed 1

Osier relief lifeboat

2008	Apr 5	Fishing vessel Matthew Harvey, craft brought in
	23	Fishing vessel Telesis, 3 persons and craft brought in
	28	Powered boat My Mate, 1 person and craft brought in

Pride of the Humber lifeboat

2008	May 1	Yacht Cautious 2, 3 persons and craft brought in
	3	Recover a body from the sea, landed a body
	May 20	Injured man on board rig standby vessel Britannia Conquest, landed 1
	June 2	Fishing vessel Misty Blue, 2 persons and craft brought in

Pride of the Humber and Cleethorpes ILB assisting the former fishing vessel Corsair in the river on 23 July 2009. (By courtesy of Dave Steenvoorden)

5	Yacht Noy, 2 persons and craft brought in
6	Yacht Brynbella, 2 persons and craft brought in
8	Yacht Piglet II, gave help – took tow from Skegness lifeboat
13	Yacht Freebooter, landed 2
26	Fishing vessel Lindisfarne, 3 persons and craft brought in
29	Powered boat Garmin Racer, stood by
July 15	Fishing vessel Wayfarer, 2 persons and craft brought in
22	Powered boat Pelcomb Lady II, 3 persons and craft brought in
27	Yacht Antagus, 2 persons and craft brought in
31	Car ferry Cervantes, stood by
Aug 5	Tug Defence, 7 persons and craft brought in
	Humber sloop Phyllis, landed 7 and craft brought in
16	Yacht Laria, 3 persons and craft brought in
21	Fishing vessel Aleyna, 2 persons and craft brought in
22	Yacht Caradi Mor, escorted craft
	Yacht Night Watch, saved craft and 2
25	Bomb target pontoon, gave help – towed from local bombing range clear of shipping lanes
30	Fishing vessel Thalassa, 2 persons and craft brought in
Sep 14	Yacht firebird, escorted craft
28	Powered boat Predator, gave help and escorted craft
Oct 11	Kayak, gave help
12	Fishing vessel Aleyna, 2 persons and craft brought in

Roger and Joy Freeman relief lifeboat

2008	Oct 17	Yacht Calax-of-Lolworth, escorted craft
	30	Sick person on board ferry Pride of Hull, landed 1 and 1 person brought in
	Nov 3	Sick person on board bulk carrier Salamena, landed 1

Pride of the Humber lifeboat

2008	Nov 16	Fishing vessel Shepherds Lad, 4 persons and craft brought in
	Dec 2	Fishing vessel Black Jack, escorted craft
	8	Sick man on board fishing vessel Shepherds Lad, landed 1, 1 brought in, assisted to bring in craft
2009	Feb 6	Bulk carrier Saline, gave help
	Apr 8	Sick man on board cargo ship Boreas Scan, landed 1 and 2 people brought in
	13	Yacht Haven Voyager, landed 3 and craft brought in

Daniel L. Gibson relief lifeboat

2009	Apr 26	Yacht, 1 person and craft brought in
	May 3	Sick man on cargo vessel Matsusaka, landed 1
		Yacht Aquila, gave help – took tow from Skegness lifeboat
	4	Fishing vessel Sweet Waters, 4 people and craft brought in

Pride of the Humber lifeboat

2009	May 24	Powered fishing boat Impossible, gave help – passed tow to Withernsea ILB
	30	Fishing vessel Shepherds Lad, 4 people and craft brought in
	31	Yacht Lady Scarlet, gave help – illuminated scene
		Yacht Lady Scarlet, gave help
June 14		Yacht Beowolf, landed 2 and craft brought in
	21	Sick person on standby vessel Putford Sky, landed 1
July 3		Sick man on board standby vessel Putford Guardian, landed 1
	6	Sick man on ferry Pride of York, landed 1
	15	Powered boat Blue Dolphin, 2 people and craft brought in
	23	Powered boat Corsair, assisted to save craft and 3
	27	Passenger vessel Ferry Queen, 2 people and craft brought in
Aug 3		Fishing vessel Nuevo-Virgen-de-Lodairo, escorted craft
	6	Fishing vessel Misty Blue, 2 people and craft brought in
	7	Yacht Arbitrator, 2 people and craft brought in
	16	Sick crew man on board fishing vessel Shepherds Lad, landed 1
	20	Yacht Foxy, gave help – refloated casualty
		Fishing vessel Black Jack, stood by
	28	Fishing vessel Fruitful Harvest, 3 people and craft brought in
Sep 9		Yacht Cariad, landed 3 and saved craft
	16	Harbour launch Humber Surveyor, 2 people and craft brought in
	19	Fishing vessel Black Jack, 2 people and craft bought in
	24	Powered boat Pied Piper, 2 people and craft brought in
	27	Yacht Bessie, escorted craft
Oct 18		Powered boat Hogwash, gave help – recovered anchor
	19	Powered boat G and T, escorted craft

Earl and Countess Mountbatten of Burma relief lifeboat

2009	Nov 1	Powered boat Moggy, saved craft and 2
	2	Sick man on board tanker Eagle Seville, landed 1

Pride of the Humber lifeboat

2009	Dec 20	Powered boat Lady 3, landed 1, 1 person and craft brought in
	22	Tug Centrica Pride, gave help

D · PERSONNEL SUMMARY

Masters/Superintendent Coxswains

John Coulter	14.7.1810 never served
Robert Richardson	25.8.1810-3.12.1841
Joseph Davey	4.12.1841 – 13.2.1843
Robert Brown	25.2.1843 – 31.10.1848
Michael Welburn	1.11.1848 – 4.1853
John Calvert	4.1853 – 17.12.1853
George Grant	18.12.1853 – 31.7.1856
William Long	Mate acted as Master
Richard Parrott	1.10.1856 – 30.7.1857
William Willis	1.8.1857 – 30.9.1865
Fewson Hopper	1.10.1865 – 31.12.1877
Thomas Winson	1.1.1878 – 1.3.1894
David Pye	14.3.1894 – 7.1912
Robert Cross	7.1912 – 15.2.1944
John Edmund Mason	15.11.1943 – 1.1949
William S. Anderson	1.1949 – 1.1959
Robertson Buchan	1.1959 – 9.1973
Neil Morris	9.1973 – 2.1975
Brian Bevan	16.2.1975 – 11.11.2001
Robert White	12.11.2001 – 5.2003
Ian Firmin	5.2003 – 7.4.2004
Dave Steenvoorden*	7.4.2004 –

*Acting Coxswain from 10.9.2003

Mechanics

Denby Dunley	1919 – 8.1920
E. S. Woodhouse	8.1920 – 11.1921
W. A. Neal	11.1921 – 5.1925
S. Solomon	5.1925 – 11.1926
Walter Harding	11.1926 –
John Major	
Claude Richards	6.1943 – 9.1944
Douglas Shead	9.1944 – 3.1947
Claude Richards	3.1947 – 10.1951
Leslie Willis	10.1951 – 4.1955
Bob Appleby	4.1955 – 10.1965
John Sayers	10.1965 – 2.1969
Barry Sayers	2.1969 – 1.1980
Roger Hallett	1.1980 – 10.1980
Robert White	10.1980 – 1990
Peter Thorpe	11.2001 – 2002
Rod Stott jnr	2001 – 2003
David Lane	2003 – 7.2008
Colin Fisk	17.7.2008 –

Second Coxswains

F. S Kendall	12.1920 –
Richard Mason	24.3.1947 – 16.5.1947
Sidney Harman	10.6.1947 –
Robertson Buchan	– 1959
Dennis Bailey Snr	– 11.1987
Ian Firman	29.11.1987 – 9.1990
Robert White	21.9.1990 – 11.2001
Dave Steenvoorden	23.11.2001 – 4.2004
Richard Dougherty	4.2004 – 11.2005
Martyn Hagan	28.11.2005 –

Coxswain Robert Cross

Robert Cross was one of the best-known Coxswains ever to serve at the Humber. When he retired as Coxswain in February 1944 aged sixty-seven, he had gained a remarkable record of service during his time at Spurn Point, and become one of the most famous Coxswains in the country. He was appointed Coxswain in 1912 and stayed in the post for thirty-one years, during which time he helped to save 403 lives. He was awarded two Gold, three Silver and two Bronze medals for gallantry by the RNLI, as well as getting the George medal. He died aged eighty-eight on 14 June 1964.

Coxswain William Anderson

Captain William Anderson, Coxswain for a decade during the post-war years, worked as a master mariner for most of his career and applied for the job at Spurn 'to settle down ashore' after a lifetime at sea.

Coxswain Robertson Buchan

Robertson Buchan, Coxswain from 1959 to 1973, originally came from Peterhead, where he worked on trawlers before 1939. He served in the Royal Navy during the war, for a time mine-sweeping from Fowey. (Robertson Buchan Collection)

Coxswain Brian Bevan

Superintendent Coxswain for more than twenty-five years, Brian Bevan became one of the most famous British lifeboatmen for the medal-winning rescues in which he was involved during the winter of 1978/79. (RNLI)

Coxswain Dave Steenvoorden

David Steenvoorden was appointed as Coxswain at Spurn in April 2004 having been acting in the post for seven months. He was appointed a full-time crew member in 1990 having previously served as a volunteer on Cleethorpes ILB. (RNLI)

E • INSHORE LIFEBOATS AT THE HUMBER

During the early 1960s an inflatable inshore rescue boat (IRB, later known as inshore lifeboat or ILB) was operated at Spurn Point. Small inflatable lifeboats were first introduced into the RNLI's fleet in 1963 to deal with inshore incidents involving casualties such as yachts, cabin cruisers, bathers and dinghies, and IRBs were sent to a number of stations in the early 1960s. The boats were 15ft 6in in length, built of neoprene-proofed nylon and driven by a 40hp outboard engine, giving a top speed of over twenty knots. In May 1964 one was sent to the Humber to supplement the offshore lifeboat, but stayed for just one summer. During this time, the boat completed only a handful of services, the first on 28 May after two boys had been reported missing in a small boat near the Haile Sands Fort. The ILB's services were not needed on this occasion, and she returned to Spurn at 2.20 p.m.

The IRB was used again on 23 August 1964 when she launched at 11.10 a.m. to the yacht *Veronique*, which was in difficulties a mile south-west of the Bull lightvessel in choppy seas and a force five south-westerly wind. The IRB escorted the yacht to safety and returned to Spurn at 11.30 a.m., only to be launched again at 6.20 p.m. that day. This time she went to the aid of the yacht *Dolphin*, which was in trouble 400 yards offshore, opposite the lifeboatmen's cottages. The IRB crew helped the yachtsmen out of trouble and returned to station at 6.35 p.m.

Two days later the IRB was launched on service again, putting out at 5 p.m. on 25 August after the Coastguard had - that a person was drifting out to sea on an air-bed off Withernsea, in a south-westerly breeze. But no effective service was performed and the IRB returned to station at 7 p.m. after what proved to be its last rescue. The boat was withdrawn at the end of the summer season, on 31 October 1964, and never returned as it was deemed the offshore boat was more suitable to the demands made on the station.

Coxswain Robertson Buchan shows the Archbishop of York, the Lord and Lady Mayoress of Bradford, the Bishop of Hull and Alderman Hind of Bradford the inshore lifeboat that was based at Spurn Point in 1964. (Robertson Buchan Collection)

Instead the RNLI established a new IRB Station in 1965 near Cleethorpes, initially called Humber Mouth, and this proved a more effective way of providing inshore cover to the waters of the Humber Estuary. Two ILBs served this station. The first was D-56, from 1965 to 1972 and the second, D-211, from 1973 until 1980. In March 1980 the station was closed because of a decline in the number of incidents in their areas, and the coverage of the 54ft Arun *City of Bradford IV*, with her Y-class inflatable, was deemed adequate.

However, by 1986 the number of services suited to an inshore lifeboat in the area warranted the reopening of the Cleethorpes station on the west side of the Humber estuary. An ILB house was built at the southern end of the Promenade and a relief D-class inflatable, D-182, was placed on station in May 1986. The following year a new ILB was built for the station, D-325 *Tricentrol II*, which arrived on 30 June 1987 and served until 1994. In 1994 the station became the sixth to benefit from the *Blue Peter* TV Appeal and the ILB D-454, which was placed on station on 22 February, was named *Blue Peter VI*. Her replacement, D-618, was also funded by Blue Peter viewers, and she was placed on service on 5 July 2004. The most outstanding rescue performed by the Cleethorpes ILB crew was to the fishing vessel *Dollard* on 26 February 2004, described on page 123.

(Above) The inflatable inshore lifeboat D-65, an RFD PB16 type, off the slipway at Spurn Point, June 1965. (Robertson Buchan Collection)

(Below) The current Cleethorpes inshore lifeboat D-618 Blue Peter VI on exercise in the Humber in 2004. (Nicholas Leach)